PLAYBACK+
Speed • Pitch • Balance • Loop

INSIDE ROCK GUITAR

by Dave Rubin

To access audio visit:
www.halleonard.com/mylibrary

Enter Code
1557-8038-9644-6817

ON THE COVER:

CHUCK BERRY: Photo by Harry Davis, Courtesy Bill Greensmith/Cache Agency
ERIC CLAPTON: Photo © Brannon Tommey/Cache Agency
JIMI HENDRIX: Photo Courtesy Good Times/Cache Agency
JIMMY PAGE: Photo by Peter Sherman/Cache Agency
EDDIE VAN HALEN: Photo by Jon Sievart/Cache Agency
ZAKK WYLDE: Photo © RTNGDP/MediaPunch

ISBN 978-1-4584-1346-8

HAL•LEONARD®
CORPORATION

7777 W. BLUEMOUND RD. P.O. BOX 13819 MILWAUKEE, WI 53213

In Australia Contact:
Hal Leonard Australia Pty. Ltd.
4 Lentara Court
Cheltenham, Victoria, 3192 Australia
Email: ausadmin@halleonard.com.au

Visit Hal Leonard Online at
www.halleonard.com

TABLE OF CONTENTS

PREFACE

These 30 select, legendary guitarists warrant individual volumes, and indeed, they are available through Hal Leonard. My goal is to give an overview of the most significant elements of their music in an easily accessible format for the guitarist who wants to possess a wide variety of rock guitar techniques. Learning most, if not all of them, will provide the broadest education upon which an inclusive, personal style may be built.

DEDICATION AND ACKNOWLEDGMENTS

I would like to dedicate this book to Chuck Berry, whom I have had the distinct pleasure and honor to back up on two special occasions. With all due respect to all the great blues, country, and rockabilly guitarists who preceded him, true rock 'n' roll guitar begins with him. Thanks to Scot Kaufman; George White, the author of the definitive Bo Diddley biography; and everyone at Hal Leonard who contributed to the planning, editing, and publishing of this book.

ABOUT THE AUDIO

The accompanying audio includes demonstration tracks for every example in the book. For instant access to the audio, simply go to **www.halleonard.com/mylibrary**, and enter the code found on page 1.

INTRODUCTION: JUST GIVE ME THAT ROCK 'N' ROLL MUSIC

It could reasonably be argued that 1955 was the official birth of rock 'n' roll music and the advent of the wild guitar playing and "jungle music" that drove teens to delirium—and their parents to distraction. Chuck Berry, Elvis guitarist Scotty Moore, and Bo Diddley, three of the most inventive and prominent early pickers, mixed a dangerous brew of the forbidden blues, country music, and even swing jazz to create a new music that featured the guitar as both the lead and driving rhythm instrument.

Historically, any number of songs could qualify as containing the first rock 'n' roll guitar—a great topic for discussion and debate beyond the scope of this book. However, Arthur "Guitar Boogie" Smith and his "Guitar Boogie" (1945) could certainly qualify as a starting point, particularly in light of the countless take-offs that followed in the '50s, including the Virtues' virtual duplication, "Guitar Boogie Shuffle" (1959), and the Rock-A-Teens' "Woo Hoo" (1959).

It is fair to say that boogie woogie music is one of the granite cornerstones of rock, a fact heard regularly through the '60s, '70s, '80s, and beyond courtesy of songs like Norman Greenbaum's "Spirit in the Sky" (1969), ZZ Top's "La Grange" (1974), and Van Halen's "Hot for Teacher" (1984), among others. The game-changer in rock music, however, was Chuck Berry. His groundbreaking "Maybellene" (1955) revealed his country music influences while containing a howling, distorted blues solo that is still striking today due to its raw energy. Of even greater significance, however, was his utilization of the bass-string cut-boogie patterns popularized by Robert Johnson on songs like "Sweet Home Chicago" (1936). His "Roll Over Beethoven" (1956) and "Johnny B. Goode" (1957) subtly altered the swing feel of the boogie blues into a more driving, straight 4/4 meter while still maintaining a limber lilt that is often missing in the countless imitations that followed.

Concurrently, two other prominent pioneers of rock guitar were storming the ramparts of conservative, contemporary pop music, particularly the music featured on the TV show *Your Hit Parade*, which "paraded" the lamest music of the '50s each week. In Memphis, Scotty Moore backed Elvis regularly from 1954 until "the King" was inducted into the Army in 1958, and less frequently thereafter. His hybrid-picked accompaniment style, influenced by hot country pioneers Merle Travis and Chet Atkins, combined with his background in Southern music and a love of the blues, helped to create an early, energetic subgenre of rock 'n' roll known as "rockabilly." His Sun Records recordings with Elvis (1954–56), including covers of bluesman Arthur "Big Boy" Crudup's "That's Alright Mama" and "My Baby Left Me," and RCA singles that followed, are classics that contributed to the teen revolution of the era.

Meanwhile, in Chicago a big, bad bluesman was bending the genre to fit his unique vision of rock 'n' roll rhythm. Bo Diddley cut a single that literally helped to create the seismic shift from the blues to rock 'n' roll. "I'm a Man," famously covered and reworked by the Yardbirds ten years later, is a monochord shuffle blues, while the flipside, "Bo Diddley," debuted the famous "Bo Diddley beat" in all its funky, booty-shaking glory. The latter became the inspiration for Buddy Holly's "Not Fade Away" (1957), the Strangeloves' "I Want Candy" (1965), and the Who's "Magic Bus" (1968), among many others. Additionally, George Thorogood has based a good chunk of his career on the music of Bo Diddley.

Despite a brief window of opportunity for instrumental rock courtesy of Duane Eddy, the Ventures, Johnny and the Hurricanes, and others in the late '50s and early '60s, in addition to surf music in the latter period of time, American rock 'n' roll settled into a fallow stretch. Buddy Holly and Ritchie Valens had died prematurely in a tragic plane crash, Chuck Berry went to jail for a second time on trumped-up charges, Jerry Lee Lewis sent his career into a tailspin when he married his 13-year-old cousin, Little Richard forsook "Miss Molly" for the ministry, and Bo Diddley had exhausted his beat. "Hootenanny," folk, and pop music featuring the insipid "Bobbys" arose to take their place. However, across the Atlantic, young bands gearing up for the British Invasion had fallen hard under the spell of American blues and '50s rock 'n' roll. Great guitarists emerged from the Yardbirds, Beatles, Rolling Stones, and the Who—Eric Clapton, Jeff Beck, George Harrison, Keith Richards, and Pete Townshend—and rock guitar evolved dramatically. Incorporating heavy distortion and emotionally charged phrasing derived from the blues, along with dynamic high volume and even intentional feedback, they helped kick off the rock renaissance of the '60s with blues rock and psychedelic music, including, chronologically, songs such as "I Ain't Got You" (1965), "Over Under Sideways Down" (1966), "Paperback Writer" (1966), "I Can See for Miles" (1967)," and "Sympathy for the Devil" (1968). Stateside, the incomparable Jimi Hendrix was virtually rewriting the "book" with even more extraordinary volume and distortion, in addition to his creative use of effects as heard on "Purple Haze" (1967) and "All Along the Watchtower" (1968). In the process, he turned the blues and psychedelia into literally a new form of extreme expression that can be heard in the playing of countless contemporary rock and blues guitarists.

A second wave of British rock guitarists followed hot on the snakeskin boot heels of their predecessors in the late '60s. The brilliant blues-rocker and tonemeister Jimmy Page used his position of power in the last incarnation of the Yardbirds to morph into the mighty Led Zeppelin for "Dazed and Confused" (1968), David Gilmour replaced Syd Barrett in Pink Floyd for "Careful with That Ax, Eugene" (1968), and Ritchie Blackmore drove Deep Purple from classical rock to hard rock with "Speed King" (1970). As the '70s wafted in on the fumes of the '60s, yet another group of young lions were eager to flaunt their blues-powered chops. Both Carlos Santana and Rick Derringer had actually staked their claims to "rock god" status in the '60s before breaking large with "Black Magic Woman" (1970) and "Rock and Roll Hoochie Koo" (1973), respectively. Joe Perry and Aerosmith came rocking out of Boston with "Walking the Dog" (1973) as America's answer to the Rolling Stones, while AC/DC's Angus Young made a bid from "down under" with primal blues rock like "Baby Please Don't Go" (1976). However, British band the Police, with classically trained Andy Summers on the strings for "Message in a Bottle" (1979), were one of the first new wave bands in the late '70s to make it big without a blues base to their music. Also getting their start at the end of the decade were Van Halen, with the revolutionary Eddie Van Halen challenging all with "Eruption" (1978), Dire Straits, with the roots and blues-rocking Brit Mark Knopfler coming to bat with "Sultans of Swing" (1978), and the retro rockabilly Stray Cats, with the bopping Brian Setzer channeling Eddie Cochran on "Rock This Town" (1981). All three enjoyed long, productive careers while building on their original music.

As seems to happen in regular cycles in rock music, a new crop of virtuoso guitarists broke through in the '80s, even as the audience split demographically into various, and sometimes competing, camps. Rush had actually been around since the late '60s, and their progressive rock had created a loyal if cultish following. *Permanent Waves* (1980), a nod to new-wave music and featuring "The Spirit of Radio," gave Alex Lifeson and his trio a higher commercial profile. When Randy Rhoads combined classical guitar technique with Van Halen-inspired hard rock, he helped Ozzy Osbourne score a hit with the classic "Crazy Train," from *Blizzard of Ozz* (1980). Even more classically influenced rock guitar arrived in the '80s courtesy of shredding virtuoso Yngwie Malmsteen, particularly with his song "Black Star" from *Rising Force* (1984).

After serving as resident virtuoso with Frank Zappa for two years, Steve Vai went on his own in 1983, recording *Flex-Able* (1984), featuring the standout "Attitude Song," and then replacing Yngwie Malmsteen in Alcatrazz in 1985 before continuing forward with various projects. As heavy metal became a major counter force to the prevailing pop music in the decade, thrash metal heroes Metallica, with lead guitarist Kirk Hammett, reached their acknowledged peak with *Master of Puppets* (1986) and tracks like "Battery." In the late, "big hair" '80s, a trend towards more melodic hard rock was led by Bon Jovi and their album *Slippery When Wet* (1986), with guitarist Richie Sambora driving "You Give Love a Bad Name," "Livin' on a Prayer," and "Wanted Dead or Alive." Joe Satriani, who had taught Steve Vai and Kirk Hammett, among others, and previously backed a number of stars, bolted to the top of the virtuoso heap when he released his landmark *Surfing with the Alien* (1987), which included "Satch Boogie" and displayed his talent for songwriting and shredding. Likewise, Nuno Bettencourt led Extreme beyond the metal leanings of their debut album to the far more radio-friendly *Extreme II: Pornograffitti* (1990), which featured the hit acoustic ballad "More Than Words." In 1996, Ozzy Osbourne guitarist Zakk Wylde began his solo career with *Book of Shadows*, which included the song "Between Heaven and Hell" and showcased a far wider diversity of styles, including southern rock, than most of his heavy rock contemporaries.

The '90s experienced further fracturing of the rock guitar audience, cracks that began in the '70s and '80s. The established heavyweight fret-busters who began frying speaker cones in the '80s continued servicing their hardcore fans. Meanwhile, Nirvana occupied the top of the grunge heap until Kurt Cobain's suicide in 1994. Post-grunge and punk-pop from L.A. competed with other, various regional styles even as heavy metal flourished while begetting a dizzying array of hyphenated subgenres.

"Rock 'n' Roll Will Never Die," of course, nor will rock guitar and the unending desire to express oneself by connecting the head and heart to fingers on amplified strings.

(**Note:** Chart positions are from the *Billboard 200* unless otherwise specified.)

—Dave Rubin
NYC, 2015

Chuck Berry performing in 1973.

(Photo by Ian Dickson/MediaPunch)

CHUCK BERRY
(1926–)

The combination of a resonant, hollowbody Gibson ES-350T with hot P-90 pickups and a tweed Fender amp grind heard on "Maybellene" in 1955 sent out a clanging clarion call to the emerging post-WWII youth culture, and in particular, provided guitarists with a blueprint. Raw to the bone, revolutionary, and a bit threatening in a way that was attractive to teens ripe for rebellion, "Maybellene" heralded a man who embodied the synthesis of the blues and country music that produced early rock 'n' roll. While Elvis had been the white messenger who brought the blues into the commercial world a year earlier, Chuck Berry was a "brown-eyed handsome man" incorporating his love of hillbilly music with the blues and R&B while appealing to middle-class teens. He was the first rock guitar hero to sing and write his own songs, as well as play rhythm and lead. In the process, he created an immortal, influential style and a catalog of songs that are an endless source of inspiration for aspiring rock guitarists.

Charles Edward Anderson Berry was born October 18, 1926, in St. Louis, Missouri, to Martha and Henry. The middle-class family lived on Goode Street, in an area known as the "Ville," in a city and time of strict segregation and crushing racism. Berry was often around music growing up, especially the religious variety, and was encouraged to sing in the church choir at age 6. An all-consuming and lifelong obsession with the opposite sex compelled him to try to attract girls by singing Jay McShann's "Confessin' the Blues" in high school in 1941, backed by his friend Tommy Stevens on guitar. The experience inspired him to begin playing, and another friend lent him a four-string tenor instrument. He took to it with much exuberance, so much so that his growing instrumental skills soon surpassed his vocal ability. By 17, he was playing for soldiers at USO shows. Berry realized that, with just three chords, he could play most blues, and Nick Manoloff's *Guitar Book of Chords* provided enough knowledge to play most popular songs to accompany his singing at backyard parties. Ira Harris, whose brother gave haircuts in the neighborhood, and who was an accomplished jazz guitarist and devotee of Charlie Christian, showed Berry "rhythm changes." This enabled him to expand his repertoire of standards considerably, as he took every opportunity to play for people, especially young ladies.

In 1944, however, while still in school, Berry was sentenced to 10 years in a reformatory for committing a string of robberies and stealing a car. He performed in a singing quartet and did a little boxing while imprisoned, but was released after three years for what would be the first of three incarcerations. In 1948, he married Themetta "Toddy" Suggs and supported her and their daughter, Ingrid, born in 1950, by doing factory work, becoming a janitor, and training to be a beautician. By the early '50s, he had become proficient enough on the guitar to supplement his income by performing with local East St. Louis bands. His earliest musical influences stemmed from his attraction to boogie woogie, particularly Tommy Dorsey, swing, and the blues of Tampa Red, Lonnie Johnson, Arthur "Big Boy" Crudup, Muddy Waters, and T-Bone Walker. Later on, Nat "King" Cole, Charles Brown, and especially Louis Jordan (whose guitarist Carl Hogan, along with Ira Harris, would provide the firmest foundation for his style) loomed large in his development.

Curiously, it was his acquaintance with "hillbilly" music, popular among whites in St. Louis, that propelled Berry forward to stardom. In 1952, Tommy Stevens, who had a steady gig at a local club, invited him to sing and play rhythm guitar in his trio, which covered the blues and popular music within the black community by artists such as Nat Cole and Harry Belafonte. Always looking for ways to liven up the act, Berry would sometimes throw in a country & western song to the great surprise of the African-American audience. Over time, he and the band incorporated additional novelty material and routines. The showmanship worked, helping to make the band popular and the club owner happy. Gradually, his name got around, too, and in December, he got a call from piano player Johnnie Johnson of the Sir John Trio to join his band on New Year's Eve at the Cosmopolitan Club. It was a big move up in all ways and would be the break Berry was seeking to match his confidence and ambition. The gig was a great success due to the impact the charismatic young man had on the audience and the club owner, and he eagerly took his place as the frontman in the band, which mostly played popular black music. In time, he would battle Johnson for leadership of the band, actually coming to blows at one point and leading him back to Tommy Stevens in 1954 for an even bigger and better gig at the Crank Club. During his tenure with Stevens, Berry was approached to play guitar at a recording session behind a local singer known as Calypso Joe. The songs contained humorous references to cars and girls, and the experience would have a profound effect on Berry's ideas about songwriting and the desire to make his own records, though the producer on the date was not interested. Following the session, Berry received an attractive offer from Johnnie Johnson to rejoin his band. Berry accepted under the conditions that he would be the bandleader and that they would pursue a recording contract. Johnson, who was an excellent blues and boogie piano man but lacked the ambition of Berry, had no clue about recording, and St. Louis lacked the opportunities at any rate.

What followed is a treasured tale from the annals of rock 'n' roll. In the spring of 1955, Berry made a trip to Chicago with the hopes of scoring a recording contract. He met his idol, Muddy Waters, in a club, asked who he should see about making a record, and was famously told, "Go see Leonard Chess at Chess Records." Chess was impressed with Berry's business demeanor and asked him to go back to St. Louis and return with a band tape. What he brought back a week later contained the undistinguished slow-blues instrumental "Wee Wee Hours" and a C&W number named "Ida Red." To Berry's surprise, Chess was more intrigued by the latter, as he had presciently realized that his audience was getting younger, more diverse, and R&B was ready to cross over. The song had a history that dated back to 1928, and it is likely that Berry had heard a more contemporary version by Bob Wills, as well as one by Bumble Bee Slim. In reality, though the titles were identical, Berry's "Ida Red" has a much more inventive, clever, contemporary, and even poetic lyric and story line. With Johnson, Chess bassist Willie Dixon, drummer Jasper Thomas, and Jerome Green (from Bo Diddley's band) on maracas, on May 21, it took 35 takes to achieve the result Chess struggled to get. Amazingly, it occurred only weeks after Bo Diddley cut his monumental first tracks. Adding to the legend of the groundbreaking rock 'n' roll classic's combination of country music and blues is the way Leonard Chess changed the name from the "too rural"-sounding "Ida Red" to "Maybellene," after having spotted a bottle of Maybelline mascara in his office and changing the spelling to avoid a potential legal infringement with the cosmetics manufacturer. With help from the constant promotion of pioneer rock DJ Alan Freed on his New York City radio show, and a buzz that built from urban center to urban center, "Maybellene," backed with the slow blues "Wee Wee Hours," hit #1 on the R&B charts and #5 on the pop charts.

Between 1956 and 1960, Berry enjoyed a remarkable and unprecedented run of classic rock 'n' roll guitar hits on the *Billboard* Pop Singles Charts, including "Roll Over Beethoven" (#29, 1956), "School Day" (#5, 1957), "Oh, Baby Doll" (#57, 1957), "Rock and Roll Music" (#8, 1957), "Sweet Little Sixteen" (#2, 1958), "Johnny B. Goode" (#8, 1958), "Beautiful Delilah" (#81, 1958), "Carol" (#18, 1958), "Sweet Little Rock and Roller" (#47, 1958), "Jo Jo Gunne" (#83, 1958), "Run, Rudolph, Run" (#69, 1958), "Merry Christmas, Baby" (#71, 1958), "Anthony Boy" (#60, 1959), "Almost Grown" (#32, 1959), "Little Queenie" (#80, 1959), "Back in the USA" (#37, 1959), "Too Pooped to Pop" (#42, 1960), and "Let It Rock" (#64, 1960).

Berry's success in 1958 afforded him the resources to invest in real estate and open a nightclub called Club Bandstand in the white business district of St. Louis. The next year, he brought back from Mexico a 14-year-old Apache waitress named Janice Escalanti to work as a hat-check girl in his club. However, after he fired her, she was arrested for prostitution, implicated him, and charges were leveled at him for violating the Mann Act, which forbids the transportation of minors across state lines for immoral purposes. In 1961, he was sentenced to 20 months in prison in what was seen by some as being "railroaded" by the St. Louis community for being "uppity." When he was released in 1963, he picked up his hit-making ways with "Nadine" (#23, 1964), "No Particular Place to Go" (#10, 1964), "You Never Can Tell" (#14, 1964), "Little Marie" (#54, 1964), "Promised Land" (#41, 1964), "Dear Dad" (#95, 1965), "My Ding-a-Ling" (#1, 1972), and "Reelin' and Rockin'" (#27, 1972).

People who knew Berry before his stretch in prison describe him as a changed man, bitter and distant. On the bright side, the musical landscape had changed advantageously in his absence. The Beatles and the Rolling Stones, in particular, among other British rock bands, had discovered his music as a prime source for their music, and he was hailed in Europe and the U.S., appearing in the landmark *T.A.M.I. Show* in 1964 and becoming a fixture on the oldies circuit. The downside was that audiences only wanted to hear his "oldies" and, over time, he became cynical and lackadaisical about his performances, going so far as to no longer front a regular band, preferring local pickup bands instead, leading to his reputation for erratic performances. Outside of the numerous reissues and collaborations, his last two albums of new material were *Back Home* in 1970, containing "Tulane," and *Rock It* in 1979—the same year he was invited by President Carter to perform at the White House and served two months in jail for tax evasion (due, in part, to his propensity for being paid in cash). In 1972, he had his only #1 hit, the childish, sexual sing-a-long "My Ding-a-Ling" (from the *London Chuck Berry Sessions*), while in 1977, "Johnny B. Goode" was included on a disc of cultural artifacts called *Sounds of Earth,* which was attached to the Voyager 1 satellite. In 1978, Berry appeared as himself in the film *American Hot Wax*, which was based on the life of Alan Freed.

In 1986, Berry was accorded the honor of being in the original group inducted into the Rock and Roll Hall of Fame. That same year, Keith Richards, his No. 1 protégé, organized a 60th birthday bash for him with guest artists at the Fox Theater in St. Louis, which was filmed and released as *Hail! Hail! Rock 'n' Roll* in 1987, followed in 1989 by the release of his autobiography and a triumphant appearance on *The Tonight Show*. But, as happened with regularity in his career, trouble rose up in 1990, when a group of women brought a class-action suit against him for allegedly filming them in the restroom of his Southern Air restaurant in Wentzville, Missouri. Though a police raid at his house supposedly found incriminating videotapes, including one involving a minor, the charges were never proved in court and Berry reportedly paid over a million dollars in a settlement with 59 women. In 1993, he performed at President Clinton's private inauguration party, but in 2000, Johnnie Johnson brought charges against Berry, claiming that he was the co-author of over 50 songs, including "Roll Over Beethoven," "Sweet Little Sixteen," and "No Particular Place to Go." In a "turnaround" in his legal travails, and a defeat for the underappreciated Johnson, the judge ruled that too much time had elapsed and the case was dismissed the same year Berry received a Kennedy Center Award at the White House.

In 2008, Berry toured Europe, and most recently, was playing once a month at Blueberry Hill in St. Louis, which is owned by his loyal friend Joe Edwards. At a New Year's Day concert in Chicago in 2011, he collapsed and passed out from exhaustion and had to be led offstage, but was reported to be in good health. In July 2011, a statue of him was unveiled and dedicated across from Blueberry Hill in University City, Missouri, an ironic gesture from an area that, in the past, often proved hostile to his ambition and accomplishments. Nonetheless, Chuck Berry's standing as arguably the "Father of Rock 'n' Roll" and one of the most influential rock guitarists of all time will outlast even bronze monuments.

THE GUITAR STYLE OF CHUCK BERRY

Similar to "Roll Over Beethoven" and "Johnny B. Goode," the four-measure unaccompanied intro contains a selection of the signature elements that would appear, to varying degrees, in many of Berry's other rock 'n' roll masterpieces. The stuttering 4ths in measure 1 are derived from electric slide guitar à la Elmore James. Measure 2 utilizes the blues scale, while measure 3 employs the A major pentatonic scale, leading to conclusive resolution in measure 4 via the E/C♯ (5th/3rd) double stop and tonic note, A.

Chuck Berry 1

Here is a classic I (A) chord "response" fill, following the "call" of a lyric line as found in tunes like "School Days" or "No Particular Place to Go." Using 4ths and 3rds from the composite blues scale, the phrase derives a potent dollop of bluesy grit from the E/C (5th/♭3rd) dyad that precedes resolution to the root (A).

Chuck Berry 2

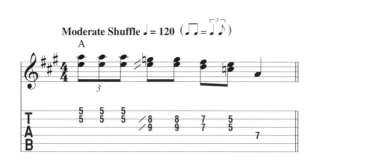

The Chuckster's bend of the 4th (D) to the 5th (E) on string 3, following the fretted 5th on string 2, is a maneuver popularized by T-Bone Walker. He creates a fat, dynamic harmony by adding the root (A) above the 5th, which exemplifies his penchant for dyads.

Chuck Berry 3

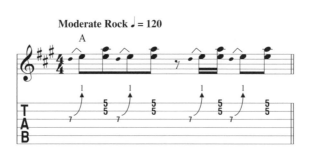

Hip harmony of both consonant (swing music) and dissonant (blues) variety is provided by dyads plucked from a creative, pioneering combination of notes from the composite blues scale. The surging effect adds substantial musical weight to accelerate the pull of gravity down to the root (A) for resolution.

Chuck Berry 4

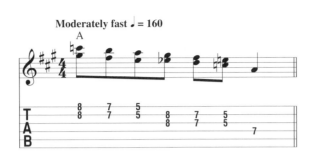

Similar to the signature riff in "Johnny B. Goode," 4ths and 3rds mix freely in a finger-friendly arrangement that, again, shows Berry bringing his particularly pungent flavor of the blues to rock 'n' roll. Observe how the pattern does not resolve to the tonic chord due to the presence of the suspended 4th (D) in the last dyad, D/A; instead, it encourages forward motion.

Chuck Berry 5

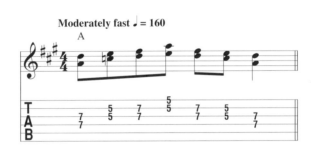

Similar to the opening riffs of "Carol," the major triad and dominant triple stop for the I (A) and IV (D) chords, respectively, are classic chordal forms in the blues and related music. The slinky, tension-producing double-string bend in measure 4 is a prime Berry characteristic that he may have nicked from pedal steel players in his beloved C&W music.

Chuck Berry 6

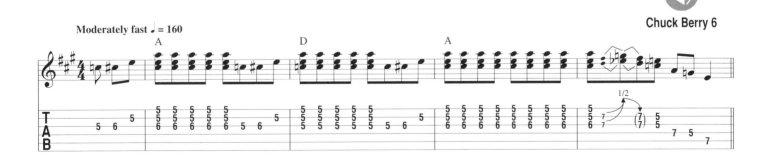

"Ringing like a bell," the augmented chord (D+) clangs the alarm to listen up in "School Days" and "No Particular Place to Go"—a new sheriff is in town! Perhaps no chord in popular music engenders more musical tension clamoring for resolution than the augmented triad.

Chuck Berry 7

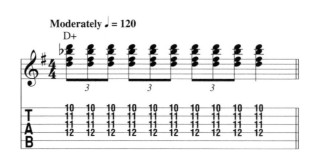

Here's another attention-grabbing intro riff that uses the F# (6th) from the major (or major pentatonic) scale to emphasize the song's major key. Similar to "Around and Around," the riff bursts with the energy and urgency for which Berry is justly famous.

Chuck Berry 8

Berry may well have been the originator of the variation on the cut boogie pattern heard in "Memphis." When Lonnie Mack got ahold of it for his instrumental version in 1963, a Top 10 hit, he performed it similarly to the figure below. Notice how it is moveable, in parallel fashion, on either strings 6–4 or strings 5–3. In addition, it is most efficient to barre with the index finger when accessing the four-note embellishment on beat 4 of each measure.

Chuck Berry 9

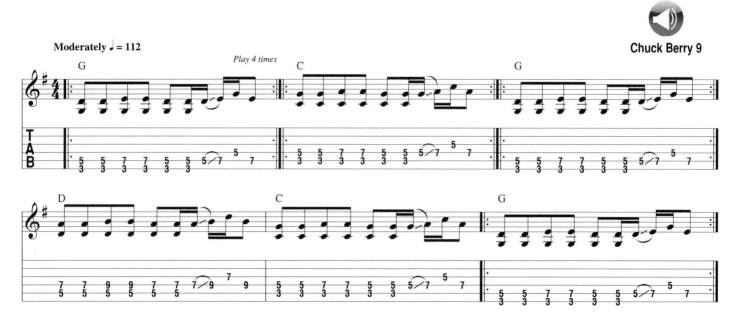

Swing jazz, Western swing, and rockabilly all employ composite blues scale riffs to indicate chord changes. Berry was likewise fond of the riffs, which use minimal note changes to follow the harmony. Notice how he drops the major 3rd (C#) down a half step, to C, in measure 3 to function as the ♭7th of the IV (D) chord. Curiously, he utilizes the same riff for the V (E) change, where C functions as the ♭6th. However, the same move can be heard in other I–IV–V progressions such as "Night Train" (1951) by R&B tenor sax great Jimmy Forrest. Equally cool, blues-approved, and Berry-sanctioned is the appearance of A/E dyads over each of the chord changes, where they function as root/5th (I), 5th/9th (IV), and 4th/root (V).

Chuck Berry 10

SCOTTY MOORE
(1931–)

Scotty Moore qualifies as a charter member of the "Unsung Heroes of Rock Guitar" club, as his historical, groundbreaking playing in the mid-'50s was overshadowed by the larger-than-life celebrity and hysterical adulation for Elvis Presley. Nonetheless, his proto-rockabilly, hybrid-picking technique and seamless synthesis of clean country music and "dirty" blues, filtered through Merle Travis and Chet Atkins, altered rock and country guitar almost overnight. The title of one of his solo albums, *The Guitar That Changed the World*, is no idle boast.

Winfield Scott Moore III was born December 27, 1931 to Winfield Scott and Mattie on a farm between Gadsden and Humbolt, Tennessee, and received his first guitar from his brother Ralph at the age of 5. He would initially learn to play from family and friends, including his neighbor Rip Brown, who taught him "Little Brown Jug." His three older brothers and father all played instruments and performed together, but as the youngest by 14 years and with the least experience, they would not allow him to join in, to his great consternation. However, Moore played constantly with his older friend James Lewis, and both gained valuable instruction from Oscar Tinsley, another farm neighbor who would book time on the radio in hopes of being discovered by the Grand Ole Opry. A tune Moore and Lewis played over and over was called "Hillbilly Boogie," and they would often argue about the tempo of pieces they were trying to play, with Moore always wanting to play faster.

By 10th grade, he was bored and restless with his lot in life, even as he had become obsessed with playing the guitar, initially influenced by Les Paul, and then Chet Atkins. In 1948, at age 16 he quit school and joined the Navy, as his brother Ralph had done previously, for a four-year tour of duty. But he was underage and his father had to lie to the recruiter, telling him that his son was 17. Coincidently, Moore was assigned to the USS Kent County, which had sailed down the Mississippi, past Memphis, when he was in the eighth grade. When he was sent to China and Korea, Moore took his guitar with him and stole away to play on the ship when he had time. In 1950, he returned to the States and was stationed in Bremerton, Washington, to wait out the lengthy time it took for his ship to be decommissioned. While there, he formed a couple of bands with shipmates and played clubs and parties, as well as a weekly 15-minute radio show. By springtime, he was married and expecting his first child, assigned to the aircraft carrier USS Valley Forge, and promptly sent back to Korea in response to the start of the Korean War. While on the carrier, he jammed with a harmonica player and a black singer, and even recorded a version of "Under the Double Eagle," which he played with expertise. Meanwhile, the carrier saw heavy action in the war and Moore was honored with two service medals.

When he was honorably discharged from the Navy in 1952, he returned to the family farm in Tennessee to rejoin his wife and newborn baby girl, whom he had sent to live with his parents. Seeking employment in Memphis, he moved his family to the city and worked in a small engine shop before ending up at the dry cleaners owned by his brother Carney. After settling in to his new routine, he went out and bought a new Fender Esquire and Deluxe amp and practiced on his lunch hour and at home after work. Before long, Moore was playing in pickup bands in the rough-and-tumble honky tonks, or "bottle clubs," around Memphis. One night, upright bassist Bill Black came by and asked to sit in for what was the beginning of a productive musical relationship.

In 1953, his marriage broke up and he got a new wife, whom he had met in the clubs. Moore also got a new guitar when he traded his Esquire for a Gibson ES-295. It all coincided with him wanting to put a serious band together, record, and go out on the road. Late in the year, he formed the Starlite Wranglers with Doug Poindexter singing lead and playing guitar, Bill Black on bass, a fiddle player, steel guitarist, and a third guitarist, but no drummer—perhaps in recognition of the Grand Ole Opry in Nashville forbidding them at that time. His experience with regimen and responsibility in the Navy provided Moore with the confidence and resolve to manage the band in a business-like manner, enabling him to get bookings and a radio appearance. Knowing that a record had to come next, he hawked Sam Phillips at Sun Records until he finally relented and recorded the band. Unbeknownst to Moore, a young truck driver fresh out of high school, with long greasy hair, loud clothes, and the burning desire to be a professional singer was also spending time at Sun Records, cutting a number of demos and looking for his chance. In the spring of 1954, the Starlite Wranglers recorded the single "My Kind of Carryin' On" b/w "Now She Cares No More for Me," co-written by Moore. Though it got some regional airplay, sales were weak. Moore was understandably discouraged, but continued to stop by the studio literally every day after work to talk music with Phillips, looking for any sort of break. Unbeknownst to anyone, one would come in the summer and be bigger than anything he could have hoped for or ever imagined.

Elvis Presley with the Blue Moon Boys, Scotty Moore (at left) and Bill Black, in 1957.

(Photo: © Pictorial Press Ltd./Alamy)

On July 4, 1954, Scotty Moore and Bill Black showed up at Sun Records at Sam Phillips' request. After fruitless hours trying to come up with something different from the countless ballads Presley knew, they goofed around with and recorded a rocked-up version of bluesman Arthur "Big Boy" Crudup's "That's Alright, Mama." The fireworks it would set off would be more spectacular and long lasting than any Independence Day celebration and a recording contract for Presley was inked with Sun Records. When local DJ Dewey Phillips played it on his radio show, the response was unprecedented. Moore and Black quit the Starlite Wranglers and the trio became the Blue Moon Boys, with Moore serving as manager for one year. Presley playing rudimentary but propulsive acoustic rhythm guitar with the combination of country (or "hillbilly") and blues, dubbed "rockabilly," offended conservatives in the segregated South, many of whom thought Presley was black due to his voice, phrasing, and choice of music. However, young people, especially girls who saw his controversial onstage gyrations, reacted to him with the kind of uninhibited excitement not seen since Frank Sinatra in the early '40s and not encountered again until the Beatles appeared 10 years later.

The band released "Blue Moon of Kentucky," "Good Rockin' Tonight," and "I Don't Care if the Sun Don't Shine" in 1954, followed by "Baby Let's Play House," "I Forgot to Remember to Forget," "I'm Left, You're Right, She's Gone," "Milkcow Blues Boogie," and "You're a Heartbreaker" in 1955. They played on the *Opry* just one time, to tepid response, but toured extensively and had a recurring engagement on the *Louisiana Hayride* for a year, where they were augmented by drummer D.J. Fontana, who would eventually join and make them a quartet. At one point, after Presley had acquired a new manager, he told Moore that he wanted to give him and Black a generous share of recording royalties. In a move that he would come to regret, Moore believed it too generous and suggested a much lower figure, but it was never put in writing and never honored. By the end of 1954, several major record labels were clamoring to sign Presley and the prize went to RCA for the then unheard of sum of $40,000. He was only 20 years old.

The year that sent Presley's popularity skyrocketing was 1956, as he created a sensation on national TV shows and in person. With a studio band added to the former Blue Moon Boys, along with the backing of the Jordanaires vocal group, RCA released "Heartbreak Hotel" (#1), "Blue Suede Shoes" (#20), "I Want You, I Need You, I Love You" (#1), "Hound Dog"/"Don't Be Cruel" (#1), and "Love Me Tender"/"Anyway You Want Me" (#1), followed in 1957 with "Too Much" (#1), "All Shook Up" (#1), "(Let Me Be Your) Teddy Bear" (#1), and "Jailhouse Rock" (#1). From the beginning, Moore was the only electric guitarist and featured soloist on the Sun sessions, and the crucial, early success of Presley is unimaginable without him. He still contributed substantially and immeasurably to the RCA singles, in conjunction with other guitarists like Hank Garland, but his role in the band would diminish precipitously after "Colonel" Tom Parker became Elvis' manager. Money that was once split three ways among "Elvis Presley, Scotty, and Bill," as they were formerly credited at Sun Records, Parker now paid Moore and Black as hired sidemen. The business arrangement extended to their participation in the movies that Presley began making in Hollywood, starting with *Love Me Tender* in 1956. As their income dwindled, Moore and Black became alarmed, culminating when a proposed album of Presley instrumentals with them was shot down by Parker. In the fall of 1957, they decided to quit and wrote letters of resignation to Presley. He called Moore and asked what it would take to make him happy, replying that he would think about his modest request. When the news of the disagreement was reported in the press, though, with Parker obviously pulling the strings, Presley used it as an excuse to accuse them of not dealing directly with him and he accepted their resignations in an open letter to a Memphis newspaper.

Parker had won by ending the relationship he always feared challenged his authority. But when Presley was dissatisfied with their replacements, Moore and Black were contacted by Parker's company within a month of their resignation and offered a substantial raise if they would rejoin the band. They agreed as long as they were paid on a per diem basis. Presley was glad to have them back. Unfortunately, following a number of wildly successful shows on the West Coast and in Hawaii, in December 1957, Elvis received his draft notice from the Army. While he was in the service, Moore and Black were, once again, left to wonder whether they would be taken care of. Much to their chagrin, they were cut loose in 1958 and would go their separate ways, with the latter forming the successful Bill Black Combo before dying in 1965. Meanwhile, Moore scuffled for work, but his luck changed when he entered into a partnership with the fledgling Fernwood Records and helped produce the million-selling, #1 pop hit "Tragedy" in 1959.

When Presley was discharged from the Army in 1960, he contacted Moore and Fontana for the *Frank Sinatra Special* TV show, and they would work together, on and off, on recordings and for personal appearances through the '60s, though Black refused to be involved. Moore also began working for Sam Phillips at Sun Records until he was fired in 1964, when he recorded instrumental versions of Presley hits for *The Guitar That Changed the World.* Unfortunately, his timing was bad, as there was little to no interest in him without Presley, and the record sank out of sight despite his precise, tasty renditions. He then moved from Memphis to Nashville to engineer and produce, with clients including Ringo Starr, Tracy Nelson, and the Holy Modal Rounders. In 1968, he appeared with Presley on his historic *Comeback Special* TV show. It would be the last time Moore would see the man who he had looked upon protectively as a younger brother, despite their financial differences. The following year, when plans fell through over money for him and the Jordanaires to join Presley at an engagement in Las Vegas, Moore had reached the end of the road. Disgusted and disillusioned, he put his guitar in its case and would not perform again in public for 24 years, except for one time in 1991, when he met Keith Richards at the Stones guitarist's request, and the two of them stayed up all night drinking and jamming.

In 1992, following his declaration of bankruptcy, Moore accepted a booking to play with Carl Perkins in Memphis. Further gigs followed, including in England, and more offers for his talents came from adoring musicians like Stray Cats bassist Lee Rocker. In 1994, Moore, Fontana, and the Jordanaires appeared in a huge Presley tribute show in Memphis, and Moore continued doing shows with Perkins. In 1997, he wrote his autobiography, as told to James Dickerson, called *That's Alright, Elvis,* setting the record straight on many issues. That same year, he recorded *All the King's Men* with Fontana, Keith Richards, Jeff Beck, Ron Wood, and Levon Helm in Woodstock as a tribute album to Presley. Since 1990, there have been two miniseries and a documentary in which Moore has been portrayed by various actors. Gibson released a limited-edition signature ES-295 guitar and, in 2000, he was finally inducted into the Rock and Roll Hall of Fame. In 2002, Moore won the Orville H. Gibson Lifetime Achievement Award for his dedication to playing Gibson guitars. Continuing to be sought after by young musicians, in 2003, he and Fontana recorded with Alvin Lee of Ten Years After fame and, in 2005, he made a DVD at Abbey Road Studios in London with Eric Clapton, Mark Knopfler, Bill Wyman, David Gilmour, Ron Wood, and Albert Lee. In 2007, at the age of 76, Moore stated that his appearance at the "Last Man Standing" show in Memphis during the 30th Anniversary of Elvis Week would be his final public performance.

For a sideman who missed out on deserved publishing compensation beyond the realm of all but a few, Scotty Moore is remarkably free of bitterness or rancor. By any reckoning, he lived a fantasy life in the fast lane for the better part of a decade that few will ever know and his honored place in rock music history is secure. Despite living in the immense shadow of "the King," his brilliant playing made Keith Richards say, "Everyone else wanted to be Elvis; I wanted to be Scotty." So did countless others.

THE GUITAR STYLE OF SCOTTY MOORE

If he was not literally the first, Scotty Moore was the first *prominent* trio guitarist in rock 'n' roll. On the early rockabilly sides with Elvis, he basically carried the whole show in conjunction with bassist Bill Black, though he would be the first to acknowledge the contribution the former Memphis truck driver made on rhythm guitar. Observe his utilization of the open second string in measures 1–2 to fatten up the I (A) chord harmony before he lays out tasty A composite blues scale (blues scale plus Mixolydian mode) licks in measures 3–4, which contain both the major 3rd (C♯) to confirm the major tonality and the gritty ♭3rd (C) for blues appeal.

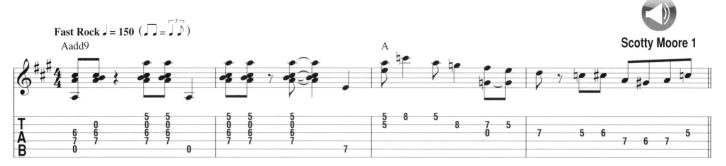

Moore is conversant in a number of blues and pentatonic scales and was known to gracefully integrate more than one in a solo. Check out the way he uses the A composite blues scale to indicate the all-important I–IV (A–D) move in measures 1–2, and then contrasts tension-inducing double and triple stops in measure 3 with the consonant A major pentatonic scale in measure 4 for release, as well as a dash of melody and country flavor.

Performance Tip: Try bending the C/G double stop in measure 3 with either the ring and pinky fingers, low to high, or by pushing up, Chuck Berry fashion, with the fleshy area of the ring finger where the fingerprint resides.

The hollow Gibson guitars Moore favored produced a rich, lower-register tone that he showed off on several Elvis hits. In measures 1–3, he employs the C minor pentatonic scale, phrased in a pattern not unlike the sound of a V-8 Ford rumbling to life, as a way of simultaneously creating tension and building momentum in the beginning of his solo. In measure 4, acceleration is achieved via the ascending, harmonious C composite blues scale resolving to the tonic (C) note.

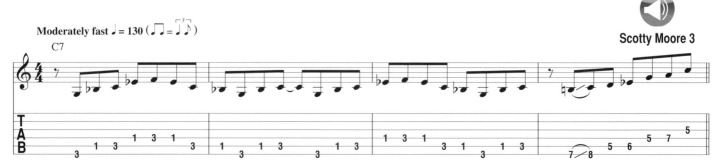

As one of the primary pioneers of rockabilly music, Moore was unsurpassed in utilizing his Chet Atkins and Merle Travis fingerstyle chops to invent classic riffs and patterns. This classic two-measure increment is brilliant in its simplicity as "The Guitar That Changed the World" forges an unforgettably propulsive and swinging hook from an open-position A7 chord.

Performance Tip: Moore used a plastic thumbpick, as did Atkins and Travis. If either the flatpick or the bare thumb is chosen, the index finger should be incorporated into the pick-hand technique. If hybrid picking is the option, the middle finger may be utilized to access the higher strings while the thumb and index hold the pick. Forming the A7 voicing with the index, middle, ring, and pinky fingers (low to high), starting on string 4, will facilitate efficiency, as the pinky may be lifted off to pick the open first string.

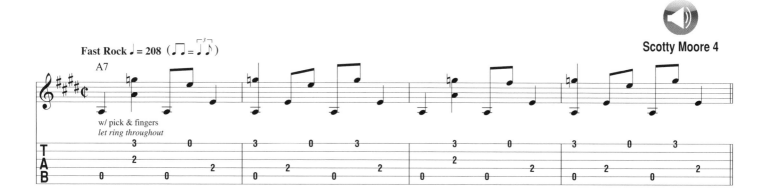

The V–IV patterns in measures 9–10 of 12-bar progressions occur at a critical juncture and constitute one of Moore's signature licks. The broken chords contain the root, 3rd, 5th, and ♭7th of the B7 and A7 chords, respectively, picked in sprightly and swinging quarter- and eighth-note rhythms, leading smoothly and logically to measures 11–12 of the turnaround (not shown).

Performance Tip: See the previous figure for the pick-hand technique. Also, be aware that the B7 chord should be voiced with a six-string barre, with the pinky accessing the A note on string 2. The index finger should also be employed as a barre on strings 6–2 for the A7 chord. In measure 3, bend the G note on string 2 with the pinky while simultaneously plucking the G note on string 4, held down by the index-finger barre. Likewise in measure 4, play the low A note on string 6 with the index-finger barre while nailing the G note on string 2 with the pinky.

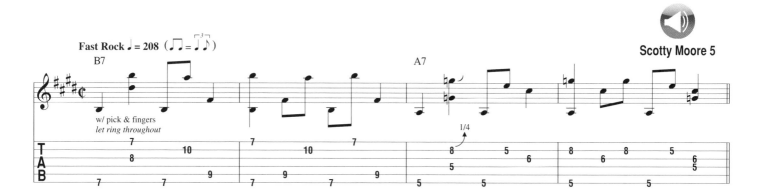

Bo Diddley in Chicago, Illinois, June 1986.

(Photo by Bill Greensmith/Cache Agency)

BO DIDDLEY
(1928–2008)

The lead guitarist has hogged the spotlight for so long now that it may be difficult to remember there was a time in the '50s, at the official birth of rock 'n' roll, when it was the "jungle rhythm" that drove people crazy. As noted, boogie woogie—from "Rocket 88" on through Chuck Berry, Scotty Moore, and many others—continued the attraction to the irresistible, swinging rhythm begun between WWI and WWII. The syncopated rhythms that Bo Diddley sprung on the unsuspecting youth culture, however, had even deeper roots, going back to Africa and perpetuated in the children's rhymes heard in the Chicago ghetto and rural Mississippi. The result was a revolutionary cornerstone of rock guitar technique, intensified by his innovative use of distortion and tremolo effects.

Ellas Bates was born December 30, 1928, in McComb, Mississippi, to Ethel Wilson and Eugene Bates, but was raised by Ethel's first cousin, Gussie McDaniel, leading to some confusion about his given name. Indeed, he himself has contributed to the confusion about the derivation of his professional name. In 1934, McDaniel moved her extended family to Chicago and young Ellas had his name legally changed to Ellas B. McDaniel. Sometime after the age of 7, he began being tutored on classical violin in the church and incurred the teacher's wrath when he kept trying to play blues. His sister gave him a guitar as a Christmas present when he was 12 and he would learn to transfer violin technique to the guitar, including playing up and down the fingerboard on one string, fast strumming to try to imitate the legato sound produced by bowing, and muted, choppy rhythms that pre-date funk. In addition, through his study of the violin he also discovered alternate tunings, which eventually led to him playing in open E like country blues guitarists. One of his classmates was Earl Hooker, with whom he would cut classes and who himself would go on to fame as a legendary Chicago electric blues guitarist. While in vocational school, McDaniel built a violin and developed his woodworking skills and the curiosity to know and learn about all things mechanical and electrical.

McDaniel began boxing around 1942 and recalled that it was the first time he was called "Bo Diddley," a name that likely refers to a "bully" or "bad dude," though he did not adopt it following his exit from the ring. Having seen Earl Hooker making money on street corners, around 1943, McDaniel was encouraged to play acoustic guitar on the streets of the South Side of Chicago in a duo with his classmate Roosevelt Jackson on washtub bass and later with Samuel Daniel, who was a Billy Eckstine imitator, contributing "sand dancing" for percussion and passing the hat. It was also at this time that McDaniel quit school. First known as the Hipsters, the casual group would eventually expand their territory into the famed Maxwell Street Market as their growing chops got attention from the public and their fellow blues musicians.

In 1948, the group began playing clubs and McDaniel bought his first amplifier and played electric guitar in order to be heard over the din. One day around 1950, neighborhood harmonica player Jody Williams met McDaniel at an amateur talent show and joined him and Jackson to form a trio, playing rudimentary bass lines on the guitar in open E tuning as instructed by the leader. Also in 1950, McDaniel was approached by blues harp blower Billy Boy Arnold to join the group now called the Langley Avenue Jive Cats. Arnold had been mentored by the late John Lee "Sonny Boy" Williamson and fit in well, but left the group in 1952 when he realized that McDaniel did not have the same professional aspirations. However, his leaving coincided with the guitarist finally becoming more serious about his music and just as important, his sound, which was inspired in part by hearing John Lee Hooker's groundbreaking "Boogie Chillun." Having made an amplifier from a radio while in school, McDaniel now experimented with guitar amps, including the Fender Bassman, by putting the guts into larger enclosures with more speakers. In addition, he wanted a way to break up his sound, and invented a primitive tremolo circuit that would later on become a signature element in his music. Just as significant was the addition of Jerome Green on maracas to make up for the lack of a drummer in his group. By his own admission, the constant battles he had with his second wife, who would smash his guitars and steal the tubes out of his amp, only hardened his resolve to advance his career.

In 1954, the group underwent major changes. Roosevelt Jackson and Jody Williams left and Billy Boy Arnold was invited back in, with Clifton James added on drums. Arnold, who had recording experience, encouraged McDaniel to make a record and a demo, and "I'm a Man" and "Uncle John" were cut at home on a wireless Webco recorder. The first place McDaniel and Arnold tried to shop it was Vee-Jay Records, where it was unceremoniously rejected. Fortuitously, in February of 1955, they went to Chess Records, where Muddy Waters and Little Walter were signed. After getting past Walter, who tried to discourage them, they ran into Phil Chess, who knew Arnold, and arrangements were made for the band to come in and play for label president Leonard Chess. Chess was looking for something different, as the blues market was shrinking, and he liked what he heard, as did Waters and Walter. The way Ellas McDaniel became "Bo Diddley" is a story that may never be conclusively confirmed. Bo himself told conflicting versions, but the one that seems to contain the most veracity is that Arnold suggested it at the rehearsal. Chess was concerned that it might be a derogatory term, but was assured that it referred to a type of comical character in the black comunity. In addition, prewar newspaper accounts refer to a "Bo Diddley and band," as well as other mentions of the name over the years. Based on these accounts, it appears that Ellas McDaniel did not become *the* Bo Diddley until he went to Chess Records.

On March 2, 1955, Bo, Jerome Green (maracas), Billy Boy Arnold (harmonica), Otis Spann (piano), Clifton James (drums), and James "Cornbread" Bradford (upright bass)—replaced by Willie Dixon at Leonard Chess's insistence—recorded the epochal "I'm a Man" and "Bo Diddley," a rewritten version of "Uncle John." The former, a one-chord shuffle stomp boasting of sexual prowess, became a classic that was also recorded by Waters. In his namesake song, Bo incorporated the lyrics of a traditional nursery rhyme and introduced the world to the "Bo Diddley beat." In short order, the song spawned "Willie and the Hand Jive" (1956) by Johnny Otis and "Not Fade Away" (1957) by Buddy Holly. Also waxed that day at Universal Studios were "You Don't Love Me" (retitled from "The Surf-Soppers Hop"), along with "Little Girl," "I'm Sweet on You Baby," and "You Got to Love Me Baby," on which Arnold sang lead.

"Bo Diddley" b/w "I'm a Man" was the proverbial smash, reaching #2 on the R&B charts, and would likely have scored high on the Top 100 charts if not for the segregation that still occurred in music. Famed DJ Alan Freed, as he would for many of the original black rock 'n' roll artists in the '50s, became an enthusiastic supporter and promoter of his music. Though fearful of leaving his family to go out on the road, Bo commenced touring, breaking attendance records at the Apollo Theater in Harlem and making a controversial appearance on the *Ed Sullivan Show*, where he refused to sing "Sixteen Tons," substituting "Bo Diddley" instead.

From 1955 to 1967, Bo scored on the R&B charts with "Diddley Daddy" (#11, 1955), "I'm Sorry" (#17, 1959), "Crackin' Up" (#14, 1959), "Say Man" (#3, 1959), "Say Man, Back Again" (#23, 1959), "Road Runner" (#20, 1960), "You Can't Judge a Book by the Cover" (#21, 1962), and "Ooh Baby" (#17, 1967). "Who Do You Love" (1956), arguably his most famous composition, with Jody Williams playing a stinging solo, did not chart, nor did other revolutionary classics such as "Hey Bo Diddley" b/w "Mona" (1957), "Before You Accuse Me" (flip side of "Say Boss Man," 1957), and "Ride On, Josephine" (1960). The only Top 40 crossover hit Bo ever had was "Say Man" (#20, 1959), a proto-rap number featuring him and Green goofing with "the dozens," somewhat foretelling Chuck Berry's success with "My Ding-a-Ling" in 1972. From 1958–63, Bo released 11 albums on the Chess/Checker label, including the best-selling *Bo Diddley* (1962), at a time when 45rpm singles still ruled the charts. Besides containing a heretofore unheard variety of syncopated and shuffle rhythms, his songs utilized the humor, jive slang, and speech patterns of the black community in a way that his peers Chuck Berry, Little Richard, and Fats Domino never did.

When Jody Williams was drafted into the service, Bo made a startling decision, perhaps inspired by Mickey & Sylvia, to include women guitarists in his band. The first was Peggy "Lady Bo" Jones (1957–61 and sporadically for decades thereafter), followed by Norma-Jean "The Duchess" Wofford (1962–66), and bassist/band leader Debbie Hastings (1984–2008)—all of whom also recorded—with lead guitarist Jones appearing most prominently. Cornelia "Cookie" Redmond sang backup (1965–73). Not merely "eye candy," they all could really play or sing and added considerably to his music and stage presentation. In 1963, Bo and "The Duchess" made a triumphant tour of the U.K. with the Everly Brothers and Little Richard, though his peak creative years were fading. He would have an especially profound influence on the young Rolling Stones, who opened for him and had yet to break into the U.S. market. As the '60s wore on, his recorded output tapered off even as rock bands covered his songs or appropriated the "Bo Diddley beat" for their own music, including "I Want Candy" (1965) by the Strangeloves and "Magic Bus" (1968) by the Who.

From 1971–78 Bo lived in New Mexico, where he served as a deputy sheriff for two years. In 1972, he performed with the Grateful Dead at the Academy of Music in New York City and saw "Bo Diddley" included on the soundtrack of *Fritz the Cat*. With his reputation still influential in Great Britain, the Clash picked him for their opening act on their 1979 U.S. tour. Stateside, as baby boomers moved into positions of power in film and the media, they began to incorporate the music and the artists from their youth. In 1983, Bo had a small but prominent cameo in *Trading Places*, which starred blues fan Dan Ackroyd. In 1987, he was inducted into the Rock and Roll Hall of Fame, inexplicably being overlooked in the inaugural year (1986), and in 1989, he appeared in a famous Nike ad campaign called "Bo Knows" with baseball and football star Bo Jackson, while also writing the music and playing on the soundtrack to the "Cross Training" ads.

He was filmed in Spain in 1991 for *Legends of Guitar*, which also featured B.B. King, Albert Collins, Les Paul, and George Benson. In 1994, Bo played "Who Do You Love" with the Rolling Stones on a pay-per-view concert broadcast from their *Voodoo Lounge* tour. In 1996, he cut his last album, the surprisingly bluesy *A Man Amongst Men* (#8, Blues Albums). The recording was produced by famed British blues producer Mike Vernon and featured Debbie Hastings and a wide range of guest artists—everyone from Billy Boy Arnold to Johnny "Guitar" Watson, Keith Richards, Ron Wood, and Richie Sambora. Bo appeared as a band member with B.B. King and Eric Clapton in *Blues Brothers 2000*. With an indomitable will and a strong constitution, he was still going strong in 2005 and celebrated his 50th anniversary in music with a world tour. The following year, he played at the 20th anniversary of the Rock and Roll Hall of Fame.

Bo Diddley died of heart failure in his home in Florida on June 2, 2008. He was 79. The outpouring of affection and respect for him was worldwide, with previous acknowledgment of his cultural contribution having even come from a member of the House of Representatives in 2003. As one of the true pioneers of rock 'n' roll, Bo clearly earned the title "The Originator."

THE GUITAR STYLE OF BO DIDDLEY

Bo Diddley regularly tuned to open E (E–B–E–G♯–B–E, low to high), known as "Sebastopol" when in open D (one step lower), and to open G (D–G–D–G–B–D, low to high), referred to as "Spanish tuning." However, it is easier and more practical for most guitarists to perform his music in standard tuning, as the secret to his unique, revolutionary rock 'n' roll style is in the right-hand rhythms. Case in point is the following four-measure example, which features only an open-position E major chord and the signature "Bo Diddley beat," driven by subtle rhythmic syncopation.

Performance Tip: Of paramount importance are the muted strings, which are best accessed by releasing pressure with the fret hand while allowing the tips of the fingers to remain in contact with the strings.

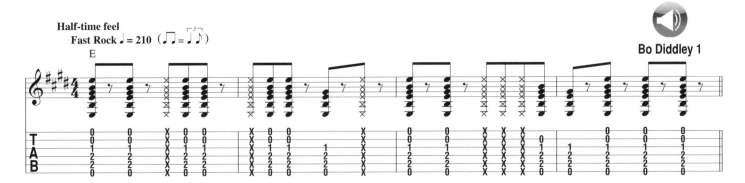

Though not quite as well-known as his classic tracks, Bo also composed blues-based songs outside his signature rhythm. The figure below is condensed to show the I (E), IV (A), and V (B) chord changes similar to those contained in one of his 12-bar arrangements, with the V-chord harmony appearing in both measures 9 and 10. Measures 11–12 in the complete progression would repeat the I-chord pattern twice without resolving to the V chord.

Performance Tip: Bo was one of the earliest rock guitarists to exploit some of the sound effects possible with a distorted electric guitar. Measure 4 shows one of his favorite short glisses used to create tension before resolution to the I chord. Play the slides with either the middle or ring finger.

The "Who Do You Love" rhythm has been successfully interpreted in many ways over the years. One version in particular has found favor and is a great crowd pleaser. Similar to patterns that Bo employed in several tunes, the following example utilizes "call and response" dynamically for rhythmic and harmonic variety.

Performance Tip: Start with a downstroke and alternate downstrokes and upstrokes in each measure to make the syncopation "kick."

Bo Diddley 3

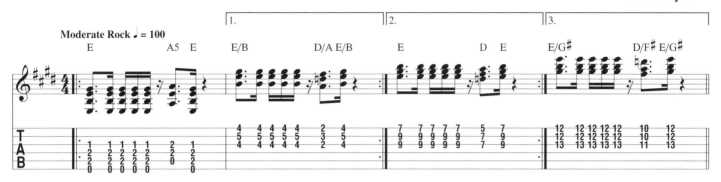

One of Bo's pet chord combinations moves dramatically from the I (A) to the ♭VII (G) and has been appropriated countless times since the '50s. He most often used voicings on the top three strings to cut through the other instruments and because that approach was the most advantageous way to access major chords in open E or open G tunings. In open G, the voicings for A and G (measures 1–2) can be played with an index-finger barre at frets 14 and 12, respectively. However, the standard-tuned voicings function perfectly as stand-ins for open-tuning chords, while allowing for effective variations, as seen in measures 3–4 for the I chord.

Bo Diddley 4

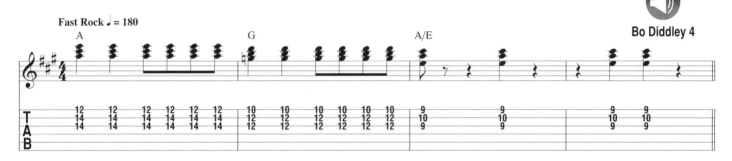

This world-famous riff in 3rds likely has long roots back to the Delta, long before it appeared on record in 1955. Though other musicians have utilized it for I–IV–V changes by moving the riff up the neck in parallel fashion, its primal power is its ability to be repeated endlessly and hypnotically.

Bo Diddley 5

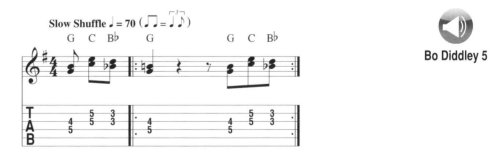

This variation on the previous figure reflects the way the dyads can be voiced in open G tuning and provides another viable alternative using both 3rds and 4ths.

Bo Diddley 6

ERIC CLAPTON
(1945–)

Though he was briefly called "Slowhand" in the Yardbirds due to his propensity for breaking strings in concert, followed by the slow, rhythmic clapping that would emanate from the impatient audience, Eric Clapton has never really needed a nickname. Just as Chet Atkins being called "Mr. Guitar" was redundant for a legend whose given name was enough to bespeak "country guitar," Clapton's is synonymous with blues-rock heroics. With the blues as his constant "rider," he has gone from mod London in the swinging '60s to sunny Miami in the laidback '70s, from intense, private woodshedding on the electric guitar following his stint with the Yardbirds to the very public display of his acoustic chops on MTV. Compared to the other great guitarists of his generation, Clapton's many accomplishments, stature, and sheer longevity are nothing short of remarkable, with the legions of guitarists that he has personally inspired second to none.

Eric Patrick Clapton was born on March 30, 1945, in his grandparent's home in Ripley, in Surrey, England. His 16-year-old mother, Patricia Molly Clapton, had an affair with Edward Walter Fryer, a 24-year-old Canadian soldier stationed in England, and Eric ended up being raised by his mother's parents, Jack and Rose Clapp. Rose had conceived Patricia with her first husband, Reginald Cecil Clapton. She played piano while Jack and an uncle were big-band fans. Fryer, who sometimes played piano professionally, had returned to his wife back in Canada before his illegitimate son was born, and Patricia Clapton would go on to meet and marry another Canadian soldier, Frank McDonald, following him and his career to Canada and Germany. Young Eric grew up with the illusion that his grandparents were his parents, despite the difference in his and their last names. When he was nine, Patricia, whom he had been brought up to think of as his older sister, returned to England for a visit with Eric's half-brother Brian. The shock of the revelation as to her true relationship to him would change the good, polite, and artistically inclined student into a withdrawn child with a loss of identity.

His grades suffered and he was shuttled from school to school, including the Holyfield Road School for art. In 1961, he entered the Kingston College of Art to study the art of making stained glass, but was expelled after only two months for playing his guitar in class. His interest in the blues, R&B, and rock 'n' roll had become an all-consuming passion. In 1958, he had asked for a guitar for this 13th birthday upon hearing an album by Big Bill Broonzy and his discovery of the rock 'n' roll of Chuck Berry and Bo Diddley. Finding that it took too much effort to play the steel-string acoustic with which he was presented, however, he put it down until he began college and his grandparents helped finance a Kay copy of the Gibson ES-335. Ever the student of American roots music, he became obsessed with the acoustic country blues of Robert Johnson, Blind Boy Fuller, Son House, Skip James, Blind Lemon Jefferson, and then the electric stylings of Muddy Waters, Buddy Guy, and the three Kings—B.B., Albert, and Freddie.

Flush with some proficiency, Clapton formed the Roosters with future Rolling Stones guitarist Brian Jones and future Manfred Mann members Tom McGuinness and Paul Jones. Within two months, however, the Roosters were history and Clapton had joined Casey Jones and the Engineers, a Mersey beat band from Liverpool. In a move that would be repeated over and over throughout his career, he left the "pop" group after two weeks, as they offended his purist sensibilities. Meanwhile, the Rolling Stones, with ex-Rooster Brian Jones, had out-grown their local gig at the Crawdaddy Club in Richmond by 1963, leaving a void to fill for the up-and-coming Yardbirds. The Y-Birds had just axed their lead guitarist, Anthony "Top" Topham, and tapped Clapton for the post in October. By that time, Clapton had a style based on a variety of sources, including Chuck Berry and the West Side of Chicago blues of Otis Rush, Magic Sam, and Buddy Guy. Short, stinging phrases, often beginning with a spiky bend, flowed from his Telecaster. Though not yet 20 years old, he already had a smooth, sensuous vibrato that would elicit praise from B.B. King (the inspiration) and Free's Paul Kossoff (the inspired, whom Clapton once asked

Eric Clapton performing at Hammersmith Odeon in London on June 8, 1988.

(Photo by Ebet Roberts/Cache Agency)

in response to *his* rapid vibrato, "How do you do that?"). When the Yardbirds backed up Sonny Boy Williamson in 1963, Clapton backpedaled to T-Bone Walker for a role model, though Sonny Boy would probably have wished to hear something more along the lines of his illustrious sidemen at Chess Records, the muscular and swinging Robert Junior Lockwood or the ripping Luther Tucker.

Though Clapton got to flash his hard-won blues licks on Chicago-style numbers like Billy Boy Arnold's "I Ain't Got You" and the original instrumental "Got to Hurry," Yardbirds lead singer Keith Relf had his eye on the "pop" prize. In March 1965, after just 18 months, Clapton was gone, just as the band was hitting the charts with "For Your Love." With his reputation growing among London's underground blues community, however, a month later he was asked to join John Mayall's Bluesbreakers and history was made. Concurrent with the gig was a paradigm change of instruments. While the trebly Tele had served him well in evoking the bright and reverbed West Side sound, he now played a sunburst 1960 Les Paul Standard with PAF humbucking pickups. In perhaps a happy accident, Clapton thought he was emulating Freddie King, who in the 1950s had actually wielded a circa 1955 Les Paul Goldtop with single-coil P-90 pickups. When Clapton mated the 'burst to a 1965 Marshall JTM 45 combo amp with two 12-inch speakers, the fatter, warmer, higher output 'buckers helped create a sound that rocked the guitar world. The result was almost magical as a thick, singing lead sound thrilled fans and fellow guitarists alike. Along with Mike Bloomfield back in the States, who was making a similar discovery with his "Lester," Clapton set in motion a demand for "old" Les Paul guitars that would eventually mutate into the vintage guitar market. In addition, though traditional blues guitarists were not as turned on to the LP/Marshall combination, rock guitarists dug the raw vibe and a whole musical trend would spring out of it in the '70s.

The power and glory unleashed on *John Mayall and the Bluesbreakers featuring Eric Clapton* in 1965 established him as a bona fide guitar hero of major proportions and convinced many a young, aspiring blues guitarist to approach their instrument with more aggression. His take on "All Your Love (I Miss Loving)" by Otis Rush displayed the same serpentine lines that would ignite envy in countless budding string benders, while "Ramblin' on My Mind" gave the guitarist a chance to play *and* sing the Robert Johnson classic his own way. Such was the feverish pitch of adulation for him that fans began scrawling "Clapton is God" graffiti on walls and buildings in old London town that would come to haunt him. Though he always bemoaned that kind of idolatry, he did nothing to discourage it with his next project. In June of 1966, a casual event occurred that would shift the rock world on its axis. Drummer Ginger Baker sat in with Mayall's band, joining the recently hired bassist Jack Bruce in the rhythm section. Clapton had a musical epiphany and asked Bruce and Baker to follow his "lead" in forming the heavy blues-rock power trio Cream, which contained the "world's greatest guitarist, bassist and drummer." With their voluminous Marshall stacks, lengthy (some would say self-indulgent) onstage jams, and cocksure attitude, they gave everyone on both sides of the Atlantic Ocean the opportunity to hear one of the guitar's most enduring "voices" when *Fresh Cream* was released in December. Retiring the Les Paul Standard (though he manhandled a black Custom in the studio), Clapton now flaunted a cherry-red 1963 ES-335, a psychedelic, rainbow-painted Gibson SG, a Les Paul Special (with P-90s), and even a Gibson Firebird.

Besides giving him room to stretch his improvisations beyond the natural boundaries governed by the traditional 12-bar blues format *and* John Mayall's orthodoxy, being in Cream compelled him to develop his rhythm chops. Of course, a critical jab from Jimi Hendrix—that Clapton "did not play rhythm guitar"—also helped to convince him to expand his vocabulary beyond basic open and barre chords. Despite the delirious reception of the fans (and record company execs who loved the infusion of cash that they brought), Cream was together for only three years and three classic albums of burning blues-rock riffing, though it was way longer than any other Clapton band before or since. The group collapsed under the weight of its own hype and the competing egos engendered by three full-time "soloists," and "gave up the ghost" in 1969. Jumping from the proverbial frying pan into the fire, however, Clapton allowed himself to be seduced into forming another "supergroup," Blind Faith (how ironic a name!), with Steve Winwood, Ginger Baker, and bassist Rick Grech from Family. Their one self-titled LP from 1970 had some tantalizing moments and signaled Clapton's continuing desire to expand his horizons beyond the blues. For example, the folk rock of "Can't Find My Way Home," a nylon-string guitar duet with Winwood, can now be seen as the seed for the MTV *Unplugged* session some 20 years off. Before the year was out, "blind faith" was not enough to keep the super egos from clashing. Blind Faith broke up after a pressure-filled, sold-out American tour, and Clapton deserted, taking yet another career turn and recording his first solo album. Bereft of blues and guitar heroics (to the utter dismay of many fans), the album nonetheless showed his developing vocal chops and songwriting ability, including "Let It Rain," a composition that would foreshadow the epic "Layla" two years hence. Produced by southern rocker Delaney Bramlett, the album also contained the American musicians who would become the Dominos behind "Derek." As an interim step, though, Clapton went on the road and recorded with Delaney and his wife, Bonnie, in a loose aggregation known as Delaney & Bonnie and Friends. Not insignificantly, Clapton had made a seismic guitar switch, moving to the Strat, which was reflected in his thinner, brighter sound.

In that busy and seminal year of 1970, the now "solo" Clapton put together Derek & the Dominos. Their one studio album, the monumental *Layla and Other Assorted Love Songs*, was a thinly disguised (thanks to the gossip in the rock press), bittersweet valentine that sprung from his unrequited (at the time) love for Patti Harrison, the wife of his good buddy George. It also provided the opportunity for Clapton to meet and become friends with Duane Allman, who shared drugs and swapped epic solos (and contributed the signature rhythm riff to "Layla") on the unparalleled artistic highpoint of Clapton's career. Again, Clapton failed to hold a band together. After a live album and an unsuccessful attempt to record a follow-up studio album, the Dominos fell apart. Crushed by the commercial failure (at the time) of *Layla* and nursing a broken heart while he carried a flame for Patti Harrison (whom he would marry in 1979 and divorce in 1988), Clapton descended into isolation and the living hell of heroin addiction for the next three years. Going so far as to sell his guitars to finance his habit, he still managed to record demo tapes at his country estate and was lured back into performing again by Pete Townshend in 1973, at the Rainbow Theater in London. A year later, he went to Miami, Florida, and tracked the #1 charting *461 Ocean Boulevard*, with the #1 single, reggae legend Bob Marley's "I Shot the Sheriff," debuting his new, clean, streamlined Southern sound and his new addiction, alcohol. Struggling with the disease that negatively affected his music and life for almost a decade, he was hospitalized for ulcers from excessive consumption of brandy and painkillers, finally getting straight in 1982 after controversial electro-acupuncture treatment suggested by Townshend. Clapton toured and recorded with regularity and, while no longer the stone bluesman of yore, the live *E.C. Was Here* (1975) *was* a thrilling slice of the old Slowhand. It literally burst with long, spectacular blues solos fueled by thick, Gibson humbucker distortion, though he would quickly return to his new main squeeze, the ubiquitous Fender Stratocaster. In 1985, he was a big hit at *Live Aid*, adding to his loyal fan base a new, younger, pop/rock-oriented audience.

In a cruel twist in which blues clichés about suffering become reality, tragedy entered Clapton's life in a big way in the '90s. In August of 1990, Stevie Ray Vaughan and members of Clapton's road crew died in a helicopter crash following a gig in the midst of an all-star tour that also featured Buddy Guy and Robert Cray. Then, in March of 1991, Clapton's five-year-old son, Conor, died after falling out of a window at an apartment building in Manhattan. Fortunately, rather than turning to substance abuse for solace, Clapton turned his grief into the Grammy-winning "Tears in Heaven," which appeared on the Grammy-winning, #1 album *Unplugged*. More importantly, for his mental health and his legacy, in 1994 he finally recorded the all-blues album for which fans had been waiting an eternity. The #1 *From the Cradle*, though conservative by the standards that virtuoso Stevie Ray Vaughan and his followers had established, was a loving tribute to his blues heroes, containing classics by Freddie King, Muddy Waters, Elmore James, Charles Brown, Lowell Fulson, and others.

In 1998, the Grammy-winning *Pilgrim* was his first album of new material in nine years and again showed the pop side of his personality that has warred uneasily with his bluesman's soul since the Yardbirds. In between, however, he realized another long-held goal when he recorded the #1 *Riding with the King* (2000) with B.B. King. A stunning commercial success with generally positive reviews, it proved once again the rap on Clapton—that he often needed a little competition to bring out his best, whether it be from Steve Winwood, Duane Allman, Albert Lee, or "the King" himself.

Not slowing down as he entered the 21st century, lest the "hellhounds" catch him, Clapton released the pop-flavored *Reptile* in 2001 and immersed himself in a number of worthy projects. In 2002, he was the musical director for a tribute concert in honor of George Harrison, who had died the previous year. He released CDs and DVDs in 2004 covering the music of his legendary guitar hero, Robert Johnson. It was also the year that he convened his first *Crossroads Guitar Festival* (followed by ones in 2007, 2010, and 2014) featuring many of the greatest rock, blues, and pop guitarists, to benefit his Crossroads Centre, a drug treatment facility in Antigua. In 2005, after a wait of nearly 40 years by his loyal fans, he finally agreed to reunite with Jack Bruce and Ginger Baker for a series of Cream concerts in London and the U.S. While the British shows had some memorable moments, by the time the band arrived in New York City to play three nights at Madison Square Garden, it became clear that Clapton was nowhere near as dedicated to the project as Bruce and Baker, and he gave uninspired, perfunctory performances. A new album of original material, *Back Home*, was also released in 2005. The following year, he commenced a productive relationship with Derek Trucks that resulted in a world tour, as well as the record *The Road to Escondido*, which featured one of his idols, J.J. Cale. In 2007, he released his self-titled autobiography and also found out detailed information about his father, the absence of which had bothered him for most of his life.

Continuing to reconnect with former musical comrades, in 2008, Clapton performed and recorded a double-set with Steve Winwood at Madison Square Garden, played on Winwood's *Nine Lives*, and joined him for a U.S. tour in 2009. He also guested with the Allman Brothers at their 40th anniversary gig at the Beacon Theater in New York City and then sat in with young American bluesman Joe Bonamassa at the Royal Albert Hall in London. In 2010, he headlined in London with Jeff Beck as his opening act and then at Madison Square Garden, followed by a short U.S. tour. In a great treat for guitarists and guitar fans, some musical sparks flew when the two jammed the blues after each solo performance. The year 2010 would prove a busy year for Clapton, as he went on an extended U.S. tour with Roger Daltrey as his opening act. He then went back out with Winwood and, after his third *Crossroads Festival*, released *Clapton* at the end of the year, hitting #1 on the Top Rock Albums chart. The album contained an exceptionally diverse selection of cover tunes, including ones by Fats Waller, Hoagy Carmichael, and Irving Berlin, as well as Little Walter, Rev. Robert Wilkins, and J.J. Cale. It also featured a wider range of guest artists than one would normally encounter on a Clapton album, with Cale, Sheryl Crow, Allen Toussaint, and jazz trumpeter Wynton Marsalis contributing their various talents. At the end of the year, Clapton appeared at the charitable *Prince's Trust* rock gala at the Royal Albert Hall. In 2011, he performed in Italy with Italian world-music artist Pino Daniele and then played a unique and historic two nights at Lincoln Center in New York City with Wynton Marsalis, resulting in *Play the Blues: Live from Jazz at Lincoln Center*.

In a class by himself, Eric Clapton, the sometimes reluctant blues guitar hero and suave, Armani-suited pop star, is still a major force to be reckoned with after 50 years. As the only triple-inductee into the Rock and Roll Hall of Fame (with the Yardbirds, Cream, and as a solo artist), his immortality is assured in the public arena and in the hearts of guitar lovers everywhere.

THE GUITAR STYLE OF ERIC CLAPTON

One of the most astute observations about Eric Clapton was made by none other than Les Paul, who said: "Every time he solos, he tells a little story." Simply put, it could be described as creating tension, followed by a musical narrative that leads to resolution. With the blues always at the heart of his emotionally expressive phrasing, he begins with a classic unison bend of the root note (E) in the root-octave position of the E minor pentatonic scale. In measure 3, brief resolution to the tonic (E) is a tease until "Slowhand" ends on the major 3rd (G#) on beat 4 of measure 4 to confirm the major tonality of the progression.

Eric Clapton 1

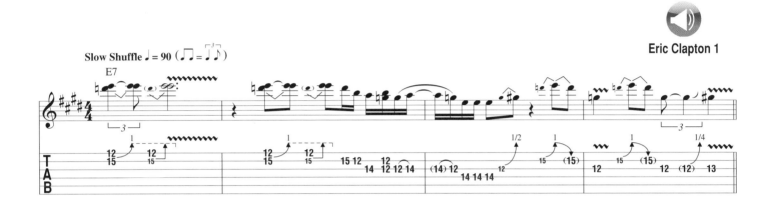

With a figurative tip of his English bowler, Clapton acknowledges his debt to Albert King with a jaunt in the "Albert King box," or upper extension of the minor pentatonic scale. Observe the half-step bend to the major 3rd (C#) in measure 1, followed by the tension-inducing one-and-a-half-step bend to the ♭3rd (C) across the bar line. Slinky vibrato, an E.C. hallmark, on the ♭7th (G) juices the blues vibe in measure 3, along with brief respite on the root (A). Choice bends, including the ear-bending double-string bend on beat 3 of measure 4, resolve neatly to the root on beat 4.

Performance Tip: Clapton and Chuck Berry would likely execute the double-string bend by pushing up with a small ring-finger barre over both strings. However, another option would be to use the ring and pinky fingers, low to high, for a cleaner sound and more control.

Eric Clapton 2

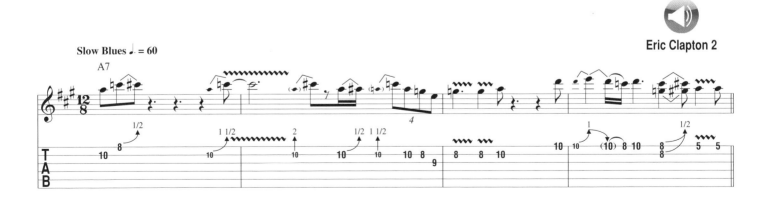

Thanks to the influence of one of his main mentors, B.B. King, Clapton has likewise become skilled at the major pentatonic scale. One of its several advantages is the availability of the major 3rd of the I, IV, and ♭VII chords to conclusively define the major tonality of each. Clapton proves it in measure 1 with the G♯ over the E (I) chord and in measures 2 and 3 with the F♯ over the D (♭VII) chord.

Performance Tip: Keep the long resolution in measure 4 going on the tonic note (E) via vibrato, with the wrist and hand quickly pulling the locked index finger down and returning to pitch.

In measures 1–2, Clapton opts to walk right up the A minor pentatonic scale and establish his key with long, fluid vibrato on the root note (A). However, in measures 3 and 4, he ramps up the energy quotient by pounding the root note in conjunction with the ♭7th (G). Clapton introduces the 5th (E) to his repetitive licks in measure 4 and keeps the tension percolating until resolution is achieved with the root (A) on beat 4.

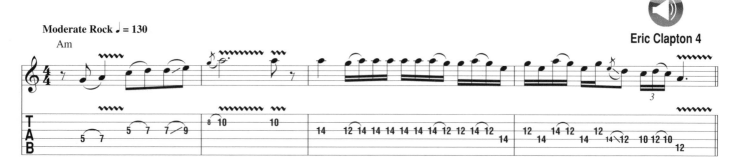

Like his peers, Clapton has resorted to fast, repetitive hammer-on/pull-off patterns to crank up the excitement level. This blues-rock classic utilizes the root (A), ♭7th (G), and 5th (E) from the root-octave position of the A minor pentatonic scale for a bluesy vibe that concludes in measure 2 with a run down the scale. Instead of resolving to the root, however, Clapton chooses to end on the gritty ♭3rd (C) to keep momentum going into the next measure (not shown).

Performance Tip: Barre strings 2–1 at fret 17 with the index finger and access the G note with the ring finger.

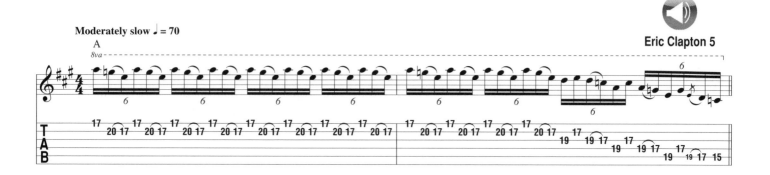

GEORGE HARRISON
(1943–2001)

As the "quiet Beatle," George Harrison contributed more timeless licks and riffs on any one Beatles album compared to what many of his more highly regarded guitar hero peers did in their entire careers. In addition, among his many accomplishments, he introduced the 12-string electric guitar and sitar into popular music. Unfortunately, he was held back by Lennon and McCartney from developing his considerable songwriting skills within the confines of the band, but as a solo artist, he blossomed while further exploring Indian music and engaging in an array of varied projects. Even if he just wrote "Something," a song Frank Sinatra hailed as "the greatest love song of the past 50 years," his legacy would be insured.

George Harrison was born on February 25, 1943, in Liverpool, England, to Harold and Louise, who encouraged him to pursue his interest in music. However, he did not consider playing the guitar until he heard Elvis's "Heartbreak Hotel" in 1956, when he was 13. He would later describe the experience as an "epiphany," as he lost interest in his school work, sat in class drawing guitars, and finally bought a Dutch flattop acoustic. To the consternation of his teachers, he let his hair grow, adopted rocker clothes, and became obsessed with practicing his guitar. Being inspired by Lonnie Donegan and his version of "Rock Island Line," like many of his fellow Brits of the era, he would form a skiffle band called, appropriately, the Rebels. American rock 'n' rollers like Carl Perkins, Duane Eddy, and Eddie Cochran, however, would soon become even more important to his development.

Harrison became friends with Paul McCartney, another guitar player who was a year ahead of him in school and, along with John Lennon, was a member of the Quarrymen. Impressed with his younger friend's growing skills, McCartney had him "audition" for Lennon in 1958 by playing the American rock instrumental "Raunchy" while the three rode on the upper deck of a Liverpool bus. Though it took years for the haughty Lennon to fully accept the "kid" as an equal, Harrison began playing with the Quarrymen on an irregular basis as a fill-in for their several regular lead guitarists. After the group fell apart in early 1959, Harrison began performing with the Les Stewart Quartet and quit school. When a dispute within the quartet occurred and Les Stewart refused to play as promised at the new teen hangout the Casbah Coffee Club, their guitarists, Ken Brown and Harrison, joined Lennon and McCartney as the "new" Quarrymen. The group functioned as the house band for a brief period of time in the early fall, after which Brown was summarily dismissed.

The three remaining members performed as Johnny & the Moondogs for a short stretch just before they headed into 1960, a most significant year in their history. By this time, Harrison was a full-fledged member and the group would go through a succession of name changes from the Quarrymen as their gig schedule expanded. Stu Sutcliffe, a friend of Lennon, who was a better artist than musician, was brought in to play bass and suggested the "Beatals," as he was a fan of Buddy Holly's backing band, the Crickets. Next were the "Silver Beetles" and then the penultimate "Silver Beatles" as they went through a succession of drummers. In August, their unofficial manager, Allan Williams, booked them in Hamburg, Germany and they needed to have a steady drummer in both senses of the word. They fortuitously stopped by the Casbah one night and heard Pete Best, son of the owner, playing with his band, the Blackjacks, who coincidentally were getting ready to break up. He passed his audition with the "Beatles" and was on his way with them across the English Channel within a week.

From August to November, the Beatles played in two different clubs in Hamburg's notorious red light district under daunting conditions. The brutal string of gigs consisted of long, multiple sets daily that sharpened their chops incrementally while the living accommodations were next to squalid and toughened their road chops. Late in their stay, they would alternate sets with Rory Storm and the Hurricanes, whose drummer was one Ringo Starr. For the 17-year-old Harrison, it was a rite of passage like few others, as he was exposed to hookers, pimps, and transvestites and the rough trade that patronized them, along with gangsters and other lowlifes. Eventually, his youth would undo the Beatles' German excursion, as he was deported for being underage. When McCartney and Best set fire to a condom in their room, they were accused of arson and were likewise sent home, as was Lennon. Sutcliffe opted to stay behind since he had fallen in love with German photographer Astrid Kirchherr, and he did not return to Liverpool until early 1961, during which time a substitute bassist was employed.

The Beatles would return to Hamburg three more times, resulting in their first recordings as a backup band for Tony Sheridan. Lennon, McCartney, and Harrison improved dramatically, which was made startlingly evident to Liverpudlians each time they returned to England. After the second trip, Sutcliffe quit so he could stay in Hamburg with Kirchherr and pursue his art career, resulting in McCartney reluctantly taking over on bass. Upon arrival for their third excursion, in April of 1962, they were informed that Sutcliffe had died of a brain hemorrhage—news that hit Lennon hard. The Beatles fourth and final "apprenticeship" in Hamburg was in November, by which time Ringo Starr was playing drums and Brian Epstein was their new manager, having taken them on in 1961 after seeing them at the Cavern Club in Liverpool where they were creating a sensation. More importantly, he secured a contract for the group with EMI/Parlophone in the summer of 1962. Following their first recording sessions, producer George Martin suggested that they sack Pete Best in what still remains a controversial move, and Starr was hired. Shortly thereafter, in September, they recorded "Love Me Do" b/w "P.S. I Love You"—ironically, with session drummer Andy White sitting in at Martin's insistence. It reached #17 in the U.K. and was followed by "Please Please Me" (#2, 1963) and an album with the same name recorded in one day (#1, 1963). "From Me to You" and "She Loves You" likewise zoomed to the top of the U.K. charts, as would 13 others through to 1969. "Beatlemania" was sweeping the U.K. and Europe as the band toured and appeared to screaming fans on numerous TV shows.

With the Beatles (#1) was released prior to the single "I Want to Hold Your Hand" (#1) in late 1963 in hopes it would break them in the U.S., as the previous singles had not been enthusiastically received in the States. When a *New York Times* music critic began taking the band seriously and lauding them in a series of articles, the groundwork was laid for their first trip to the U.S. in February 1964. In a heretofore unseen "harmonic convergence," the baby boomer youth were totally primed for a musical "British Invasion." A national trauma had followed the assassination of JFK in November of 1963, and the pop music scene, save for Motown and soul music, had been in the doldrums for years. The "Fab Four" took '50s American rock 'n' roll and transformed it into their own image. Along with their trend-setting "mop top" haircuts and cheeky, irreverent humor, it was just what the emerging counterculture needed for a soundtrack to their coming revolution. Another plus was the fact that the older generation hated and feared the Beatles.

From 1963–70, Harrison would contribute immeasurably to the language of rock music with his creativity and choice of instruments in the Beatles. His "Don't Bother Me," from *With the Beatles* (*Meet the Beatles* in the U.S.), revealed a subtle, melancholy tinge as a preview of things to come, and his jazzy nylon-string solo on "Till There Was You" showed musical sophistication beyond his years. Lennon's "You Can't Do That," from *The Beatles' Second Album*, contains what may be the first use of a funky 7#9 chord in pop music, a chord that shows up again on "Tax Man," from *Revolver*. Harrison introduced the Rickenbacker electric 12-string guitar to popular music on "A Hard Day's Night," which profoundly inspired Roger McGuinn of the Byrds. In addition, the opening Gsus2 chord would baffle guitarists for years. His 12-string would likewise appear on "Ticket to Ride" (#1). *Rubber Soul* would be a step forward as a showcase for his talents, particularly the sitar on "Norwegian Wood" and his compositions "Think for Yourself," featuring innovative fuzz-tone lines, and "If I Needed Someone," with its jangly 12-string. On *Revolver*, a landmark recording both sonically and compositionally, Harrison would indulge his musical curiosity on three tunes, including

George Harrison of the Beatles, circa 1965.

(Photo Courtesy CEA/Cache Agency)

"Love You To," with sitar and tabla drums that revealed his growing interest in Indian music and Hinduism. He continued in the breakaway direction on the monumental, genre-busting *Sgt. Pepper*, with his "Within You, Without You" featuring sitar and Indian musicians from London. The soundtrack to the ill-fated TV special *Magical Mystery Tour* contained more classics, as well as Harrison's haunting psychedelic paean to the hippie era, "Blue Jay Way," and only suffered in comparison to its predecessor.

The Beatles had been gradually growing apart for years as the crushing strain of their celebrity—and often competing interests—led to acrimony. The apogee was reached on the *White Album,* which is essentially a sprawling, spectacular two-disc collection of individual tracks recorded by four individuals. Harrison was still only "allowed" two songs per disc, including the epic, dramatic "While My Guitar Gently Weeps," on which Eric Clapton plays the uncredited solo, the novelty "Piggies," the trance-like, devotional "Long Long Long," and the wry R&B dessert fantasy "Savoy Truffle," featuring a fuzzed-out solo. He would be unquestionably vindicated, however, on *Abbey Road*. The last gasp at "getting back to where they once belonged," *Let It Be*, with accompanying documentary graphically showing the tension in the studio, led to Harrison actually quitting the band for two weeks. The album was released last, though *Abbey Road* was actually the last recorded, with "Here Comes the Sun" and "Something" conclusively demonstrating his right to be in the company of Lennon and McCartney, particularly the latter.

It was the literal and symbolic end of an era when the Beatles officially broke up in 1970. Though he had previously released the soundtrack *Wonderwall Music* (#49, 1968) and *Electronic Sound* (1969), the break up would be liberating for Harrison, as a backlog of compositions burst from him and he became involved with numerous musical and film projects. The six-times-platinum *All Things Must Pass* (1970) contained the #1 hit "My Sweet Lord," which would eventually lead to Harrison losing a copyright suit regarding the Chiffons' hit "He's So Fine." The album is considered his finest effort, much as *Layla* is for Eric Clapton. In 1971, Harrison organized the charitable *Concert for Bangladesh* in response to a plea from his friend Ravi Shankar. The hit *Living in the Material World* (#1, 1973), which showcased his guitar playing (especially on slide), was followed by the critically panned, India-centric *Dark Horse* (#4, 1974), an album he recorded following the loss of his wife, Patti Boyd, to his "friend" Clapton and while he was suffering from laryngitis. Likewise, his first solo tour, plagued by his vocal problems, was, to his great embarrassment, slagged by critics and discouraged him from touring the U.S. again. *Thirty Three & 1/3* (#11, 1976) renewed his reputation for melody and songcraft, though *George Harrison* (1979), which followed his marriage to Olivia Trinidad Arias and the birth of their son, Dhani, has been dismissed as slick L.A. pop.

In 1980, Harrison became the only former Beatle to write an autobiography, *I, Me, Mine*. That same year, the murder of John Lennon hit him especially hard, as he had incurred Lennon's wrath by barely mentioning him in the book. However, he rewrote the lyrics to "All Those Years Ago" (#2), from *Somewhere in England* (#11, 1981), as a tribute to the man he claimed to have always looked up to, and both McCartney and Starr joined him on the recording—the closest thing to a Beatles reunion ever. *Gone Troppo* (1982), rushed out to fulfill his contract following previous battles with his record company, seemed to also reflect his distraction with Formula One auto racing and film production and, along with his cocaine habit, is considered the low point of his career. It would be five years before his next record. Nonetheless, he came back swinging with the platinum *Cloud 9* (#8, 1987), which contained a rocking cover of "Got My Mind Set on You" (#1) and his wistful Beatles remembrance, "When We Was Fab" (#23). In 1988, the same year the Beatles were inducted into the Rock and Roll Hall of Fame as charter members, Harrison formed the Traveling Wilburys with Bob Dylan, Roy Orbison, Tom Petty, and his buddy Jeff Lynne from the Electric Light Orchestra. *Vol. 1* (#3) would be one of the highlights of his later years, though the death of Orbison in 1988 seems to have cast a pall over *Vol. 3* (there was no *Vol. 2*), which was released in 1990 and reached #11. In 1992, Harrison became the first recipient of the Billboard Century Award for his significant body of work.

In a belated and token tribute to his main influence, in 1996, Harrison appeared on one track of the Carl Perkins all-star *Go Cat Go*, two years before the pioneering rockabilly star would die. Harrison's last solo album of rock music would be *Brainwashed* (#18, 2001), which was completed posthumously in 2002 by his son Dhani and Jeff Lynne, and featured the Grammy-winning "Marwa Blues." Harrison had died on November 29, 2001, following a long battle with lung cancer, an ironic twist of fate indicative of his personality. His avowed Hinduism and its shunning of the material possessions was in marked opposition to his lavish, English manor lifestyle and multiple worldwide residences. Likewise, continuing to smoke cigarettes while practicing vegetarianism was a curious contradiction. Nonetheless, there is no mistaking his enormous musical contributions with the Beatles and as a solo artist, in addition to his dedication to the guitar as an instrument of profound personal expression. In 2002, Clapton organized the "Concert for George" and, in 2004, Harrison was posthumously inducted into the Rock and Roll Hall of Fame as a solo artist. Martin Scorsese released the bittersweet documentary *Living in the Material World: George Harrison* in 2011.

THE GUITAR STYLE OF GEORGE HARRISON

As opposed to the bluesier British Invasion bands, the Beatles did not feature extended, improvised guitar solos early in their career, even though they had an excellent lead player in George Harrison, not to mention Paul McCartney. Hence, his extraordinary skills at placing tasty, iconic fills were exploited in service to the group. Note how the 4ths, derived from the G blues scale, add a gritty touch to the smooth G6 harmony. The rich, vibrant bass tones emanating from his Gretsch Country Gentleman contributed to the effect.

Performance Tip: Execute the gliss with the ring finger.

George Harrison 1

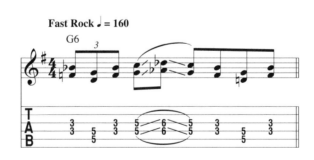

This fill connects the V (D) and VI (E) chords simply and logically with root notes while including the D♯ as a fluid passing tone.

George Harrison 2

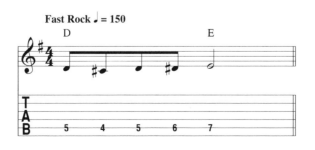

Though definitely nowhere near a blues guitarist like his pal Clapton, Harrison certainly knew the form and would utilize the licks, if not the deep expression for which they stand. Ensconced in the root position of the C minor pentatonic scale in a 12-bar solo, he builds typical bluesy tension and release by repeatedly bending the 4th (F) to the 5th (G) over four measures of the I (C) chord before dynamically dropping down the scale to resolve to the root (C) note on string 6.

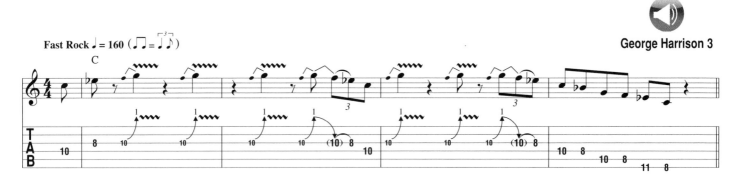

Harrison ably shows how he could "tell a story" like Clapton by skillfully manipulating the root and extension ("Albert King box") positions of the A minor pentatonic scale. With the ♭7th (G) providing anticipation and forward momentum in measures 2 and 4, he creates a self-contained musical statement with a beginning and an end, as well as one that flows to the next section.

The Beatles did not employ as many I–IV vamps in their songs as the Rolling Stones, for example, but when they did, Harrison was ready, willing, and able to navigate them skillfully. Check out his utilization of the ♭7th (G) on the "and" of beat 4 of measure 1 as a musical boost to the IV (D) chord in measure 2. Though he does nick the root (D) briefly in measure 2, his greater goal is forward motion, which is encouraged by emphasis on the 5th (A). In measure 3, over the I (A) chord, he not only dynamically ascends the scale, but resolves to the root with a soaring bend from G to A. In measure 4, he ends his phrase on the ♭7th (C) to encourage movement to the next measure.

Commensurate with his propensity to favor melody over bluesy licks and riffs, Harrison was comfortable in the friendly confines of the major pentatonic scale. Notice how he creates gentle musical tension in the beginning of measure 1 in order to enter his solo with momentum before resolving to the root (C) on the "and" of beat 4. Harrison opts to keep musical tension going in measure 3 by emphasizing the D (2nd) and A (6th) notes in particular, before resolving conclusively to the root (C) in measure 4.

Performance Tip: Bend the D note on beat 1 of measure 3 by pulling *down* with the ring finger, backed by the middle and index fingers, which will also put the hand in an advantageous position to access the C note at fret 3 with the index finger.

George Harrison 6

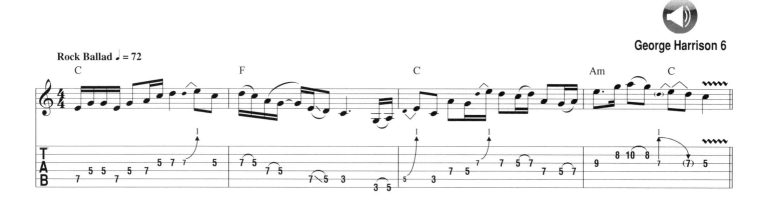

Keith Richards performing with the New Barbarians at Madison Square Garden in New York City on May 7, 1979.

(Photo by Ebet Roberts/Cache Agency)

KEITH RICHARDS
(1943–)

Chuck Berry in the '50s and Keith Richards in the '60s: two of the most influential rock guitarists of their respective eras, masters of rhythm and the riff, and stone blues players. Not coincidentally, Richards is Berry's No. 1 acolyte and his greatest fan. As the Rolling Stones developed within the British blues scene in London in the early '60s, Richards looked beyond the postwar electric legends for his muse. Instead, he went directly to the deep Delta blues of Muddy Waters, where the *groove* and *feel* is the deal, as opposed to the instrumental virtuosity that Clapton, Green, Beck, and Page sought in the three Kings, in addition to Otis Rush and Buddy Guy. In the process, Richards invented a unique style of "team" guitar playing with Brian Jones, Mick Taylor, and for over 35 years, Ron Wood. Based on the "telepathic" rhythmic interplay of Muddy and Jimmy Rogers in the classic Waters band of the early '50s, it has been the spawning ground for countless blues-inflected riffs, inspiring countless followers. As many people consider Richards to be the heart of the Rolling Stones, their story is his story.

Keith Richards was an only child, born on December 18, 1943, in Dartford, Kent, England, to Bertrand and Doris Richards. When he was less than a year old, with his father away in the army, he and his mum had to be evacuated from their home due to Nazi bombing during the waning years of WWII. Upon their return after the war, they found it demolished and had to find a new residence. In 1948, Richards went to Westhill Infants School and enjoyed playing football (rugby) with his father, as well as going on outings to the Isle of Wight. From the beginning, he was apathetic about school, though he liked drawing and painting, along with history and English. Saturday morning movies really held his interest, however, especially American westerns. Roy Rogers was a particular favorite; he wanted to be just like him and play the guitar. In 1951, he went to Wentworth Junior County Primary School, where he met Mick Jagger for the first time. Jagger shared Richard's interest in the guitar, but not in Roy Rogers.

Richard's maternal grandfather, Gus Dupree, played guitar, fiddle, saxophone, and piano and when the young Richards went to visit him, he was always drawn to the guitar. Finally, in 1958 for his 15th birthday, his mother bought him a cheap acoustic on the condition that he actually "play it." His grandfather obliged by teaching him a few chords. By 1959, he was listening to Little Richard and playing hooky from school, with the poolroom his hangout of choice. A year later, he was asked to leave school due to truancy, but the headmaster took sympathy on the rebellious youth and enrolled him in Sidcup Art School to study advertising. At Sidcup, Richards met Dick Taylor, who played guitar with Jagger in an amateur R&B band. Unbeknownst to Jagger, Richards and Taylor started playing together in a C&W band and Richards bought his first little amp to electrify his guitar.

In 1961, Jagger started attending the London School of Economics while Richards was still at Sidcup, and the two happened to meet by accident at the Dartford Railway Station one day and renewed their friendship. In what has become part of the lore of the Stones, the two talked about the Chuck Berry and imported R&B records that Jagger had with him and made plans to get together again to listen to each other's record collection. On the following occasion, they realized that Dick Taylor was a mutual acquaintance and the fateful decision was made for the three to join together in a band. Richards acquired a Hofner electric, and when Jagger heard him and Taylor play, he decided to move away from the guitar and concentrate on his singing and blues harp playing instead. Taylor switched to drums, Bob Beckwith shared guitar duties with Richards on a tiny, six-watt amp, and Allen Etherington shook the maracas. They played Chuck Berry and Jimmy Reed tunes and called themselves Little Boy Blue and the Blue Boys. Band members would come and go, but Richards and Jagger always remained as the core of the group.

In the spring of 1962, Jagger and his boys went to Ealing, outside of London, to see Cyril Davies and Alexis Korner's Blues Incorporated at the Ealing Blues Club (formerly the Ealing Jazz Club). Brian Jones, who had been playing guitar with Paul Pond (later Paul Jones, leader of Manfred Mann), had been sitting in regularly and on this occasion played "Dust My Broom." Jones, who had taken to calling himself "Elmo Lewis" in tribute to his idol, Elmore James, is credited with being one of the first to play electric slide guitar in England, and he certainly impressed Richards and Jagger. After the show, Jagger spoke to Jones and informed him that he was planning to start a band. In the meantime, Jagger sent a tape of his band to Korner. He was promptly invited to join Blues Incorporated, which included drummer Charlie Watts and bassist Jack Bruce, for gigs in Ealing and at the Marquee Club in London. Concurrently, he still practiced regularly with Richards and Taylor.

Jones put an ad in *Jazz News* looking for musicians to join his R&B band, and piano player Ian Stewart responded first. Geoff Bradford, a respected and excellent "pure" blues guitarist who was also into Elmore James, Muddy Waters, and John Lee Hooker, was personally invited into the group. In the summer of 1962, Jagger attended one of Jones' rehearsals and then started bringing Richards and Taylor along for twice-weekly sessions. However, Bradford left when the band began playing Chuck Berry and Bo Diddley covers and straight-ahead Chicago blues. Mick Avory, later of the Kinks, filled in on drums and in July, the band, now dubbed the "*Rollin'* Stones" by Jones, got their first big break when they subbed for Blues Incorporated at the Marquee Club, followed by engagements at the Ealing Blues Club. (*Note:* Dave Godin, a friend of Jagger's, told Bill Wyman that the name came from "Mannish Boy," in which Muddy sings, "Ooh, I'm a rollin' stone," not from the single of the same name from 1950.) It was Jones' band from the beginning and he exercised his authority for years until his self-destructive and bizarre nature caused his rapid decline and Jagger maneuvered into position.

Meanwhile, Richards graduated from Sidcup Art School and the Stones needed a permanent drummer as they scuffled. In the late summer of 1962, Jagger and Jones moved into a flat in Chelsea together and were joined shortly thereafter by Richards. Discouraged with their lack of gigs and progress, they decided to give it one more year to pan out, even as Jones unsuccessfully tried to replace interim drummer Tony Chapman (late of the Cliftons, Bill Wyman's group) with Charlie Watts from Blues Incorporated. Drummer Carlo Little, who played with Screaming Lord Sutch, and bassist Ricky Fensen were often called upon for rhythm-section duties, but mainly the Stones just rehearsed and listened to records, though an underground buzz about their sound was developing without their knowledge. In the fall, the band played a gig without a drummer and, not long after, Taylor left to finish his studies at the Royal College of Art. The split was amicable and Taylor would go on to play in the Pretty Things and achieve a measure of success.

With the Stones in need of a bass player and a permanent drummer who satisfied them, Chapman, the good sport (!), approached Bill Wyman (whose real name was Bill Perks), his old bandmate from the Cliftons, in December of 1962 about auditioning. Apparently, the group was not impressed with Wyman's lack of blues experience, though they were keen on his substantially more professional equipment. In addition, Wyman felt that the Stones could not survive "playing 12-bar blues all night." After a few more rehearsals, however, he threw in with the group and played his first gig on December 14 at the Ricky Tick Club in Windsor.

The year 1963 began as 1962 had ended: with the Stones still struggling for gigs and Richards, Jagger, and Jones literally starving in their Chelsea digs. Charlie Watts was approached again and basically told that he was in the band whether he liked it or not. Despite his major reservations about them making a go of it, he was coming around to R&B music, as opposed to the swing jazz that was his great love, and he went along with their request. On January 12, Jagger, Jones, Richards, Ian Stewart (piano), Wyman, and Watts played their inaugural gig together. (*Note:* The name went back and forth between "Rollin'" and "Rolling" for some time for apparently no rhyme or reason.) They continued to work regularly for the same low wages, but a type of snobbish blackballing occurred, as the "Jazz Mafia," Chris Barber and Cyril Davies, thought they were "too poppy" and "inauthentic," thereby costing them gigs at the Marquee and the Flamingo. At the end of January, though, the band received a reply from the BBC concerning their application for an audition in April for the "Beeb's" *Jazz Club* show.

Two important contacts at this time were Giorgio Gomelsky, an influential promoter and club owner, and Glyn Johns, an engineer at IBC Studios who encouraged the Stones to record a demo tape. Gomelsky provided more and better-paying gigs and Johns set up a recording date for March. The Stones recorded Bo Diddley's "Road Runner" and "Diddley Daddy," Muddy Waters' "I Want to Be Loved," and Jimmy Reed's "Honey What's Wrong" and "Bright Lights, Big City." Jones was proud of the results and especially happy that they were able to capture the Jimmy Reed sound so authentically, an unheard of concept in England at that time. An IBC exec shopped the tape around to a half-dozen labels, but it was uniformly turned down for not being commercial enough. The Stones were discouraged, but on the upside, a real blues scene was developing around them, with more bands and an audience receptive to the wild, sensual energy that emanated from the aggressive way the music was being interpreted. Their gigs increased in frequency as the crowds increased in number and enthusiasm. A steady engagement at Giorgio Gomelsky's Crawdaddy Club in Richmond got them a sizeable review in a local paper and would prove a major stepping stone. Another major move would be the acquisition of 19-year-old Andrew Loog Oldham as the Stones' manager.

Oldham's limited experience was in pop PR, but he immediately got what the Stones were about: sexual energy that made them both dangerous and alluring. A three-year contract was signed. The next thing Oldham did was insist that the burly Stewart stop performing live with the band—"six faces were too many for the fans to remember"—and become the road manager while only playing in the studio. On May 10, the Stones cut their first single, Chuck Berry's "Come On" b/w "I Want to Be Loved." Later in the month, they found out that they had failed the April 24 audition for the BBC show, which was performed with Carlo Little and Ricky Brown subbing for Watts and Wyman, who still had day gigs. The BBC felt the singer sounded "too black," but *were* interested in having the band back touring U.S. acts on the radio, an offer that was laughingly ignored. On May 14, however, Oldham met with Decca Records and quickly released "Come On" on June 7. Though the recording had also been rushed and the Stones were so unhappy with it that they fought with Oldham over playing it live, it differentiated them from the Mersey Beat's pop sound, which was becoming the "mod" rage courtesy of the Beatles and other British acts.

The single only reached #26 in the U.K., but positive press was starting to build. In August, the Stones made the first of 20 appearances on the influential and popular *Ready, Steady, Go!* TV show while breaking attendance records at the Crawdaddy Club and virtually everywhere else they appeared. Jones' somewhat erratic behavior and incredibly bad leadership (he had considered letting Jagger go at one point, as well as replacing Wyman and Watts) encouraged Oldham to consolidate his position of power. At the end of September, the Stones were excited to be booked on a 30-date tour with the Everly Brothers, Bo Diddley, and Little Richard. Diddley was so impressed with *them* ("Brian was the only white cat that got my rhythm") that he wanted them to back him up on tour, which they respectfully declined. On October 7, they went back in the studio to record Lennon and McCartney's "I Wanna Be Your Man" b/w "Stoned," which reached #12 on the U.K. charts. In an ironic payback for the generous "gift" of the composition, the Stones began outdrawing the Beatles at some venues. At the same time, they took something else from the "Fab Four": the revolutionary idea of taking a side trip from their cherished blues and writing original material.

The next year (1964), the growing madness continued with screaming girls, a brutal round of sold-out shows, and hyper press that either loved or hated them. The long hair was an issue, as was the "bad boy" image brilliantly cultivated by Oldham. A sign of things to come was the recording of the first Jagger/Richards original composition, "Will You Be My Lover Tonight" b/w "It Should Be You." More significantly, however, was the January recording of Buddy Holly's "Not Fade Away" b/w the original "Little by Little." In May, it became their first U.S. single and, with "I Wanna Be Your Man" as the flip side, it made a respectable showing (#48). In February, the Stones recorded their first self-titled LP, which mostly consisted of blues and R&B covers and reached #1 in the U.K., edging out the Beatles and remaining on the charts for 51 weeks. In May, it was released in the U.S. where it hit #12. That same month, they tried to meet their idol, Chuck Berry, when he toured the British Isles with Carl Perkins, but were inexplicably blown off. In June, the first Jagger/Richards original song to get into the U.K. Top 10, "As Tears Go By" (as recorded by Marianne Faithful), was released.

In June of 1964, the Stones made their first, epochal cross-country tour to the United States, where they were met with a combination of hysteria, shock and, in some cases, ignorant American behavior about their hair and dress. The highlight for the band had to be going to Chess Records in Chicago and recording what would be their second album. Bobby Womack's "It's All Over Now" (with the infamous line "half-assed games" that radio stations regularly censored) b/w the original "Good Times, Bad Times" was cut and released as a single, reaching #1 in England and #26 in the U.S. In addition to meeting Buddy Guy and Willie Dixon, as well as a friendlier (!) Chuck Berry the second time around, they got the thrill of their lives when Muddy Waters helped carry in their equipment for the session and later coolly said of Jones: "That guitar player ain't bad."

In August, the Stones' *Five by Five* EP was released and climbed to #1 in the U.K. Irma Thomas' "Time Is on My Side" b/w the original "Congratulations" rose to #6 in the U.S. after a September release and featured Keith's best Chicago blues guitar solo to date. *12 X 5,* an expanded *Five by Five*, was put out as an album in the U.S. only and exemplified the Stones' ever-growing popularity by going all the way to #3. In November, they reached back to their ever-present blues roots with the Willie Dixon-penned Howlin' Wolf classic "Little Red Rooster" b/w the original "Off the Hook," which promptly strutted to #1 in the U.K. On a tremendous roll, they also released their best original to date, "Heart of Stone" b/w "What a Shame," and watched it rise to #19 in the U.S.

The Rolling Stones No. 2, a collection of mostly R&B covers, began the pivotal year of 1965 by easily reaching #1 in the U.K. Their third American album, *The Rolling Stones, Now!*, a mix of tunes from the previous U.K. album and other covers, scampered up the charts to #5 after a February release date. Later that same month, "The Last Time" b/w "Play with Fire" arrived containing Richards' and the Stones' catchiest riff to date, reaching #1 in the U.K. and #9 in the U.S. Though both tunes were credited to the up-and-coming songwriting team of Jagger/Richards, the A-side was actually based on "This May Be the Last Time" (1955) by the Staple Singers. In May however, the No. 1 Richards/Stones riff of all time—and possibly in music history—was captured for posterity when "(I Can't Get No) Satisfaction" b/w "The Spider and the Fly" were put to tape in Chicago while the band was in North America on yet another riotous tour. The story of how Richards awoke in the middle of the night with the riff in his head and recorded it on a portable tape player before going back to sleep is another part of the band's mythology. It naturally zoomed (the fuzz-tone guitar sound that Richards employed to such devastating effect was called a "zoom bass") to #1 in England, but more importantly, it was the Stones' first #1 single in the U.S. A little over a year after their first American release, the Stones had conquered the "colonies" on the strength of their love and dedication to the blues by bringing America's only indigenous art form back home and flaunting it in the face and ears of an unwitting public.

Fifty years after they began, the Rolling Stones are still at it as performers, with only three changes in personnel. *Beggars Banquet* (1968), arguably their greatest album, was unfortunately the swan song for Brian Jones. Among many ironies, it is their bluesiest, rootsiest recording, but prompted him to bemoan the "fact" that the Stones had gotten too far from the blues for his tastes. In truth, his increasingly unpredictable behavior, fueled by outrageous alcohol and drug use, had led to a life of utter decadence and his considerable musical talents had declined precipitously. He was at odds with the band in every way and was preventing them from touring in the U.S. due to a previous drug conviction. On June 8, 1969, it was bilaterally announced that he was leaving the band, to be replaced by 20-year-old Mick Taylor from John Mayall's Bluesbreakers. Three weeks later, on July 2, Jones was found dead in his swimming pool at the age of 27. Meanwhile, Richards had his own drug demons to face down and in the early '70s, after he was put in jail by the British authorities, Jagger almost fired him from the band. Fortunately for him and all concerned, he beat the rap and has been mainly an abuser of only alcohol and cigarettes ever since.

Taylor was—and still is—a brilliant lead blues guitarist and his tenure in the band, from *Let It Bleed* (1969) to *It's Only Rock 'n' Roll* (1974), took the Stones to an instrumental place that they had never been, even with Jones. In the process, it freed Richards to really hone his patented rhythm style with the open G tuning that he learned, along with others, in 1968 from Ry Cooder and Gram Parsons (the Byrds and Flying Burrito Brothers) and that took hold from *Let It Bleed* on. In December of 1974, however, Taylor amicably left the band for "personal reasons." The band was dismayed, particularly Richards, who was a true admirer of the younger man's musicianship, saying, "No one leaves the Stones alive."

Ron Wood, late of the Faces (with Rod Stewart), took his place, effectively becoming an interchangeable guitarist with Richards, as they both played an intertwining rhythm/lead style that once again harkened back to the early Muddy Waters band *and* the early Rolling Stones. Richards had been hanging out with "Woody" for over a year and had played on his *I've Got My Own Album to Do,* as did Taylor, and they had also performed together as the New Barbarians.

In December 1985, the Stones' longtime "invisible" piano player, Ian Stewart, died at the age of 47. A year later, due to a row with Jagger over the direction of the band (Mick wanted "pop" and "Keef" wanted rock, of course), a hiatus resulted, during which Richards went out on tour with the X-pensive Winos and released his first solo effort, *Talk Is Cheap*, in 1988. It far outpaced Jagger's solo vanity recording, *Primitive Cool,* both critically and commercially, going gold in the process, and he followed it up with *Live at the Hollywood Palladium* in 1991. After the smashing success of the Stones' *Steel Wheels* tour in 1989, however, the "Glimmer Twins" reconciled and agreed to put the Stones fortunes ahead of their solo projects, including Richards' second outing, *Main Offender* (1992). In 1993, Bill Wyman retired from the band to pursue his interest in documenting the blues and performing and recording with his blues band, the Rhythm Kings, and Darryl Jones became their touring bassist, though not an official "Stone."

"The World's Greatest Rock 'n' Roll Band" showed no sign of letting up as they commenced spectacular world tours in 1997, 1998, 1999, and 2002–03. A planned 2006 European tour was temporarily interrupted when Richards fell out of a tree in Fiji and required cranial surgery. In 2007, he appeared as the father of Johnny Deep in *Pirates of the Caribbean*, a role he reprised in 2011. After signing a lucrative book deal in 2007 to write his autobiography, *Life* was published in 2010 to great anticipation and generally positive reviews regarding his candid admissions and wry commentary. Though he was unambiguous in his praise for Mick Jagger's musical abilities, he was just as clear in his criticism of his lifestyle and "Peter Pan syndrome." Even as rumors of a Stones tour in 2012 swirled in late 2011, Jagger formed Super Heavy with Dave Stewart, Joss Stone, Damian Marley (son of reggae legend Bob), and A.R. Rahman. Their self-titled album was released to tepid response and appears to be one of those side vanity projects that Jagger feels compelled to do every so often in between Stones recordings or tours.

Still spry as he turned 70, the seemingly indestructible "old pirate" Keith Richards is as committed to the music and the life it entails as he ever was, rocking out and playing the blues with the energy and passion of a man *one third* his age. Long may he wave his Tele.

THE GUITAR STYLE OF KEITH RICHARDS

Richards's guitar style may reasonably be divided into two eras: pre- and post-*Beggar's Banquet*. In the Stones' first five years, he creatively assimilated riff ideas from classic R&B, which traditionally relates directly to each chord change in a progression. The bluesy E minor pentatonic scale or the E Mixolydian mode could be seen as the source for the I (E) chord riff, while the ones for the ♭VII (D) and IV (A) chords are derived from the D major pentatonic scale and A Mixolydian mode, respectively. Be sure to avoid the ♭3rd when utilizing the pentatonic scale or Mixolydian mode relative to a major chord.

Keith Richards 1

Sometimes, Richards merely added a short, simple embellishment to "dress up" a standard chord change on the Stones' early recordings, often in the guise of a diatonic bass line. Observe the way the line comes right out of the I (C) chord to resolve handsomely to the root of the V (G) chord.

Keith Richards 2

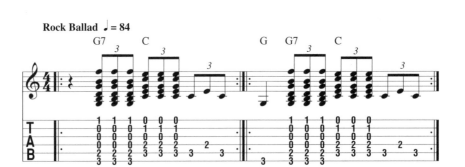

Beggar's Banquet (1968) was the official debut of Richards' new and revolutionary rhythm guitar style based on open tunings, which considerably extended his evolving R&B-based chord melody. Mostly centered on open G, a favorite of blues, folk, and country guitarists, it opened an entirely new world of songwriting for Richards and the Stones. Essentially, the G tuning allows for quick I–IV moves derived from an open A chord-type barre with the index finger at any fret position. "Street Fighting Man," "Brown Sugar," and "Start Me Up" are just three of many classics featuring the dynamic technique. Of significant importance is the ability to play a very reasonable facsimile of Richards' style conveniently in standard tuning inasmuch as strings 4–2 are the same in both open G and standard. The root on string 5 is lost, but the important harmony is conveyed.

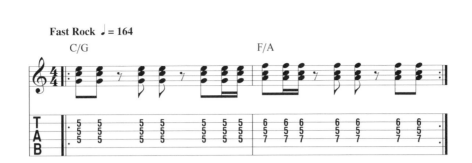

Though "less is more" is an overworked expression in all of the arts, in this case, it is entirely appropriate. Notice how first-inversion (3rd on bottom) and second-inversion (5th on bottom) C triads convey similar harmonic information through minimal means, yet sound much different to the ear. In addition, note how the succession of inversions, characteristic of this rhythm technique, provides an infinitely hipper effect than common, root-positon major triads.

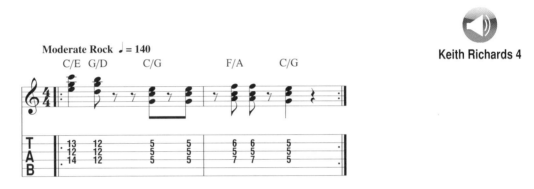

Richards neither aspired to nor has achieved his notoriety through soloing. That said, the man can improvise with aggressive expression and bluesy phrasing. Check out how both are in evidence in the four-measure phrase below, which is similar to one of his more famous instrumental forays. Though no one would confuse him with Clapton, check out how he also "tells a little story" with a beginning, middle, and end by: 1) establishing the E tonality, 2) creating tension by running up to the B note (6th of D), 3) creating more musical tension and anticipation with the bent E (5th of A), and 4) satisfying resolution to the tonic (E) note.

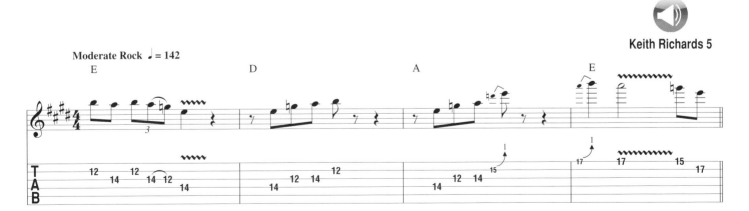

Make no mistake, Richards knows his country blues inside and out. To his credit, he is no slavish imitator; instead, he freely incorporates elements of his chord-melody style while maintaining unwavering commitment to the spirit of the music. Its essence, like the chord melody of other genres including jazz, along with that of Jimi Hendrix, depends on melody and harmony relative to each chord change.

This eight-measure intro to a country blues classic, played in 6/8 time, is a mini-tutorial on some of the expressive techniques at his disposal. Measures 1–2 and 7–8 are basic arpeggios that provide solid harmony around which Richards builds a seamless, flowing musical statement that stands on its own sans rhythm section. The highlight, however, is measures 3–4, where he combines intelligently chosen notes from the E minor pentatonic and C major scales to imply the Em (vi) and C (IV) chords, respectively.

Similar to perhaps the most dramatic intro in rock music history, measures 1–3 demonstrate how intriguing chord melody may be easily accessed with a combination of 3rds, 4ths, and 5ths. Measure 4 takes a different, bluesier tack that is derived from a fifth-string B♭ barre chord voicing, with 3rds fleshing out the change.

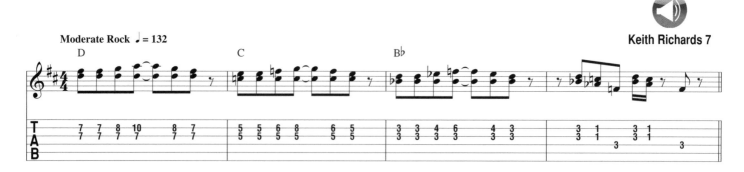

JEFF BECK
(1944–)

In case anyone missed the reference to the great Spanish Renaissance artist El Greco when "El Becko" was released on *There and Back* in 1980, his constantly evolving and masterly use of aural color and musical space should dispel any confusion. Furthermore, his revolutionary and expressionistic use of sonic distortion parallels the revolutionary and elastic visual distortions of the legendary painter. With his storied career and stature as arguably the most creative rock guitarist ever, expanding exponentially through regular tours, CD recordings, and DVDs, the time is ripe for a mini-retrospective of the magnificent Jeff Beck. The wildly inventive artist pioneered the creative use of extreme volume, distortion, and feedback, profoundly influencing Jimi Hendrix and Pete Townshend, among countless others, in addition to his innovative appropriation of Eastern-sounding modalities and "jazz" scales. He has enough righteous blues feeling to have sustained a career as a first-rate bluesman, but that would have felt confining to the restless virtuoso. On top of that, Beck continues to progress and explore the limitless possibilities on the electric guitar with undiminished vigor and enthusiasm, refusing to live in the past or rest on his Olympian laurels. As his esteemed peer and former bandmate Jimmy Page once said, "When he's on, Beck is probably the best there is," and he has been consistently spot-on for over four decades.

Geoffrey Arnold Beck was born to Arnold and Ethel on June 24, 1944, in Wellington, Surrey, England, in the waning years of deprivation during WWII. When he was eight years old, he began piano lessons at his parents urging and was forced to practice two hours a day until he ripped out a black key. Equally unproductive lessons on the cello and violin with an uncle, however, likely planted the seed for his affinity for sustain, which he would begin exploring in the early '60s. At 10, he was singing in the church choir, though it did not induce a desire to pursue a career as a vocalist. A memory from his childhood that would be recalled in the '70s was hearing a record called *Sparky's Magic Piano*, which featured a "talking piano" effect, fascinating the young boy.

When he was 12, Beck entered Junior Art School, a calling his fellow Brits Eric Clapton, Keith Richards, and John Lennon, among others, also heard. His desire to play the guitar arrived simultaneously with his discovery of rockabilly music and the release of musical comedy *The Girl Can't Help It* in 1956, which starred Jayne Mansfield and featured Gene Vincent and the wild rock guitar pioneer Cliff Gallup. The experience transformed him. Similar to one of his idols, Les Paul, but out of dire economic necessity, Beck was inspired to build an electric guitar out of plywood, followed by a "custom" one built for him, almost as rough as the one he connected to an amp made in the school workshop. As if the obsessed youngster needed any more inspiration, seeing Buddy Holly on his 1958 tour of Great Britain sealed his fate. "That'll Be the Day" was the first song he learned on the guitar.

In 1960, Beck further advanced his fine arts education when he began attending Wimbledon Art School. He also commenced his musical career by joining an instrumental group, the Bandits, who backed singers on a rockabilly tribute tour. Meanwhile, he continued to progress on the guitar as his interests broadened to include jazzers like Barney Kessel, Charlie Byrd, and especially Les Paul. At the same time, his parents encouraged an interest in classical music with Ravel's dramatic "Bolero," an interest that would play itself out in the recording studio years later. Equally (or more) important to his development, the blues entered his life via B.B. King. Around 16, Beck joined the Deltones, a local R&B outfit of older musicians who at that point were performing covers of the popular Hank Marvin and the Shadows instrumental group, even as the recordings of Gallup and James Burton (backing Ricky Nelson) provided further inspiration. The Deltones would provide his first encounter with a Telecaster, as he borrowed a 1959 model from John Owen, his school friend and the group's rhythm guitarist. By 1961, however, he had bought a new sunburst Strat on credit, the first of his future iconic guitars, even while the band was metamorphosing into the Crescents and he was again compelled to play in the manner of Hank Marvin. During his tenure, Beck appeared on a Crescents demo of a popular Deltones number called "Wedding Bells," which was likely his first recording. At the same time, Ian "Stu" Stewart, the barrelhouse blues and boogie piano player who helped found the Rolling Stones with Brian Jones, and who would sometimes play anonymously on their recordings, was "instrumental" in turning the erstwhile guitarist onto Chicago blues through his record collection. Consequently, hearing Buddy Guy and Otis Rush would come to significantly influence his exceptionally creative and expressive string bending and vibrato.

After drifting insouciantly from group to group and gig to gig (where he would sometimes literally show up unannounced and plug in), around 1961–62, Beck fell in with and possibly helped form the straight-up R&B group the Night Shift. Now fully leading the bohemian and rebellious lifestyle that came with the art school territory, he had to play on a "borrowed" 1959 Tele with rosewood neck, as he had sold his trashed Strat in order to buy a car. The band enjoyed early success, performing regularly and even having the

Jeff Beck, circa 1985.

(Photo by William Hames/Cache Agency)

Rolling Stones open for *them* one time. They recorded "Stormy Monday" b/w "That's My Story" and "Corrina, Corrina" (with an unknown flip side) for the Piccadilly label, though to Beck's dismay, the tracks did not see the light of day until 1965, when he was making rock history via every recording with the Yardbirds. What followed would be a harbinger of poor career choices that bedeviled him until the mid-'70s: he cavalierly turned down, or carelessly ignored, an offer to join the Roosters in 1962, before Eric Clapton accepted, then lacked the confidence to take the place of "Slowhand" in John Mayall's Bluesbreakers in 1966, despite repeated calls from Mayall. Years later, Beck would decide against becoming a Rolling Stone when he was asked to replace Mick Taylor in 1975, deciding their lifestyle was not for him.

At the same time, Beck was making a name for himself on the nascent British blues scene in the early '60s. The Tridents, fronted by a lead singer/harp blower, were also proving themselves an adept blues band. Beck coveted the lead guitar chair and, when their regular plectrist left, he was overjoyed to be offered the position. It would prove to be the first real chance to let his Buddy Guy-meets-Les Paul style run rampant. By 1964, the band was attracting serious attention and bookings and the main attraction was to see and hear Beck get wild on his Tele. The controlled use of feedback, which he claims to have been perfecting since 1960, became a featured part of his act, along with distortion and echo, and his legend was born. Assisting him in his early electronic experiments was bassist/vocalist Paul Lucas, who not only rewired the pickups on the Tele for a hotter sound, but also created a remarkably fat-sounding fuzz box to complete the anarchic onslaught. Three unreleased Tridents tracks from 1963–64 confirm that Beck was breaking uncharted ground for rock guitarists at least a year before his vaunted and much better known Yardbirds songs. The group recorded the Louisiana Red classic "Keep Your Hands off My Woman" b/w the equally classic 8-bar blues "Trouble in Mind," on which his slide work betrays a significant Earl Hooker influence.

The Tridents also waxed the original "That Noise" b/w the original "Wandering Man Blues" in hopes of snaring a contract. The latter 12-bar blues not only includes a fluid and authentic "West Side of Chicago" guitar solo, but also features a rare Beck recorded lead vocal, though it is reported that he was known to regularly sing the blues in concert with the Tridents, acquitting himself with surprising assurance and aplomb. One other surviving Tridents track is a live recording of the Bo Diddley number "Nursery Rhyme," on which his uninhibited attack—lightning-fast rockabilly licks, rude scraping sound effects, feedback squeals, and fast tremolo picking on the bass strings—is a startling preview of the bold, new territory into which he was going to drag rock guitar, "screaming" and "crying," in the years to come. David Bowie once commented that after seeing Beck with the Tridents at Eel Pie Island, the destination in the Thames where so many British Invasion bands like the Who incubated in the early '60s, he was never so knocked out until Stevie Ray Vaughan performed at the Montreux Jazz festival in 1982.

Advancing up the British guitar ranks at the same time was in-demand session guitarist Jimmy Page. He attended technical school with Beck's older sister Annetta, who would make the introduction between the two future rock guitar legends. They hit it off famously, jamming and trading licks and forging a fast and lasting friendship that would benefit both. A historic jam with pianist Nicky Hopkins and former members of Cyril Davies All-Stars would be taped at a recording session produced by Page and Glyn Johns in the spring of 1964. Beck "stars" on "Chuckles" and the slide tune "Steelin'"—the predecessor of the Yardbirds' "Steeled Blues"—both of which were released by Andrew Loog Oldham in 1968 under questionable conditions, on his Immediate label as *The Beginning British Blues*. Unfortunately, the first recorded version of "Jeff's Boogie" remains in the can.

As Beck's reputation started to build and spread, he, like Page, was offered studio gigs where his flash guitar left jaws agape. In fact, "Pagey" was so successful and secure doing sessions that he fortuitously turned down an opportunity to join the Yardbirds. Originally inspired by the Rolling Stones and first known as the Metropolitan Blues Quartet, in 1963, singer/harmonicist Keith Relf and bassist Paul Samwell-Smith split off and were joined by rhythm guitarist Chris Dreja, drummer Jim McCarty, and guitarist Anthony "Top" Topham to form the Blue-Sounds before settling on "the Yardbirds." Though they were quite clean cut and conservative in their fashion, the name was derived from a term Jack Kerouac had used to describe "hobos" who hung around train yards. They soon sacked Topham for not being bluesy enough and snared their first future guitar "god," Eric Clapton. Ever the purist, however, Mr. "Slowhand" eventually found the Yardbirds heading in a direction that was way too pop for his tastes. He considered splitting in early 1965, during the "For Your Love" sessions, where he simply provided the basic boogie patterns on the bridge while Brian Augur played the signature harpsichord part in the verse.

The Yardbirds first choice for a replacement was Page, who demurred and instead recommended Beck. Their manager/producer, Giorgio Gomelsky, concurred and practically kidnapped the greasy, long-haired hot-rodder. An "audition" was arranged, but hiring Beck was a done deal, though he harbored regrets about leaving the Tridents after the productive time they had spent together. While Clapton was still dithering about leaving, Beck surreptitiously laid down guitar tracks at London's Advision Studio with the band for "Heart Full of Soul," "Steeled Blues," again featuring his slide, "Still I'm Sad," and "Evil Hearted You." In March, Clapton finally ran off to join John Mayall's Bluesbreakers. Within days, Beck was playing his first gigs, including at the famous Marquee Club, where he earned a standing ovation after playing "Jeff's Boogie." Apparently, he then lost the '59 Tele from his Tridents tenure when the Yardbirds opened for the Beatles in Paris. He had to use the red Tele that belonged to the group and had been played previously by Clapton. He next bought his iconic '54 Esquire from John Maus of the Walker Brothers, with whom the Yardbirds were touring behind the Kinks. When he swapped the white pick guard for a black one, he set off a fashion trend in England among guitarists.

Whatever the initial feelings of the band towards the unkempt and seemingly undisciplined renegade guitarist, they must have altered over time, as Beck cleaned up his appearance and turned his Esquire into a sonic paintbrush featuring fuzz, feedback, tremolo, and reverb/tape delay that were light years ahead of the guitarists in the Stones, Beatles, and the Who, not to mention virtually every other Invasion and American group.

The rest of 1965 was a runaway locomotive for the Yardbirds, culminating in their first U.S. tour, where Beck, in his fringe and snakeskin boots, was accorded full rock-star status by admiring groupies. Adding to the their prestige were recording sessions at Sun Studios in Memphis, where they cut the rollicking "The Train Kept A-Rollin'" and "You're a Better Man Than I," and at Chess Records in Chicago, where "New York City Blues," the rave-up version of "I'm a Man," and the prophetic "Shapes of Things," with a controlled feedback solo, were immortalized on tape. None other than Bo Diddley himself, who penned and recorded the original "I'm a Man," described it as "beautiful." Backed with "Still I'm Sad," the song reached #17 on the charts.

The year 1966 saw continued action in concert and in the studio, including the July release of the classic album *Roger the Engineer* in Britain, which was titled *Over Under Sideways Down* in the U.S. and featured the revolutionary single of the same name. Contributing to the success and evolution of the Yardbirds' sound was the '59 Sunburst Les Paul Beck had acquired early in the year. The genesis of his rep as being "difficult" also reared its head during this time, as he became frustrated with the inadequacy of his amps and effects. In addition, though he had nowhere near the lead guitarist's instrumental ability, harmonicist Keith Relf jostled for the spotlight and, according to Beck, had the most annoying habit of noisily using an atomizer onstage for his asthma during guitar solos. Nonetheless, in early summer, rock guitar fans were bedazzled when Paul Samwell-Smith left and Jimmy Page joined the band on bass and second lead. The U.K. release in the fall of the single "Happenings Ten Years Ago" b/w "Psycho Daisies," with Dreja now on bass, gave only a hint of the Beck/Page tandem guitar possibilities, which unfortunately would never reach full fruition. Meanwhile, Beck contributed another rare lead vocal and a thrilling jolt of feedback to "The Nazz Are Blue," a "Dust My Broom" copy and the flipside of the U.S. single. For posterity, the band, with the "dream team" on guitar, appeared in new wave director Michelangelo Antonioni's *Blowup* in the fall of 1966, though they were forced to perform a hastily disguised version of "The Train Kept A-Rollin'," dubbed "Stroll

On." The director had originally wanted the Who to perform in his swinging '60s London fantasy and Beck had to reluctantly "pull a Townshend" by smashing a cheap, hollow Hofner guitar for the climax of the tune—after being seen playing his vintage and valuable Les Paul Standard in the previous shots.

Despite their close, personal relationship and mutual respect, a professional rivalry was building between Beck and Page that was manifesting itself in fierce, often unproductive onstage fireworks. Compounding the growing situation, Beck had been twice hospitalized for tonsillitis while on another U.S. tour and back in London, respectively, fueling unsubstantiated rumors that he was looking for an exit strategy in order to pursue a solo career. In October of 1966, while on tour in the U.S. with Dick Clark's "Caravan of Stars," after an astoundingly innovative, productive, and historic 18-month period, the Beck era came to an inglorious end. He and Relf had yet another nasty blow up, resulting in Beck smashing his beloved '59 'burst into pieces in a dressing room confrontation that was observed by Page. Beck then flew off in a snit to California for "tea and sympathy" from an American girlfriend. When the rest of the band caught up, he was summarily fired.

In March 1967, Beck initiated his solo career by signing a contract with pop producer Mickie Most and releasing his first singles, which featured his repaired Les Paul *and vocals* on the pop-inflected "Hi Ho Silver Lining" and "Talley Man." The B-side of the former, however, was the instrumental "Beck's Bolero." Recorded in 1966 with Jimmy Page, bassist John Paul Jones, who filled in for the absent John Entwistle, drummer Keith Moon, and pianist Nicky Hopkins, the song is considered a landmark that influenced, among many others, Hendrix's version of "All Along the Watchtower." For a brief, shining moment, Beck had fantasized it as the nucleus of a super group to end all super groups! Alas, Moon opted to remain in the Who and Page, of course, had his own ambitions, which would include Jones. Hot on the trail of a vocalist to front his band, in early 1967, Beck put the first Jeff Beck Group together with Rod Stewart and future Rolling Stones guitarist Ronnie Wood, who would soon unhappily switch to bass. The group released two guitar-centric albums, *Truth* (1968), containing "Beck's Bolero" and "Rock My Plimsoul," and *Beck-Ola* (1969). Despite an uneasy collaboration with the diva Stewart and a dearth of original material, which has plagued Beck over the years, both albums are treasured by fans and fellow plectrists, spotlighting a rich, luscious Les Paul/Marshall tone and a '54 Strat, respectively. Also suffering at this time was his repaired and stripped-finish original Les Paul, which fell off an amp. Mickie Most quickly scored the stripped '54 Strat, though Beck was not yet entirely won over from his preference for the classic 'bursts. Coming to the rescue, collector and dealer Rick Nielsen, later of Cheap Trick fame, sold him another '59 "Flametop" with a Bigsby tailpiece, known as LP #2. In yet more harrowing guitar adventures, his first 'burst was sent for repairs to Memphis, where not only a thinner, newer neck was installed, but the prized PAF pickups were swapped out (stolen?) for brand new Gibson replacements (!), all to Beck's understandable horror.

Interestingly, though thoroughly grounded in the blues, Beck's creative use of distortion, feedback, and other effects are now seen as proto-heavy metal rumblings. The tensions in the band did produce some great music, but eventually led to Stewart and Wood splitting to join the Small Faces and Beck going his own way again, even though the band was invited to play at Woodstock in August of 1969. One can only imagine how rock history would have been changed had Beck accepted. Also in 1969 during their last U.S. tour, Beck's latest Les Paul Sunburst (#2) was nicked, and while in Memphis, he bought the refinished '54 Goldtop that he changed to what he charmingly calls "oxblood," replacing the original P-90 pickups with PAF humbuckers and using a Gibson combination stop/bar tailpiece for added sustain. The guitar's exceptionally sweet but biting tone would be put to even greater use and immortalized in a few years.

An idea for a new group with Stewart and former Vanilla Fudge bassist/singer Tim Bogert and drummer Carmine Appice was bandied about, but Stewart demurred in order to pursue his own path. Then in late 1969, Beck was in a near-fatal accident in his hotrod 1923 T-Bucket Ford, fracturing his skull and recalling a quote from Jimmy Page: "He plays guitar like he drives his cars—recklessly and dangerously." Plans for the "super group" were put on ice. After Beck recovered from his injuries in the spring of 1970, his growing love for black R&B compelled him to go to Detroit's Motown Records with drummer Cozy Powell in order to cut tracks with legendary session cats like virtuoso bassist James Jamerson. The poorly planned and naive venture turned out to be a bust due to a lack of material, as well as for other reasons, but the experience would bear fruit years later.

Upon his return, Beck convened another Jeff Beck Group, featuring Powell, singer Bobby Tench, and keyboardist Max Middleton, as Bogert and Appice galloped off to form Cactus. The "new" Jeff Beck Group recorded the underrated, jazzy, funky, and prophetic *Rough and Ready* (1971), as well as the exploratory, funky, albeit uneven *Jeff Beck Group* (1972), affectionately called "The Orange Album," which was produced by Steve Cropper at Memphis' Stax Studios for that "Booker T" vibe. In addition to the blues-rocking classic "Going Down," "Definitely Maybe," the lone instrumental track on *Jeff Beck Group*, ignited audiences in concert. It would point the way towards his greatest post-Yardbirds triumph in the mid-'70s, when the rock guitarist logically gravitated towards jazz. The seed had been planted: Beck could perhaps succeed best as an instrumentalist.

In the interim, Cactus disbanded and Beck recklessly threw in with the overblown egos of Bogert and Appice for the ill-fated but tantalizing power trio Beck, Bogert & Appice. His main axe going in was the '54 Strat, before he acquired a white 1970/71 CBS Strat. However, in order to be heard above the overpowering din of the bass and drums, he soon realized that he would need to play the far more powerful oxblood LP. The result was one spotty studio album in 1973 featuring Beck singing lead on "Black Cat Moan," with the highlight being the Stevie Wonder future classic "Superstition," which had already been recorded by the Motown legend. The lack of original material and a strong, charismatic lead singer, combined with Bogert's propensity for thunderingly loud "lead bass," led to the dissolution of BBA after the recording of *Beck, Bogert & Appice Live in Japan*, which wasn't released until 1975, a year after their split.

Before moving on to what would become the next defining moment of his career, Beck heeded the call to audition for the Rolling Stones upon the departure of Mick Taylor. Sessions were held in Holland, where he played on a few tracks that have only appeared on bootlegs, and on "Black and Blue Jam," which became "Slave" on *Tattoo You,* minus his contribution. In hindsight, turning them down was one of his better career decisions. As is well known, the job went to his old buddy Ron Wood, who has proved to be a perfect fit for the Stones lifestyle and a much better mirror image for "Keef."

After the contentious experience in trying to lead a bombastic boogie rock group, in 1975, Beck released the quietly spectacular, George Martin-produced *Blow by Blow*, with Max Middleton on keys, his most consistently sympathetic bandmate. Again pushing the envelope for improvising guitarists everywhere, he made his strongest, most cohesive musical statement to date on his newly iconic and modified oxblood Les Paul. *Blow by Blow* is a stunning selection and combination of original jazz, rock, funk, and blues instrumentals, highlighted by a gorgeously melancholic version of Stevie Wonder's "Cause We've Ended as Lovers," which he dedicated to Roy Buchanan and played on a highly modified '58 Tele with Gibson PAFs that Seymour Duncan gave him in exchange for the '54 "Yardbirds Esquire." Also featured on the landmark album are the original shuffle "Freeway Jam" and a reggae interpretation of the Beatles' "She's a Woman," which contains the "talk box," among other electric guitar monuments of creativity. It was a critical and commercial success, going platinum and reaching an eye-opening #4 on the charts. In the spring, he went on tour opening for John McLaughlin and his Mahavishnu Orchestra, receiving great praise and sporting the Les Paul, the stripped Strat that he trashed in frustration onstage, and ultimately, an array of white Strats that would go on to become his sonic weapon of choice.

A year later, he gravitated whole heartedly to the white Strat and began a short, productive, and fiercely competitive association with Jan Hammer, the electronic keyboard wizard and Mahavishnu Orchestra alumnus. In 1976, Beck, with both Hammer and Middleton in tow, released the much edgier and looser *Wired,* which contained a dramatic reading of the Charles Mingus ballad "Goodbye Porkpie

Hat" as a melancholy, melodic statement analogous to "Cause We've Ended as Lovers," along with "Led Boots," a good-natured jab at Page. The album likewise struck gold at #16. Fully established now as a true *artiste* of the electric guitar to be reckoned with, Beck set off that same year on an extensive tour with Hammer, resulting in the exuberant *Jeff Beck with the Jan Hammer Group Live.* However, this too was not meant to last. Instead of butting heads with a lead singer or rhythm-section bashers, Beck now had to deal with an equally aggressive electronic keyboardist who threw strikingly authentic, synthesized "guitar lines" back in his face, along with the type of dense instrumental interplay that was lost in the arenas and stadiums at which they were booked. Nonetheless, Beck was at the top of his game and receiving long-overdue acclaim for his singular talents. In 1978, while using his new credibility as a jazz-rock guitar star, he toured Japan with bass virtuoso Stanley Clarke, keyboardist Tony Hymas, and drummer Simon Phillips, but then allowed two more years to go by before recording his own music again. This lack of consistency, or perhaps disinterest in promoting his career, would work to his disadvantage whenever the inevitable comparisons with the other, more commercially successful ex-Yardbirds star guitarists would arise.

In 1980, Beck released his first tentative foray into techno-rock, *There and Back*, featuring a reunion with Hammer, Hymas, and Phillips, as well as bassist Mo Foster, and the creation of another modern classic, "El Becko." The taut juggernaut toured extensively to much acclaim as Beck debuted a '54 Strat that was given to him by Steve Marriot of Humble Pie fame. Beck then put his personal recording career on hold for another five years as he grappled with depression, practiced playing the drums, and occasionally guested with other artists, most notably with Mick Jagger. However, he kept busy to a degree, playing with Eric Clapton at the Amnesty International-sponsored "Secret Policeman's Ball" in 1981, and in 1983, making a historic appearance with both Clapton and Jimmy Page at an ARMS concert for multiple sclerosis for Ronnie Lane, ex-bassist for the Faces.

In 1985, funk guitarist Niles Rodgers produced the pop-styled *Flash*, which featured a gaggle of guest vocalists, including the preening Rod Stewart on Curtis Mayfield's gospel-infused "People Get Ready," Beck's only hit single (#48), while "Escape" won a Grammy for Best Rock Instrumental. Also of significance, *Flash* was the first album that Beck recorded with his new, "pick-less" fingerstyle technique. True to form, Beck rested for the next four years, but returned in 1989 with the album that would pave the way for his future—and futuristic—musical explorations. *Jeff Beck's Guitar Shop*, with the high horsepower of "Big Block," featured the equally devastating chops of young master drummer Terry Bozzio (Zappa, Missing Persons) and keyboard wizard Hymas pushing Beck into grooves, riffs, rhythms, and melodies that earned them a Grammy for Best Instrumental Rock Album and produced the single "Stand on It" (#35). A memorable tour with Stevie Ray Vaughan followed, giving lucky fans a chance to marvel at two of the greatest electric blues-rock guitarists of all time duking it out. In 1992, Beck played on Roger Waters' *Amused to Death,* the ex-Floyd bassist's "comeback album," along with being inducted into the Rock and Roll Hall of Fame for the first time, with the Yardbirds. Ironically, in 1967, Beck had been considered as a replacement for original Floyd guitarist Syd Barrett, but Nick Mason recalled that, "None of us had the nerve to ask him." In 1993, Beck revisited his youth and roots with the Big Town Playboys' *Crazy Legs*, a tribute to his rockabilly hero, Cliff Gallup. A loving homage, it features unadorned, note-for-note recreations of the original guitar parts.

Following another fallow recording period, Beck, along with Tony Hymas and drummer Steve Alexander, cut *Who Else?* (1999), containing "Brush with the Blues," and *You Had It Coming* (2001), earning a Grammy for Best Rock Instrumental Performance with "Dirty Mind," and both featuring American virtuoso guitarist Jennifer Batten. Each disc found him on top of contemporary techno and dance trends, along with brutally intense rockers and heartbreaking ballads. In the summer of 2003, Beck, with bassist Dean Garcia and drummer Steve Barney, released *Jeff*, featuring "Hot Rod Honeymoon" and "Plan B," and scored another Grammy for Best Rock Instrumental Performance. He also embarked on an unprecedented tour with B.B. King, including an *A&E Live by Request* appearance and a transcendent, historical appearance at King's Manhattan club that resulted in *Live at B.B. King's Blues Club and Grill*, released in 2006.

Prominently featured is his stunning, show-stopping instrumental version of the Beatles' "A Day in the Life." A year later, as a major highlight of Eric Clapton's "Crossroads Festival" in 2007, Beck confirmed his unique mastery of the Strat to new fans, something that his loyal followers had known for years. In 2008, while building on the strong reception that his shows were receiving, especially in the U.S., Beck decided to test his viability on home turf. Recorded at the renowned London venue, *Performing This Week: Live at Ronny Scott's Jazz Club* proved his contemporary worth, with his new working band consisting of the young, female Australian bassist Tal Wilkenfeld, keyboardist Jason Rebello, and veteran drummer Vinnie Colaiuta. An accompanying DVD features guest singers Joss Stone and Imogen Heap, as well as Clapton sitting in on two blues numbers, and even Jimmy Page replicating his original contribution by playing 12-string rhythm guitar on "Beck's Bolero." Coincidentally, in 2009 Beck was inducted into the Rock and Roll Hall of Fame for the second time—this time, in recognition of his solo career.

Finally, in 2010 Beck released his first studio album in seven years, *Emotion & Commotion*, which coincided with a spring tour that he undertook with Clapton. The album is a sprawling musical canvas, ranging from classical compositions backed by a 64-piece orchestra to jazz, funk, and blues, including songs by Jeff Buckley ("Corpus Christi Carol"), Screamin' Jay Hawkins ("I Put a Spell on You"), and Harold Arlen ("Over the Rainbow"), with Beck notably playing down his explosive virtuosity. Instead, vocalists Joss Stone, Olivia Safe, and Imelda May are prominently presented. Nonetheless, it garnered Grammys in 2011 for Best Pop Instrumental Performance and Best Rock Instrumental Performance for "Nessun Dorma," the aria from the Puccini opera *Turandot*, and the original hard funk of "Hammerhead," respectively. Following *Emotion & Commotion*, two live albums offering different aspects of his music were released: *Live and Exclusive from the Grammy Museum* (2010), containing performances from the studio album, and *Rock and Roll Party: Honoring Les Paul* (2011), featuring classic rockabilly and Les Paul and Mary Ford classics with singers Darrell Higham and Imelda May, respectively. However, in the spring of 2010 while opening for E.C. on a tour of the U.S., particularly when the two jammed on the blues at the end of each concert, Beck gave his seemingly endless creativity free rein, pushing the envelope beyond even the legendary Buddy Guy with high-revving intensity and extreme emotional expression.

Thankfully for his many fans, Jeff Beck shows absolutely no sign of letting up. In addition to being a great inspiration to countless guitarists, at the age of 70, he continues to create at a level above and beyond what guitarists a third his age could conceive, let alone perform.

THE GUITAR STYLE OF JEFF BECK

Beck always had an uninhibited approach to blues and rock, a characteristic of his extraordinary creativity. Following his split from the Yardbirds, he began to stretch his wings beyond the constraints that he sometimes felt in that seminal British Invasion group. Notice the dramatic, dynamic contrast between the "sheets of sound" in measures 1–2, derived from the B Mixolydian mode, and the soaring bends in measure 3. The whiplash trill to the 5th (F#) on beat 1 of measure 4 releases the previous taut, compressed tension.

When his interest in jazz and instrumental music evolved in the late '70s, Beck was able to further indulge and develop his taste for melodies. He would eventually come to be lauded for his exceptional skill at manipulating a select group of scales. Using the "proletariat" minor pentatonic scale in C, he produces inventive, expressive lines that are intensified by the dynamic tension generated between the bass and treble registers, reminiscent of jazz saxophone.

Performance Tip: In measure 2, pull down on the E♭ note with the ring finger, backed by the middle and index.

True to his blues roots, Beck has employed slide guitar in his music on significant occasions going back at least as far as "Beck's Bolero" in 1967. Like Robert Nighthawk and Earl Hooker, he favors standard tuning and has a clean, refined touch. In measures 1–2, observe the way he promotes a degree of tension and anticipation by emphasizing the 5th (E). However, he does resolve to the root of the VI (F♯5) chord before injecting three bluesy dyads for spice. In measure 4, he zips to the upper register, where the ♭5th (C) and ♭3rd (A) clang powerfully over the F♯5 in anticipation of later, eventual resolution of the tension.

Performance Tip: Beck places his glass slider on his middle finger, as he only plays lead over accompaniment. However, wearing it on the pinky, as the country bluesmen did, is recommended in order to free the index, middle, and ring fingers for chords or fretted riffs.

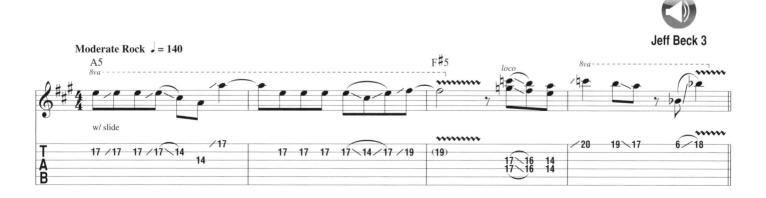

In the '90s, Beck took his penchant for sonic exploration to a new, spectacular level. In particular, his virtuosic manipulation of the whammy bar on his Strat traveled far past mere sound effects to being another expressive tool for playing melodies. The half-step dips in measure 2 are bluesy due to the presence of the notes C (♭5th) and A (♭3rd), respectively. In measure 4, the extreme lowering of string 6, along with the wildly dynamic, two-step dip from B (4th) down to G (♭2nd), followed by a quick, one-step scoop to C♯ (5th), is virtuosic rock guitar technique.

Performance Tip: As if his whammy hijinks were not enough, Beck inserts a measure of jackhammer-fast tapping in measure 3 that should be executed with the pick-hand index finger at fret 13 as the fret-hand index finger descends, in what is essentially a trilled phrase played with two hands.

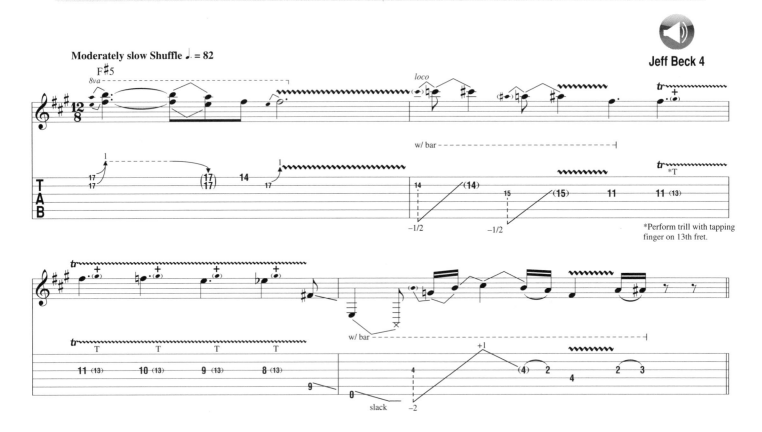

Beck has a unerring sense for "picking" cover tunes most suited to his artistic sensibilities and for turning vocal melodies into breathtaking instrumental statements. With judicious use of the whammy bar to bend his "vocal" inflections, he creates a guitar masterpiece for the ages.

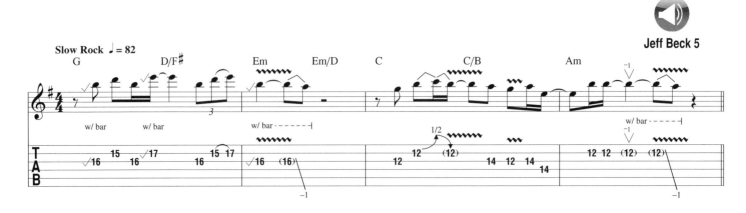

PETE TOWNSHEND
(1945–)

Like Keith Richards in the Rolling Stones, his counterpart as a chord-riff man par excellence, the story of Pete Townshend is the story of the Who. As a man with superior intelligence and sophisticated artistic and philosophical tastes, Townshend has delved deepest and most profoundly into the shamanistic effect of rock. He is the guitarist who put the most "power" in power chords while exposing his vulnerability lyrically with disarming candor. Additionally, he attacked with vehemence the hypocrisy of his "generation" following the "Age of Aquarius." Using his contrary and contradictory nature as fuel for his art, Townshend wrote fist-pumping anthems and, most famously, wildly ambitious rock operas while forging an unmistakable sound based on a rhythm machine in his right hand—like a musical machine gun.

Peter Dennis Blandford Townshend was born May 19, 1945, in London, England, to Cliff and Betty, a clarinetist/bandleader and singer, respectively. As "trad," or Dixieland, jazz aficionados, they exerted an influence on their young son at an early age, when he went out on the road with their band before he attended school. However, there was virtually no music in his house, except when his dad would practice. Townshend played the harmonica until the age of 12, when his grandmother bought him a cheap acoustic on which he preceded to break the strings. At the same time, he got a banjo, and by 14 was playing Dixieland music in the Confederates with his classmate John Entwistle on trumpet.

In 1962, Entwistle went off to play R&B bass in the Detours, which consisted of guitarist Roger Daltrey, a drummer, and a lead singer. Townshend began art college, but Entwistle convinced Daltrey to bring him in on rhythm guitar. However, coming under the influence of "Shakin' All Over" (1960) by Johnny Kidd & the Pirates, who were a guitar/bass/drums/lead singer quartet, Townshend saw the enticing appeal of one guitar playing rhythm and lead. By early 1964, Daltrey had relinquished his guitar chair to become the front man/lead singer and the group's name was changed to the Who. They would play many shows with Kidd, and Townshend would watch guitarist Mick Green with interest. Meanwhile, while at college, Townshend acquired his first record player and became immersed in jazz and blues through the music of Mose Allison, Ray Charles, Jimmy Smith, Jimmy Reed, and especially John Lee Hooker and Steve Cropper. Bill Haley, James Burton (with Ricky Nelson), and Link Wray, in particular, were some of the few rockers who impressed him.

The Who made do with session drummers until Keith Moon was recruited following his tenure in a surf music band. They began playing their rock and R&B covers on the burgeoning London club scene and proceeded to build a cult following in large part because of a fortuitous accident that occurred at the Railway Hotel in Harrow. In the course of an energetic stage performance featuring feedback, Townshend broke the headstock of his Rickenbacker model 1998 when he smacked it against the low ceiling over the stage. Thinking quickly, he pretended like it was a deliberate part of the act and smashed it to pieces before strapping on his "Rick" 12-string. Literally overnight, the "auto-destruction" became a big draw, and within a few weeks, "Moonie," never one to miss a chance for mayhem, began joining in the fun with his drums. Noticing the growing audience, their manager directed them to dress like "mods" as opposed to "rockers," and he changed their name to the "High Numbers." They recorded "I'm the Face" b/w "Zoot Suit," the A-side being a cop of Slim Harpo's "Got Love If You Want It," and would go on to anchor the bottom of a bill with the Beatles. The failure of the single to generate any attention compelled them to switch management, who advised them to go back to being called the Who and booked them into the famous Marquee Club for an extended sold-out engagement.

In early 1965, the Who released "I Can't Explain" (#8 in the U.K.), featuring session stalwart Jimmy Page, and boosted the song's chart position via an explosive performance on the British teen TV show *Ready, Steady, Go*. "Anyway, Anyhow, Anywhere" (#10), released in the spring, was the follow-up and, though released roughly six months after John Lennon had first recorded deliberate feedback on "I Feel Fine" (fall of 1964), the searing siren howl and crunching distorted chords in the instrumental break were a reflection of their stage show and a harbinger of the aural assault that would become the signature sound of the Who. In late 1965, Daltrey, in what would become a hallmark of the band, was fired for fighting with the others just a few weeks before their debut album, as the friction between he and Townshend would literally erupt into fisticuffs. After the success of *My Generation* (#5), with "The Kids Are Alright" and the title track tying the highest singles chart position the band would ever achieve (#2), Daltrey was quickly reinstated. "I'm a Boy" (#2) only confirmed their smashing debut.

In January of 1966, the Who made a historic appearance on the last *Shindig!* show in Los Angeles, followed by the release of "Substitute" (#5). Another future classic that showed Townshend's growth as a thoughtful composer, the song engendered controversy with the lyric "I look all white, but my dad was black," which was changed for the U.S. market and was involved in a complicated, convoluted legal morass with producers. Later in the year, the Who put out *A Quick One* (#4), which boasted songs penned by each member as per the decree of their new producer. In a preview of the shapes of things to come, the title track was a rather lengthy mini-opera composed by Townshend as a way to fill 10 minutes and featured each member singing a lead part. In early 1967, the album was retitled *Happy Jack* for release in the U.S. and the title track became their first American single (#24, #3 in the U.K.). Concurrently, in the early spring, the Who inaugurated their first U.S. visit by playing on a series of disk jockey "Murray the K" shows in New York City. Following the release of "Pictures of Lily" (#4 U.K., #51 U.S.), a controversial song due to the topic of masturbation featuring Entwistle's French horn flourishes, the Who went on an extensive North American tour opening for Herman's Hermits, which culminated with their literally explosive set at the Monterey Pop Festival in the "Summer of Love." In a beloved story, Townshend argued with Jimi Hendrix backstage about who would close the show, with neither musician wishing to follow the other. Finally, in exasperation, Hendrix declared that if he closed the show, he would "pull out all the stops." Grabbing his Strat, he jumped up on a chair and proceeded to blow away everyone in the room with a devastating display of virtuosity.

The Who closed out 1967 with "I Can See for Miles" (#10 U.K., #9 U.S.), from *The Who Sell Out* (#13 U.K., #48 U.S.), and Townshend's frustration with what he considered a lack of audience support would compel him to eventually create a masterpiece. Nonetheless, the Who never scored a #1 hit single, and he saw the relatively poor charting in the U.K. as a personal insult to what he considered their finest work to date, contemptuously stating, "I spat on the British public." The album had started out as an ambitious pop-art concept presented as a radio show, complete with commercial spoofs between tracks, but seems to have broken down before completion. Reportedly, the manufacturers that were parodied initiated lawsuits. Included on the album was the 12-string acoustic instrumental "Sunrise," which revealed Townshend's study of jazz through Mickey Baker books, and was created to prove to his mother that he could write "real" music. Of even more significance was "Rael," another mini-opera that contained melodic ideas that would resurface spectacularly two years later.

In the spring of 1968, the band returned to the U.S. as headliners. In the summer, Townshend learned of the Indian spiritual master Meher Baba and became a follower of the guru, as had George Harrison, and later, John McLaughlin and Carlos Santana would do the same. After the retro-mod single "Dogs" (#25 U.K.) failed to live up to expectations, the Who remained on the road, especially in the U.S., as a means to offset their declining record sales. Perhaps out of desperation or a desire to prove his worth, Townshend withdrew in order to begin writing an extensive serious work about a deaf, dumb, and blind boy. In the interim, "Magic Bus" (#25 U.K., #26 U.S.) and *Magic Bus: The Who on Tour*, a collection of

Pete Townshend performing with the Who at Maple Leaf Gardens, Toronto, Canada, in May 1980.

(Photo by Patrick Harbron/Cache Agency)

previously released material, came out in the fall in the U.S. only. The album was their first American release to chart (#39). At the end of the year, they performed in the *Rolling Stones Rock and Roll Circus*, a filmed-for-TV "circus" with an all-star lineup. The Who stole the show with a galvanic "A Quick One While He's Away," but to their detriment, it would not be shown publicly for 28 years due to the ragged performance and haggard appearance of the Stones in their closing set.

In 1969, the Who finally attained the commercial and critical status that Townshend desired, as *Tommy* (#2 U.K., #4 U.S.), the "rock opera," was released to much fanfare, publicity, and a badly needed revenue infusion. A double album containing an involved story about enlightenment and redemption, inspired by the teachings of Meher Baba and on which Townshend had long labored, *Tommy* confused some listeners and reviewers, but contained a glorious selection of dramatic, even emotionally wrenching, original rock music. "Pinball Wizard" (#4 U.K., #19 U.S.), "I'm Free" (#37 U.S.), and "See Me, Feel Me, Touch Me" (#12 U.S.) would be released as singles. To many, the Who's credibility was elevated to the level of the Beatles and Rolling Stones on the compositional skills of Townshend. Numerous performances of *Tommy*, or "Thomas," as Townshend would begin to sarcastically refer to his masterpiece, followed, though few were complete or in the original sequence. Rapt audiences did not seem to mind, however, and in August, the Who made a devastating appearance at Woodstock where they played selections from the album. Though they would come to disown their performance, the visual and audio evidence supports the praise. In between American tours, the Who played the first Isle of Wight Festival in Great Britain and closed out the year with a series of shows in European opera houses.

The year 1970 began on a sour note, as Keith Moon accidentally ran over and killed his chauffeur. However, in the spring, *Live at Leeds* (#3 U.K., #4 U.S.), one of the greatest live albums of all time, came out and picked the Who back up as they entered a new era of creativity and prosperity. In the summer, they capped another American tour by performing "Thomas" at the Metropolitan Opera House in New York City to acclaim, although again the opus was presented in a slightly truncated version. In August, they appeared at the third Isle of Wight Festival, an ill-fated affair where they were reunited with Jimi Hendrix. Like Altamont in California in 1969, the violence and rioting that occurred was seized upon by cynical journalists as yet further proof that the "Age of Aquarius" was over. The Who then capped the year in the winter with the last complete performance of *Tommy* until 1989.

Feeling the pressure to follow his triumph with another opus, Townshend set out to work on a science fiction rock opera called *Lifehouse*, which was likewise based on the teachings of Meher Baba. In early 1971, the Who began rehearsing in London and recording in New York with disastrous results. Daltrey, Entwistle, and Moon were baffled by the concept, and by springtime, the project was abandoned as Townshend experienced a nervous breakdown. Fortunately for them and their fans, however, they returned to the studio shortly thereafter to re-record many of the tracks for a new album titled *Who's Next*. The counterculture critique "Won't Get Fooled Again" (#9 U.K., #15 U.S.) climaxed a sensational set that included "Baba O'Riley," "Bargain," "Going Mobile," and "Behind Blue Eyes" (#34 U.S.). Perhaps most vindicating to Townshend was the album reaching #1 in the U.K. (#4 in the U.S.), and it remains their most popular creation. The innovative programmed synthesizers originally slated for *Lifehouse* added to the requisite bombast of a classic Who recording, and the band finished out the year re-energized with jubilant U.S. and U.K. tours.

Driven by his artistic sensibility and ambition, in 1972, Townshend released his first solo album, *Who Came First* (#69 U.S.), which contained songs relating to Meher Baba and featured acoustic guitar. He also undertook another concept album, dubbed *Quadrophenia*. A "mod rock opera" about the early London scene featuring a hero who is "quadrophenic" (rather than just "schizophrenic"), it consumed much of his time and the near nonstop touring of the band was curtailed. In early 1973, Townshend became alarmed by his friend Eric Clapton's drug dependency and seclusion, and organized a show for him at the Rainbow Theater in London. The event resulted in a classic live album (#19 U.S., #18 U.K.) and helped to jumpstart E.C.'s dormant solo career. During the spring and summer, the Who recorded *Quadrophenia*. In the fall, they toured the U.K. to perform the new rock opera and coincide with its release (#2 U.K. and U.S.), though the taped backing tracks necessary to fill out the expansive production proved unreliable. In November, they opened a U.S. tour in San Francisco, where Moon, the worst substance abuser in the band, collapsed onstage after taking a monkey tranquilizer, and a drummer from the audience was recruited to finish the show. The Who capped the year in Montreal by spending a night in jail after trashing a hotel room.

In the spring of 1974, director Ken Russell commenced work on a film version of *Tommy* starring Daltrey and an all-star cast of musicians and actors, including the Who. Moon would respond to the implication that he had allowed himself to "go to seed" by stating, "I am still the best Keith Moon-type drummer." Townshend was hired to score the sprawling, synthesizer-based soundtrack and experienced a second nervous breakdown due to the stress. Following a U.S. tour and a show at Madison Square Garden in New York, Townshend fell into a deep depression resulting from the pressure to please an audience that wanted to hear the hits and see stage antics, and his desire to continue to move forward artistically. Unfortunately, the conflict would result in a slow decline for the band. In the meantime, Townshend took a hiatus and *Odds & Sods* (#10 U.K., #15 U.S.), a collection of rarities, was released. In 1975, Moon moved to California as his hard partying accelerated and Russell's *Tommy* was released to a thorough critical thrashing in the rock press, although it was enthusiastically embraced by the fans. Daltrey's performance was singled out for praise and he would go on to play Franz Liszt in Russell's historical drama *Lisztomania*.

In the summer, the band recorded *The Who by Numbers* (#7 U.K., #8 U.S.), which contained the mildly lascivious "Squeeze Box" (#10 U.K., #16 U.S.) and "Slip Kid." A U.S. tour began in the fall that was a financial and critical success and showed Townshend full of the old fire and fury.

The Who continued touring in 1976, cementing their reputation as the most uncompromising and hardest-rocking band of their generation. Precipitously, Moon collapsed in concert in the U.S., his body bloating from excessive drinking as his health deteriorated, and the optimism diminished. In the fall, their closing engagement in Toronto would be the last official gig with their legendary drummer and coincided with Townshend's desire to give up touring. He would later reveal that he was frustrated with not being able to perform the more sophisticated songs from *Quadrophenia* and the later albums. In 1977, the band found themselves on another hiatus as Townshend considered quitting in order to focus his attention on recording and making films. Although he felt threatened by the burgeoning punk movement, he was also secure in the knowledge they would brandish the torch for rock 'n' roll rebellion that the Who had lit a decade earlier. Apparently, he was unaware at the time of the high regard and awe in which he was held by bands like the Sex Pistols, and he would write "Who Are You" in response to his dilemma. He also recorded *Rough Mix* (#45 U.S.) with Small Faces bassist Ronnie Lane as the highlight of his solo career. At the end of the year, the Who was filmed performing in a theater for the forthcoming documentary *The Kids Are Alright*.

In the spring of 1978, the band, in a studio before an invited audience, played their last show with Moon, followed in the early summer by the release of *Who Are You* (#18 U.K., #14 U.S.) to moderate response. The album (#6 U.K., #2 U.S.), though, confirmed their enduring appeal, especially in America. The elation was short-lived, however, when in September the inevitable happened: Keith Moon died from an overdose of drugs meant to counteract his alcoholism. Initially, Townshend and the band reacted by thinking that they could not go on without him, but in 1979, the Faces' Kenney Jones was hired with the unenviable task of replacing the world's greatest rock drummer. Nonetheless, the Who felt revitalized and they made their debut with Jones and keyboardist John "Rabbit" Bundrick at the Rainbow Theater. They next won the *Rolling Stone* Reader's Poll as the "Best Band of 1979," despite reservations Daltrey would always have about Jones' musicianship. The Who took to the road at the end of the year, which ended on another tragic note: 11 fans were trampled to death while trying to get into the group's concert in Riverfront Coliseum in Cincinnati.

In 1980, Townshend put out his next solo album, *Empty Glass* (#5 U.S.), with the singles "Let My Love Open the Door" (#9 U.S.) and "Rough Boys" (#89 U.S.), and it stands as his most popular album to date. However, while the Who were touring the U.K. and U.S. in 1980–81, he was battling alcohol and heroin addiction as his marriage was crumbling and he nearly overdosed. The news was a shock to his fans due to his public anti-drug stance but, *Face Dances* (#2 U.K., #4 U.S.), released in early 1981 and featuring "You Better You Bet" (#9 U.K., #10 U.S.), provided encouragement. In 1982, Townshend recorded his third official solo disc, *All the Best Cowboys Have Chinese Eyes* (#26 U.S.), which included the tracks "Face Dances Part Two" (#105 U.S.) and "Uniforms (Corp D'Esprit)" (#48 U.K.). That same year, he checked into a California rehab clinic and Daltrey told him that he would quit touring if it meant saving his friend. Emerging clean, Townshend and the Who began a "farewell tour" in the U.K. and U.S. in the fall as the appropriately titled *It's Hard* (#11 U.K., #8 U.S.), the last album with Jones, came out. For the next two years, Daltrey and Entwistle pursued solo careers, with the former enjoying a measure of success through recordings and acting. Townshend, in comparison, went off to greater acclaim, releasing the album *White City: A Novel* (#26 U.S.) in 1985—which contained a story of his upbringing—and later reluctantly reuniting the Who in order to play a set at Live Aid. Unfortunately, the performance was plagued by technical difficulties. With their 25th anniversary looming at the end of the decade, in 1987, Townshend began hyping the event to Daltrey and Entwistle. In 1989, they reformed with drummer Simon Phillips for 25th anniversary tours in the U.S. and U.K., despite the hearing issues Townshend was suffering following

25 years of "maximum R&B." In consideration of his problem, Steve "Bolz" Bolton played lead guitar while Townshend played acoustic and some electric rhythm, the stage volume was lowered, and a horn section and backing singers were added to fill out the sound. Several special performances of "Thomas" were presented with guest stars on what was being called "The Kids Are Alright" tour. Concurrently, Townshend kept at his solo career, releasing *The Iron Man: The Musical by Pete Townshend* (#58 U.S.), which was based on the *Iron Man* story that was adapted into a movie.

In 1990, the Who were inducted into the Rock and Roll Hall of Fame. However, in a surprising turnaround a few months later, Townshend sent letters to Daltrey and Entwistle stating that he was quitting the band and wishing them well if they wanted to continue on with another guitarist. In 1993, a hit version of *Tommy*, containing several new songs penned by musical director Townshend for the occasion, opened to rave reviews on Broadway. That same year, Townshend released his rock opera *Psychoderelict* (#108 U.S.), which featured both dialogue and music, and launched his first solo North American tour. In 1994, Daltrey, Entwistle, Bundrick, drummer Zak Starkey (son of Ringo), and Pete's brother Simon (guitar) went on the road and recorded *Daltrey Sings Townshend*. In the summer of 1996, the Who reunited to perform *Quadrophenia* with additional musicians, as opposed to backing tapes, at Madison Square Garden. Encouraged to play together, in the fall, the band took the show on the road in the U.S. but were met with cool response and returned home to London. In the summer of 1997, they came back and tried again with *Quadrophenia* but were pilloried in the rock press, as Townshend mostly played acoustic guitar, something he'd been doing in concert since 1982.

In 2000, as the Who came together again to tour the U.S. with drummer Zak Starkey, the designated "spiritual heir" to Keith Moon, Townshend released the *Lifehouse Chronicles*, a six-disc box set that he had been assembling on and off for decades. A year later, they played an unforgettably emotional charity benefit at Madison Square Garden in New York City for the families of the victims of the September 11th terrorist attacks, with Starkey and keyboardist John Carin filling out the band. In 2002, the Who played five shows in England, and with renewed vigor, were preparing for yet another North American tour when tragedy struck the bedrock of the band. On June 27, the seemingly indestructible "Ox," John Entwistle, died of a heart attack while in bed with a stripper at the Hard Rock Hotel in Las Vegas. Even though he had been on heart medication, traces of cocaine were found in his body. After a short period of soul searching, as a tribute to their fallen comrade, Townshend and Daltrey decided to continue with their plans to tour. Fans and critics were divided on the wisdom and appropriateness of the decision, but they played on with the hastily recruited bassist Pino Palladino.

More controversy dogged Townshend in 2003, when he was arrested in England for purchasing child pornography on the Internet. He claimed it was in the interest of research for his planned autobiography in which he was to reveal his belief that he himself had been the victim of abuse as a child. He was released on bail, given a "caution," and placed on the sex offender registry for five years even though no downloaded images were found on his computers. Throughout the ordeal, Daltrey was his strongest supporter, and the situation was credited with bringing them closer together, along with the desire to record new Who music.

On a more optimistic note, in 2004, Townshend and Daltrey recorded two new singles, with Palladino and Greg Lake on bass. The first new Who studio album in 23 years was planned for 2005. Titled *Who2*, an apparent reference to the two surviving original band members, Townshend instead turned his attention to a new mini-rock opera called *Wire & Glass*. At the same time, Daltrey continued to speak of realizing his long-held ambition of producing a biopic of Keith Moon, with comedian Mike Myers being considered for the lead role. In 2006, *Endless Wire* (#9 U.K., #7 U.S.) came out in conjunction with a 2006–07 tour and contained the mini-opera "Wire and Glass," hailed as their best work since *Who Are You*. In 2007, Townshend witnessed the performance of his solo rock opera *The Boy Who Heard Music* at Vassar College in upstate New York.

The Who embarked on Japanese and U.S. tours in 2008 and were presented with Kennedy Center Honors in Washington, D.C., followed by a southern Pacific tour in 2009. That same year, Townshend announce that he was working on a new "opera," *Floss*, containing songs that would likely debut on the next Who album. In early 2010, they played the half-time ceremony at Super Bowl XLIV with a medley of their hits edited down in a way never done before. A tour was planned, but later cancelled due to a return of the tinnitus that has plagued Townshend for years. In 2011, Daltrey and his No Plan B band with Simon Townshend performed a *Tommy* tour without Pete, by his request. However, Townshend planned to tour and perform *Quadrophenia* with Daltrey in 2012 with the hope that new in-ear monitor technology would allow him to play without further damaging his hearing. In the fall of 2011, Townshend announced he'd finished his long-anticipated autobiography, *Who I Am*, and in 2012, it was released to acclaim for his soul-baring candor. In late 2012, a *Quadrophenia* tour was announced for the next year (a Blu-ray of their last show at Wembley Stadium in the summer, titled *Quadrophenia: Live in London*, was released in 2014). Meanwhile, in the fall of 2013, Townshend had declared their final tour would be in 2015 in locales the Who had never visited. In addition, less than a year later, Townshend confirmed that the Who were considering making a new album: "I'm trying to [look] through my 20,000 hours of complete and utter disorganized music [to find possible songs]," adding, "I'll be pulling some songs out of [his long-gestating project] *Floss* to give to Roger to see if we've got enough to make an album. It might be a big waste of time, but I'm hoping there will be an album." In the summer of 2014, Townshend and Daltrey reunited with drummer Kenny Jones for the first time since 1988 at a benefit performance for Prostate Cancer U.K., appearing on the bill with Jeff Beck, Procol Harum, and Mike Rutherford.

Pete Townshend has dedicated 50 years of his life to the love of rock music and appears nowhere near the end of the line. While adding tremendously to the language of rhythm guitar, in particular, he sacrificed part of his precious hearing in order to create a magnificent, timeless musical edifice. To quote one of his raucous, rambunctious, defiant anthems: "Long live rock!"

THE GUITAR STYLE OF PETE TOWNSHEND

Townshend has always seen his role as the driving rhythm and harmonic backbone of the Who and is a master of creative rock guitar chord voicings. With the advantage of having an equally masterful bassist, the late virtuoso John Entwistle, to fill in the bottom and even the middle part of the sonic spectrum, he could indulge his taste for triads and triple stops on the top three strings. Observe the root-position and second-inversion D triad voicings in measure 1, a simple but effective way of making a progression richer and deeper.

Pete Townshend 1

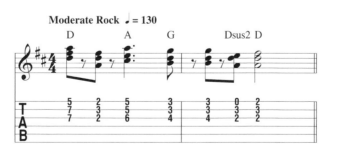

Broken chords are a useful tool for rock guitarists, as they can add forward motion, as well as diatonic melody and dynamics. In particular, notice how Townshend utilizes the classical technique known as "parallel motion" on strings 3 and 1, with the ascending "voices" creating a beautifully melodic sequence.

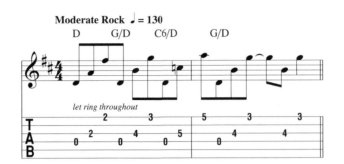

Pete Townshend 2

It has long been acknowledged that Townshend, by his choice, did not develop into one of rock's great soloists. However, he can—and has—soloed with concise, powerful expression, as shown by his skillful command of blues licks and riffs in a rock context. Unsurprisingly for a British guitarist "making his bones" in the '60s, the pervasive influence of Albert King is in strong evidence. Nonetheless, his commitment to harmonic indicators asserts itself in measure 4, where, on beat 1, he inserts a B/G dyad (the 3rd/root of G) before continuing with a blues lick from the G minor pentatonic scale and resolving to the root on beat 4.

Performance Tip: In measure 2, play the low G with the thumb and bend the E/C dyad with the middle and ring fingers, low to high. This approach will place the hand in an advantageous position for the two bends that follow, including accessing the D/B♭ dyad on beat 4 with the index finger.

Pete Townshend 3

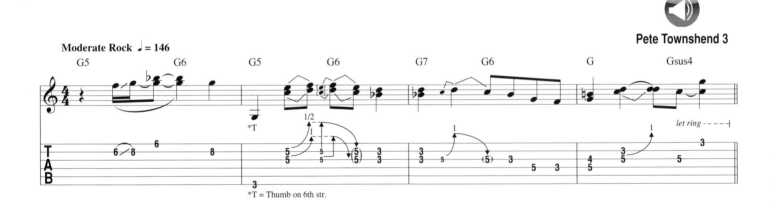

Townshend also favors chordal forms on the bass strings to fill out his palette of aural colors. In this example, he favors the "less is more" approach, with single notes, double stops, and triple stops indicating harmony in a fluid flow of musical forms.

Pete Townshend 4

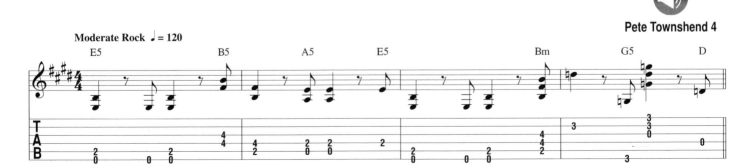

JIMI HENDRIX
(1942–1970)

Jimi Hendrix was so spiritually and physically connected to the electric guitar that his oneness with the instrument was deemed to be a supernatural union, allowing him to reach deep down inside and then soar to stratospheric heights of ecstasy. He was, and continues to be, worshipped as the No. 1 rock guitar "god," and over 40 years after his death, Hendrix's innovative use of electronics and whammy-bar manipulation are still the benchmark. Hendrix listened to his voodoo muse, and through pyrotechnics and culture-crossing fusion, conjured a world of sounds, colors, and indelible images. Though steeped in the blues, his rock music blew up tradition and clichés with wickedly bent strings, extremely overdriven amplifiers, and mind-altering use of pedals and effects.

Originally named Johnny Allen Hendrix, but changed by his father to James Marshall (how appropriate!), Hendrix was born in Seattle, Washington, on November 27, 1942, to Al and Lucille. His mother was part Cherokee Indian, an aspect of his heritage that he would eventually acknowledge in song. In 1951, Al and Lucille, who is remembered as a neglectful mother who frequented night clubs instead, divorced after a tumultuous marriage marred by fights and alcohol abuse. Lucille would die in 1958 from cirrhosis of the liver. As a child, the first music Hendrix heard was the jump blues of Louis Jordan, Roy Milton, and Big Joe Turner, with Muddy Waters and B.B. King also making appearances on the family turntable. By 8, he had become enthralled with the guitar and would play air guitar on a broom, leaving bristles all over the floor for his father to find when he returned home from work. In elementary school, Hendrix was so intent on having a guitar that school personnel felt it would be harmful to his psyche if he did not get one. He proceeded to make a cigar box guitar with rubber bands until his father acquired a one-string ukulele.

In 1956, Hendrix heard Mickey and Sylvia's "Love Is Strange" and his passion to play a real guitar escalated to a full-out obsession. In 1957, he saw Elvis play in Seattle and met Little Richard in his neighborhood, further fueling his desire until he finally received a $5 acoustic from his father the following year. The hot R&B that drove his imagination would not let him be, however, and he badgered his father until he bought his son a white electric Supro Ozark, without amp, from a local music store in 1959. In order to further bond with his son, Al Hendrix also purchased a C Melody saxophone for himself so they could play together. A natural left-hander, the younger Hendrix would always turn right-handed guitars upside down and restring them.

By 1959, Hendrix was in the Rocking Kings performing the rock 'n' roll and R&B hits of the day. At the same time, he was deeply absorbed in the blues of Jimmy Reed and Elmore James, in addition to Muddy and Hooker. Apparently, he learned many of his stage moves, including playing with his teeth, from local Seattle guitarist Raleigh "Butch" Snipes. In addition, he was profoundly impressed by guitarist David William "Guitar Shorty" Kearney, who dated his half-sister and did somersaults and flips onstage. Hendrix dropped out of high school in 1960 and scuffled at menial day gigs while living to play his guitar. He had two brushes with the law and was given the option of going to reform school or joining the Army. In 1961, he enlisted in the 101st Airborne Division as a parachutist and was stationed in Ft. Campbell, Kentucky, where he continued to play and would meet bassist Billy Cox. His Army career lasted but one year, as he was given a discharge for laxness, which he readily accepted. Nonetheless, he continued playing on and off the base with Cox in the Casuals, an informal group.

In 1962, Hendrix stopped with the Casuals in nearby Clarksville, Tennessee, to wait for Cox to be discharged and observed guitarist Alphonso "Baby Boo" Young play with his teeth. When Cox arrived, they continued on to Nashville to advance their fortunes in the music business, with Larry Lee supplanting

Young on second guitar. Changing their name to "the King Kasuals," Hendrix and Cox began finding their way around the local R&B scene. They were often called upon to back established artists like Carla Thomas and Nappy Brown and went out on tour with Curtis Mayfield and the Marvelettes. Mayfield's unique chord-melody approach, along with that of Steve Cropper at Stax Records in Memphis (whom he met while on a package tour with Sam Cooke in 1964), would have an extraordinary effect on Hendrix. Other tours on the "chitlin' circuit" sharpened his chops and included backing Solomon Burke, Jackie Wilson, and Chuck Jackson. Hendrix would also meet Bobby Womack, another R&B great with a unique lead/rhythm style. In late 1962, Hendrix went to Vancouver to visit relatives and stayed into the new year.

In early 1963, Hendrix returned to the South for another shot at making it. He resumed "cutting his teeth" backing acts associated with the Theater Owners' Booking Agency (TOBA), also sarcastically known in the 'hood as "Tough on Black Asses" due to their punitive financial policies. In 1964, he then went to New York at the urging of a promoter who recognized his latent talent and landed in Harlem. Exercising the exceptional power that he had over the ladies, Hendrix got Faye Pridgeon to take him in and bring him to the Apollo Theater, where she introduced him backstage to Sam Cooke, her former boyfriend. Hendrix was hoping to land a gig with Cooke, which did not materialize, though he did make a favorable impression on the legendary soul singer. More significantly, in early 1964, Hendrix won first prize at the Apollo Amateur Night competition. With the street savvy Pridgeon as his culture guide, he made the rounds sitting in at the clubs to the consternation and derision of the conservative musicians who had no time for his outrageous blues playing. Also contributing to his growing unhappiness was his chronic poverty, as he often had to pawn his guitar and then scramble to borrow one in time to play. However, his first real break occurred when he was offered a gig with the Isley Brothers, who encouraged him to develop his talent and showmanship. He would record "Testify" with the band but, while on tour with them later in 1964, he became restless and split while in Nashville.

In 1965, he joined Little Richard's band as "Maurice James" and wore a pencil-thin moustache. The two flamboyant artists butted heads over every detail, including stage clothes and showmanship. Nonetheless, Hendrix was quoted as saying, "I want to do with my guitar what Little Richard does with his voice." While on tour in L.A., Hendrix recorded "My Diary" with singer Rosa Lee Brooks. The song was written by singer/guitarist Arthur Lee of the band Love, who would exert an influence on Hendrix's image and vocal style. In addition, Hendrix would make his last recording on Lee's *False Start* in 1970, on "The Everlasting First." A brief stint with Ike and Tina Turner in 1965 was followed by Hendrix returning to the Isley Brothers in the summer to record "Move Over and Let Me Dance" b/w "Have You Ever Been Disappointed?" It was then a short trip from the Isley's home base in north New Jersey back to Harlem, where Hendrix met journeyman R&B singer/band leader Curtis Knight. Joining Knight would prove to be a major step upward, as he came to the attention of producer Ed Chalpin, who also recognized his talent and signed him to a three-year recording contract that would come back to haunt the young guitarist. A series of mostly mediocre recorded tracks with Curtis Knight & the Squires resulted and would come to be shamelessly exploited, with the exception of one spectacular live blues show that was recorded by Chalpin with a portable recorder on December 26, 1965 in Hackensack, New Jersey. Consisting of classics and the spectacular Hendrix original instrumental "Driving South," it displayed his already devastating virtuosity, as well as his vocals, and the first aural example of him playing with his teeth. In retrospect, it also reveals the enormous influence Buddy Guy would have on him.

Between gigs with Knight, Hendrix went out on the road for two months with Joey Dee & the Starliters (of "Peppermint Twist" fame), along with backing and recording controversial tracks with King Curtis in tandem with R&B guitarist Cornell Dupree in 1966. Similarly, recordings with saxophonist Lonnie Youngblood in Philadelphia would eventually lead to overdubs, fabrications, and legal wrangles later on. In the early summer, Hendrix formed a band in Greenwich Village under the name Jimmy James and the Blue Flame, featuring future Spirit guitarist Randy California (nee Wolfe). Their final shows together would be backing blues singer/guitarist John Hammond, Jr., as the big break loomed. Linda Keith, "girlfriend" of Keith Richards, heard and befriended Hendrix and introduced him to Animals bassist Chas Chandler, who was moving into management and production. Impressed with the Hendrix version of folkie Tim Rose's version of Billy Roberts' "Hey Joe," Chandler spirited Hendrix off to London, where he suggested "Jimi" instead of "Jimmy," exposed him to science fiction, and built the Experience around him, with Noel Redding on bass and "Mitch" Mitchell on drums. Chandler would then hand Hendrix off to manager Michael Jeffery.

It would be difficult to exaggerate the effect Jimi Hendrix had on the British rock scene in 1966. Established stars like Eric Clapton, Pete Townshend, Jeff Beck, the Rolling Stones, and the Beatles were quite blown away. His combination of outrageous showmanship (expected on the chitlin' circuit), high volume, distortion, feedback, and psychedelic blues pyrotechnics made him an overnight sensation. Tragically, his star would blaze bright for only the better part of three years, with a limited number of recordings released before his untimely death. The single "Hey Joe" (#6 U.K.) was followed in 1967 by "Purple Haze" (#3 U.K., #65 U.S.), and "The Wind Cries Mary" (#6 U.K.), and his first landmark album, *Are You Experienced?* (#2 U.K.), featured, along with the three singles, the classics "Manic Depression," "Fire," and "Foxey Lady" (#67 U.K.). The album would reach #5 in the U.S. after the Experience debuted at the landmark Monterey Pop Festival in California in the "Summer of Love," as Hendrix raised the bar to unreachable heights for virtually all rock guitarists. Fulfilling his contract with Track Records, Hendrix released *Axis: Bold as Love* (#5 U.K., #3 U.S.) at the end of 1967, an album that featured him stretching his compositional chops with the classics "Little Wing," "Castles Made of Sand," "Spanish Castle Magic," and the hippie manifesto "If 6 Was 9."

In the spring of 1968, the compilation *Smash Hits* (#4 U.K., #6 U.S.), containing the first version of "Red House," filled the void between studio albums. A single from the forthcoming *Electric Ladyland,* the landmark cover of Bob Dylan's "All Along the Watchtower" (#5 U.K., #20 U.S.), came out in the fall of 1968. In less than a month, the double album featuring guest stars Steve Winwood, Dave Mason, and Jack Casady followed and became the first to be initially released in the U.S., where it shot to #1 (#6 U.K., with a risqué cover of nude women). The single "Crosstown Traffic" (#52 U.S., #37 U.K.) hinted at a slight downward spiral in the late fall, but the album, with the experimental soundscapes "Rainy Day Dream Away," "1983… (A Merman I Should Turn to Be)," "Moon, Turn the Tides… Gently Gently Away," as well as the blues tracks "Voodoo Chile," Earl King's "Come On (Let the Good Times Roll)," and "Voodoo Child (Slight Return)," remains a classic.

Noel Redding, originally a guitarist, quit in a snit in the early summer of 1969 after years of chafing under the enormous shadow of Hendrix, who then recruited his old Army buddy Billy Cox to play bass. Opting for a larger sound, he brought in guitarist Larry Lee from the old King Kasuals days, along with percussionists Juma Sultan and Jerry Velez, to form Gypsy Sun and the Rainbows. Their debut at the historic Woodstock Festival in August was a major triumph for Hendrix, with his wildly creative solo rendition of the "Star Spangled Banner" as the centerpiece of a stunning two-hour set to close the festival. However, the band only held together for two gigs in New York and a spate of studio sessions before dissolving.

Returning to the power trio format, Hendrix enlisted drummer/singer Buddy Miles to join Cox, playing only two gigs as the Band of Gypsys including New Year's Eve at the Fillmore East in 1969. The resultant live album (#6 U.S., #5 U.K.), released on Capitol Records as payment to Ed Chalpin for violating Hendrix's original contract, gave a tantalizing look at, perhaps, the shape of things to come. Heavy funk grooves dominated, including "Who Knows," Miles' composition "Them Changes," "Power to Love," and "Message to Love," as well as the anti-war anthem "Machine Gun." After playing a disastrous show at Madison Square Garden at the end of January that consisted of just two songs with Hendrix obviously high on drugs, he ended the Band of Gypsys by replacing Miles with Mitch Mitchell. Though Redding was supposed to come back to complete the "Experience," Cox was still in tow. This "new" Experience, known unofficially as the "Cry of Love," played the Berkeley Community Center in the spring and the Atlanta Pop Festival in the early summer before embarking on a lengthy three-month U.S. tour, which featured Hendrix in top shape. Additional live selections from the Band of Gypsys and the Cry of Love band would eventually be released in 1986.

In between shows with Cox and Mitchell in the summer of 1970, Hendrix began recording material at his Electric Lady studio in Greenwich Village for a new album with the working title *First Rays of the New Rising Sun*. At the end of August, he and the band flew to Great Britain to kick off a European tour and play the Isle of Wight Festival, where his haggard appearance was the perfect image for a concert that ended in disarray and rioting. The rest of the tour went no better, and he was booed at his last concert at the Isle of Fehmarn Festival in Germany on September 6th, after which Cox quit the tour and went home to Memphis, Tennessee. Hendrix left for London and his final performance was at Ronnie Scott's Jazz Club with Eric Burdon and his band War. In the early hours of September 18, 1970, Hendrix died at the "mystical" age of 27 of asphyxiation in the London flat of his girlfriend, Monika Dannemann, under still mysterious and contested circumstances.

The final descent and end of Jimi Hendrix was as tainted and tawdry as his ascent to stardom had been glorious. Dannemann, who committed suicide in 1996, may have been at the least morally negligent in attending to him while he lay unconscious in her bed. The attending physician seems to have been guilty of malpractice and was eventually struck off the medical register. Initially, Eric Burdon claimed it was a suicide, though he recanted. Hendrix was in the process of leaving his shady manager, Michael Jeffery, who was accused of murdering his famous client, though this, too, was never proven. But nothing could ever diminish his supreme musical accomplishments and unequaled contribution to the language of the electric guitar.

Nothing sparks more discussion among rock fans than what musical direction Hendrix would have taken had he lived. By the time of the Band of Gypsys, he had grown tired and discouraged with having to recycle the same group of original hits and pull the same stage stunts. His last jams and previously unreleased tracks reveal a desire to seemingly go in a fusion or perhaps jazz direction, but intense pressure from management and his record company to keep the money-making machine going only fueled his substance abuse, which had always been substantial. Whether his unique creativity would have continued remains an intriguing question, prompted by compositions like the experimental "Cherokee Mist," which appears on several posthumous compilations.

Jimi Hendrix was posthumously inducted into the Rock and Roll Hall of Fame in 1992 and his recorded legacy includes as yet unreleased tapes for a concept album entitled *Black Gold*, which is in the possession of Experience Hendrix in Seattle. The unfinished *The Cry of Love*, featuring "Ezy Rider" and "Angel," was released in 1971 and rereleased in 1997 as *The First Rays of the New Rising Sun*. Unfortunately, there has been too much opportunistic "grave robbing" of questionable quality, though the *Live at Winterland* albums are worthwhile, as are the jazz-rock jams on *Nine to the Universe*. In 2010, Legacy Recordings and Experience Hendrix produced and released *Valleys of Neptune*, a collection of unreleased tracks from 1969 featuring the original Experience lineup that was greeted with much anticipation.

THE GUITAR STYLE OF JIMI HENDRIX

Possibly more than any of his peers and followers, Jimi Hendrix was the most complete guitarist, as evidenced by his revolutionary mastery of both lead and rhythm styles. Building on the influence of blues legends Albert King and Buddy Guy, in particular, he took advantage of the added sustain that resulted from extreme volume and distortion to "throw snakes" in his distinctive blues solos, which seem to "stretch time." Maintaining bends across bar lines creates longer, more expressively fluid lead lines. In addition, the repetition of the ♭3rd (D) as well as the one-and-a-half-step bends to the ♭5th (F) manifests in taut musical tension that is finally released on the root (B) in measure 4.

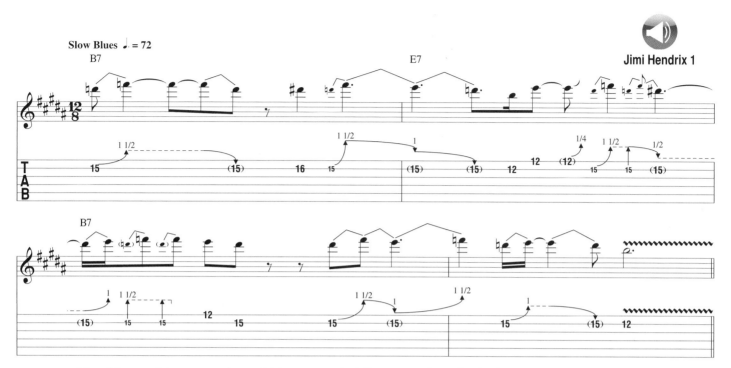

Hendrix provides a preview of his vaunted ability as a trio guitarist by establishing the key in each measure with the root (B) note. In contrast to the previous figure, he tightly compresses "time" by rapidly moving back and forth (mostly) between the root and the ♭7th (A) to produce palpable tension before final resolution to the root on the "and" of beat 4 of measure 4.

Performance Tip: Execute the quarter-step bends to the "true blue note" in between the minor 3rd (D) and major 3rd (D♯) by pulling *down* with the index finger.

Building on the pioneering chord-melody work of R&B greats Curtis Mayfield, Ike Turner, Steve Cropper, and Cornell Dupree, Hendrix fashioned his own virtuosic technique far above and beyond that of his rock guitar peers. Often, the results were relatively simple, if always appropriate to the occasion, as in measure 3 where an F major arpeggio and F major scale licks end with the defining root (F) and major 3rd (A) to outline the F major harmony. Observe the smooth, logical flow from measure to measure as he employs various techniques for each chord change, which increase in relative complexity and culminate in measure 4 with a full A major triad and a melodic fill from the E major pentatonic scale.

Similar to "Little Wing," Hendrix again establishes the root note on beat 1 of each measure in a manner that would make for an effective solo guitar intro sans bass, drums, or another rhythm instrument. Pay attention to his use of the E/C (5th/♭3rd) dyad in measure 1, confirming the minor tonality, as well as the G/D double stop and individual E and G notes, which anticipate the Em harmony in measure 2. Measure 3 blends G minor and major pentatonic notes in a rich melodic and harmonic brew over the course of only four beats. Measure 4 contains a bass string move from the 2nd (G) to the 3rd (A), resolving to the root (F) on string 4.

Each measure employs the root note and a melodic riff that consists of the 3rd, 5th, and 6th from the relative major pentatonic scale, a move Hendrix utilized to great effect in classics such as "Hey Joe," "The Wind Cries Mary," "Little Wing," and "Castles Made of Sand," among others. Check out the major triad voicings for the B and A chords, with the root notes on string 6 accessed with the thumb. Often favored by him in lieu of full six- or five-string forms, these voicings leave the hand in a more advantageous position for mixing in scale licks and riffs, as opposed to the standard voicings that require the index finger to barre across all six or five strings.

Performance Tip: Playing chord melody this way is "Hendrix 101" for major triads. Follow his system of starting on the major 3rd located four frets above the root on string 6, or the equivalent on string 5, depending on whether the E-form or A-form barre chord voicing is used.

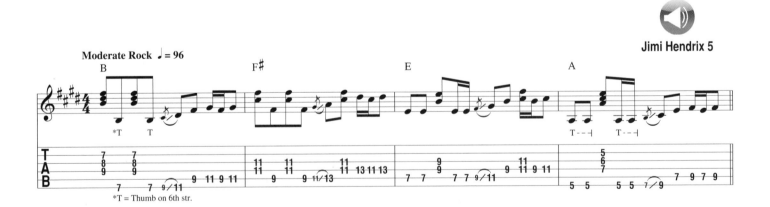

averaging 10 pop and rock sessions a week. Though there are many questions relating to the exact sessions, it is generally accepted that he backed up the Who ("Bald-Headed Woman," the B-side of "I Can't Explain"), the Kinks (their first LP, but probably not the solo on "You Really Got Me" as long rumored), Jackie DeShannon (with whom he shared a romance), the Pretty Things, the Nashville Teens ("Tobacco Road"), Brenda Lee, Lulu, Joe Cocker, Marianne Faithful, Herman's Hermits, Tom Jones ("It's Not Unusual"), and Donovan, among many others. He also recorded an exceedingly rare single in February 1965 under his own name, "She Satisfies" b/w "Keep Moving," featuring his guitar and *vocals* that unfortunately stiffed. That same year, he contributed to a series of blues jam sessions with Jeff Beck and Eric Clapton on the Immediate label for producer Oldham of Rolling Stones fame. A busy year for "Pagey," 1965 was also the year in which he received his first offer to join the Yardbirds, following Clapton's decision to leave. Content with the relative financial security of session work and afraid of offending Clapton by looking like an opportunist, he declined and instead recommended his buddy Jeff Beck.

In June of 1966, however, Yardbirds bassist Paul Samwell-Smith decide to hang it up and Beck talked Page into covering on bass until rhythm guitarist Chris Dreja could learn the instrument (though neither had any experience with it), with the idea of eventually receiving the unprecedented opportunity to perform in a dual-guitar lineup. In fact, because some time would pass before Dreja was ready, session bassists were called in to record so that Page and Beck could engage in what was, for too short a time, a rock guitar freak's fantasy come true. On "Happenings Ten Years Ago," the only official studio track with both guitar greats, John Paul Jones handled the bass chores in a tantalizing preview of what would occur in 1968. Before that, the Beck/Page tandem also appeared in Italian movie director Michaelangelo Antonioni's mod classic *Blow Up* in October 1968, miming to a version of "The Train Kept A-Rollin'" titled "Stroll On." In November, Beck was fired from the Yardbirds while they were on tour in the U.S.

Page stayed with the Yardbirds through the recording of *Little Games* in April 1967, an album that featured both Dreja and Jones on bass and debuted Page's famous violin bowing technique (on "Puzzles"). Though the songwriting and production was wildly uneven in this period, Page took the Yardbirds further into psychedelia and experimentation than had occurred even during Beck's relatively short tenure. Tours and more singles followed but, on July 7, 1968, the "original Yardbirds" played their last gig. While Page and Dreja were willing to continue and play the band's remaining bookings, singer Keith Relf and drummer Jim McCarty were anxious to move on to a new pop project. Robert Plant was brought in to sing and he, in turn, recommended drummer John Bonham. A devious trick was played on Chris Dreja, who along with McCarty, was a founding member of the group. He was aced out in favor of John Paul Jones, despite his co-ownership of the band name with McCarty! Much acrimony occurred over Page, Plant, Jones, and Bonham going out as the Yardbirds after the contractual obligations for the band had been fulfilled, but it became moot when the name change to "Led Zeppelin" was officially reported in the rock press on October 18, 1968. Though the late Who drummer Keith Moon has been credited with coining the name, the late Who bassist John Entwistle always maintained that he was the one who said the group assembled for "Beck's Bolero" was "going down like a lead zeppelin." (The spelling of the first part of the name was changed to avoid it being pronounced "leed.") Their historic first gig was November 9, 1968.

The mighty Zep, instead of going down in flames like the Hindenburg as depicted on the cover of their debut *Led Zeppelin* (#10) in 1969, soared to heights undreamed of by the Yardbirds or Clapton's blues-rock supergroup Cream and reached eight-times platinum. Starting with the two Willie Dixon-penned classics, "You Shook Me" and "I Can't Quit You, Baby," Page demonstrated his inventive, dramatic interpretations of the genre along with his genius for hammering the blues into a succession of blues-rock masterpieces, starting with "Good Times Bad Times" (#80) and "Dazed and Confused." *Led Zeppelin II* (#1) the same year was even heavier, winning a Grammy for Best Recording Package, though it was recorded on the fly while Zeppelin was on world tour. It eventually topped out at 12-times platinum while presenting "Whole Lotta Love" (#4) and the virtuoso showcase "Heartbreaker." *Led Zeppelin III* (#1, 1970), however, contained acoustic Celtic and folk music with more of an emphasis on songwriting beyond crunching blues and blues rock, though the epic slow blues "Since I've Been Loving You" can stand with any Chicago or Texas blues. In late 1971, the monumental fourth album was released, known by various names including *Led Zeppelin IV* (#2). Cited by many fans, musicians, and critics as their paramount achievement, it went 23-times platinum and would cement their status as the greatest rock band of the '70s with Page the reigning guitar hero via classic tracks like "Black Dog" (#15), "Rock and Roll" (#47), Memphis Minnie's "When the Levee Breaks," and arguably the #1 rock song of all time, "Stairway to Heaven." Balancing the overwhelming blues power is the selection of acoustic Celtic and folk tunes for which the band was likewise being lauded.

Four more studio albums of new songs would follow as Page refused to be locked in to recycling the heavy blues-rock style the band had come to epitomize and dominate. *Houses of the Holy* (#1, 1973, 11-times platinum) was the first to contain all original material, including "D'yer Mak'er" (#20) and "Over the Hills and Far Away" (#51). The two-disc *Physical Graffiti* (#1, 1975, 16-times platinum) is an expansive collection of the various styles Page and Plant were exploring, and both have named it their favorite album, as well as the peak accomplishment of Led Zeppelin. Included are the classics "Kashmir," "In My Time of Dying," "Trampled Under Foot" (#38), "Ten Years Gone," "The Wanton Song," and "Houses of the Holy," which had not appeared on the previous release. *Presence* (#1, 1976, three-times platinum) was meant to be a return to the basic heavy blues rock of their earlier career and "Nobody's Fault but Mine" (by Blind Willie Johnson, but not credited) and "Tea for One" would bear it out. Recorded under trying conditions due to Plant being confined to a wheel chair following a car accident, it nonetheless showed the ever-evolving musical and producing mastery of Page, and features his favorite song, the epic "Achilles Last Stand." *In Through the Out Door* (#1, 1979, six-times platinum) was recorded following the tragic death of Plant's five-year-old son Karac in 1977. Originally envisioned by Page as "hard-hitting and riff-based," it became a showcase for the synthesizer talents of Jones and the restrained, melodious vocals of Plant ("Fool in the Rain," #21, "All of My Love"), in part due to the substance abuse of Page and Bonham, which tended to separate them mentally and physically from their bandmates.

Following the death of John Bonham to an overdose of alcohol on September 25, 1980, at the age of 33, Page was so distraught that Zeppelin deflated and he entered a two-year period where he hardly played, while nursing the heroin habit he had acquired in the late '70s. In 1982, he released *Coda* (#6, platinum), consisting of previously unreleased Led Zeppelin studio and live tracks, including "I Can't Quit You, Baby," and he also surfaced to contribute music to the soundtracks of *Death Wish I* and *II*.

In 1984, Page combined forces with former Free and Bad Company vocalist Paul Rodgers in the Firm, but they dissolved the partnership after two albums. With drummers Phil Collins and Tony Thompson behind them, Page, Plant, and Jones reunited in 1985 for Live Aid in Philadelphia, but the rock guitar legend turned in a shabby performance. Three years later, the band came together again, with Bonham's son Jason behind the trap kit for the Atlantic Records 25th Anniversary Concert at Madison Square Garden, but the results were woefully the same. Undaunted, Page played on Plant's solo effort *Now & Zen* and released his own solo debut, *Outrider*.

Plant refused to reunite Zeppelin a few years later, so Page convened the Coverdale/Page band with former Whitesnake and Deep Purple singer David Coverdale. They kept the unit together for only one album, a self-titled release from 1993. A year later, Plant relented and joined Page, with Jones inexplicably left out, for the acoustic *No Quarter* and the similar *MTV Unplugged*, followed by a smash, sold-out world tour. In 1995, Led Zeppelin was inducted into the Rock and Roll Hall of Fame. It was an encore appearance for Page, who had previously strolled in with the Yardbirds in 1992. Page and Plant released *Walking into Clarksdale* in 1998 to little interest and the longtime collaborators called it a day. Page joined the Black Crowes for a tour and a live album, *Live at the Greek*, in 2000, though a second tour was torpedoed when

Page hurt his back. In 2001, however, he joined Plant on stage to celebrate the 60th birthday of folk artist Roy Harper. To the wildly enthusiastic response of Zeppelin's countless fans, in 2003, Page oversaw the release of separate DVD and CD box sets containing previously unreleased live performances. In 2014, he was hard at work re-mastering all nine Zep albums while searching down alternate takes and bootlegs to present his and the band's legacy as he wished it to be preserved. Meanwhile, Plant steadfastly refuses to be involved in a reunion, despite the clear enthusiasm of Page and Jones.

THE GUITAR STYLE OF JIMMY PAGE

As with his illustrious British peers, Jimmy Page traces his influences to the blues, with B.B. King and Otis Rush being only two of the legends he studied assiduously. Likewise, along with the best of his guitar buddies, he absorbed the styles of the originators and turned them into his own brilliant style. Proving the point is his combination of minor pentatonic, major pentatonic, and blues scales into a seamless flow of musical expression. Observe his unusual use of C# (6th) and F# (9th) from the E major pentatonic scale in measure 1 to create subtle diatonic tension before resolving to the root (E) on the "and" of beat 4. In addition, notice the brief appearance of the abrasive ♭3rd (G) in measure 3 (beat 4), followed by the sweet bend to the major 3rd (G#) to conclude the phrase (measure 4).

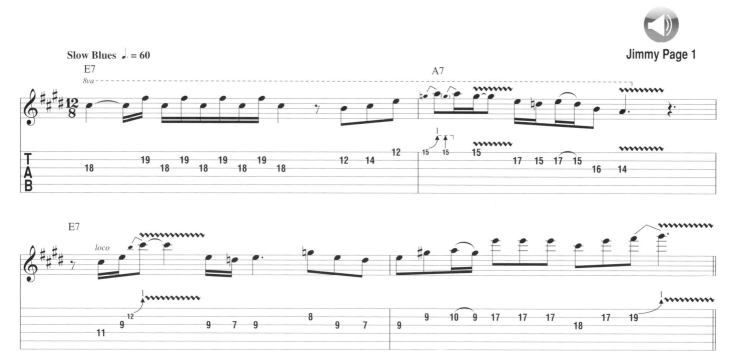

Page has an affinity for the classic West Side of Chicago blues as exemplified by Otis Rush, Buddy Guy, and Magic Sam. A hallmark of their style is minor key blues, and Page is more than adept at creating memorable forays into the dramatic tonality. In major or minor keys, Page, more than most, is intelligent about defining chord changes when he deems it appropriate, as in measures 1 and 2, where he clearly navigates the i (Cm) and iv (Fm) changes with the C Aeolian mode. In that same vein, the passage in measure 4, one of his favorite bending licks, produces an Eb/C (b3rd/root) dyad to nail the i chord.

Performance Tip: In measure 4, bend the Bb note with the ring finger, backed by the middle and index, while accessing the Eb with the pinky.

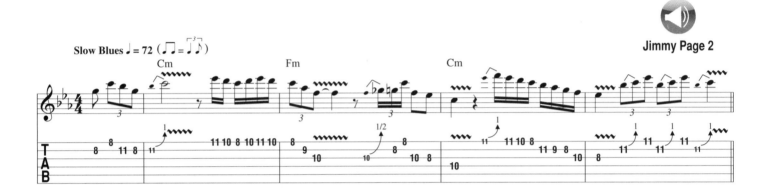

Blues and, particularly, rock guitarists, love to play fast, repetitive patterns to build tension—or to show off! The sextuplet is a favorite of Brit guitarists, and Pagey employed it to highlight his unaccompanied solo in "Heartbreaker." Though most pickers opt to play these types of licks exclusively on the top strings, check out how they can be moved down to two other sets of strings for an especially dramatic effect.

Performance Tip: Use strict, alternating downstrokes and upstrokes.

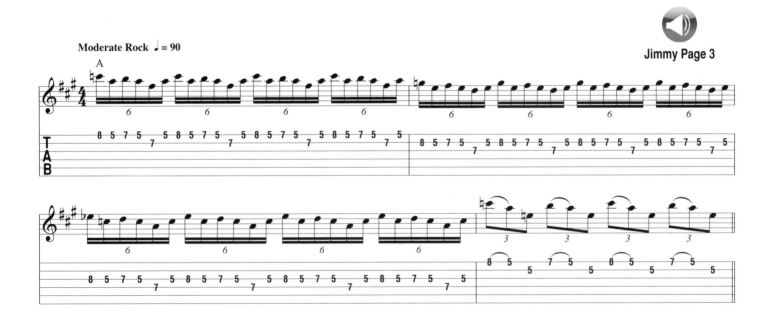

Another "fab gear" pattern of the Brits moves sequentially up and down the minor pentatonic scale, using mostly triplet phrasing.

Performance Tip: Page throws in hammers and pulls, but as a chops builder, strict, alternate upstrokes and downstrokes are recommended.

Jimmy Page 4

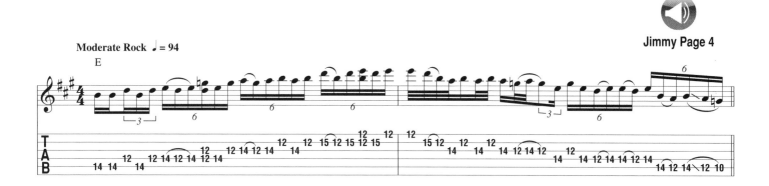

Variations of the classic flamenco descending minor key progression seems to have been "in the air" in the '60s and '70s. Prominent examples include "All Along the Watchtower," "While My Guitar Gently Weeps," "25 or 6 to 4," "Turn to Stone," and "Sultans of Swing," as well as the solo chords in the ultimate Led Zep classic, "Stairway to Heaven."

Jimmy Page 5

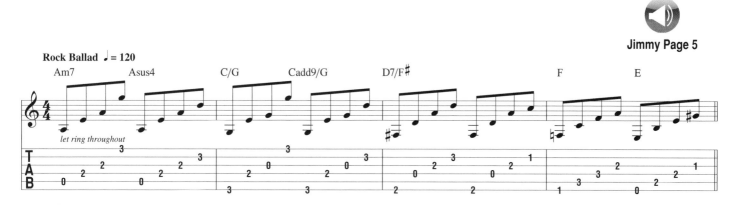

David Gilmour of Pink Floyd, in concert, 1977.

(Photo by Ian Dickson/MediaPunch)

DAVID GILMOUR
(1946–)

Despite two major changes in personnel, Pink Floyd navigated the winds of change that blew through rock music from the mid-'60s to the '90s. Their long, strange trip absorbed a rich variety of styles, from blues to early psychedelia, folk, jazz, and electronica, ultimately creating a unique form of moody, grandiose music. Though bassist Roger Waters maneuvered to become the de facto leader of the band in a bloodless coup, it is the exceptionally melodic guitarist David Gilmour who had been the steady force and guiding light through the decades of musical change and band turmoil. In his personal life, Gilmour has been involved in many charities, was appointed a CBE (Commander of the Order of the British Empire) in 2003, and was presented with the Outstanding Contribution title at the 2008 Q Awards.

David Jon Gilmour was born on March 6, 1946, in Cambridge, England, to Douglas and Sylvia. While a young schoolboy, he met Roger Keith Barrett, nicknamed "Syd," whom he would later meet up with again when both attended the Cambridgeshire College of Art and Technology. Barrett had been playing guitar in a band and a mutual interest in music brought them together, as Gilmour also began playing guitar. In addition, Barrett's childhood friend Roger Waters also took up the instrument. In 1963, Gilmour joined Jokers Wild, a group that played R&B covers, and in the summer of 1963, he and Barrett took off for France to unsuccessfully busk and travel. When they returned to Britain, Gilmour briefly hooked up with the band Flowers before rejoining Jokers Wild, who had renamed themselves "Bullitt." During that same time period, Waters was playing rhythm guitar in a group known as either Sigma 6 or the Meggadeaths with keyboardist Richard Wright and drummer Nick Mason. When their bassist and singer left, Waters switched to the four-string while Barrett and a second guitarist were brought in and the band went through a laundry list of names, finally settling on the "Tea Set" by 1964. Barrett, who came to be acknowledged as a musical genius, would assume leadership and rechristen them "Pink Floyd" in honor of American bluesmen Pinkney "Pink" Anderson and Floyd Council. By 1966, under Barrett's inspired stewardship, Pink Floyd had evolved from the typical rock and R&B of the British Invasion into the premier English psychedelic band, with mind-blowing light shows and revolutionary, experimental instrumental sound effects.

Their 1967 debut album, *The Piper at the Gates of Dawn*, made the British Top Ten and was hailed as second only to *Sgt. Pepper's* as a psychedelic landmark due to Barrett's innovative, spacey, and humorous songwriting. However, subsequent touring revealed his LSD abuse and consequent erratic behavior and he would never pen another masterpiece. In early 1968, Gilmour was hired to cover for him on lead guitar, and within months, Barrett's mental condition so deteriorated that he left to become a solo artist, releasing two albums. Eventually, his condition became so critical that his mother confined him to homecare, where he painted and tended a garden for the rest of his life.

Waters took over lead vocals and writing duties on Floyd's next album, *A Saucerful of Secrets*. In addition to Gilmour's impressive skills, it extended and expanded upon the space-travel themes of their debut. *More*, from 1969, was conceived as a soundtrack for the French hippie movie of the same name. The two-disc *Ummagumma*, containing a live disc and a studio disc, followed and presented the band in all of its otherworldly power, glory, and creativity, charting at #74. In 1970, *Atom Heart Mother* (#55) further tantalized with its orchestral pretensions and shorter pop material. *Meddle* (1971), with Gilmour taking a larger role on lead vocals and guitar, went to #70 and ends the first chapter of the Pink Floyd saga. *Obscured by Clouds* (1972) was another movie soundtrack and proved their growing pop appeal, reaching #46. Nothing, however, prepared the band, their fans, or critics for the unprecedented commercial success of *Dark Side of the Moon* the following year. Rocketing to #1, it would remain on the charts for an amazing 741 weeks and elevate Pink Floyd to superstar status worldwide. To this day, *Dark Side* remains one of the most popular albums in rock history.

Rather than building on the positive elements of *Dark Side of the Moon* and the hit single "Money" (#13), *Wish You Were Here* (1975), though containing the Barrett tribute "Shine on You Crazy Diamond," reflected Waters' morose tendencies. Nonetheless, the album still went to #1, while the even darker *Animals* (1977) reached #3. Feeling frustrated creatively, Gilmour released a self-titled solo album (#29) in 1978, as did Wright, who released *Wet Dream* in September. *The Wall* (1979) topped out at #1 while creating dissention in the ranks as a vehicle for Waters' bleak personality. Though highlighting the most successful chapter of the Pink Floyd saga via long, dirge-like songs, conflicts with Waters forced Wright out of the band, though he would be retained as a salaried sideman for the live shows. After the disappointing *The Final Cut* (1983), which was a virtual Waters solo album and the only Floyd disc without Wright, Waters stated that the band was a "spent force." With the group in apparent disarray, Gilmour released his second solo effort, *About Face* (#32), in 1984. The album featured guest musicians Steve Winwood, Pino Palladino, and Jeff Porcaro and was more accessible and pop-oriented than his first solo effort. In 1986, Waters quit and then turned around and sued Gilmour and Mason for the rights to the band name when they attempted to continue on as Pink Floyd, but lost his case.

With Gilmour running the show, Floyd minus Waters returned with a vengeance. *A Momentary Lapse of Reason* (1987), with Wright as a "sideman," was triumphant, reaching #3. With Tony Levin now on bass, the album recalled Pink Floyd's classic, early '70s sound. In what must have been particularly galling to Waters, who was plodding along with a solo career, Pink Floyd hit #1 in 1994 with *The Division Bell,* also including Wright. Several extravagant tours and live albums were produced in the '90s, which preceded the last Floyd reunion with Waters (at Live 8 in 2005) and their induction into the Rock and Roll Hall of Fame in 2006. Coincidentally, that same year, Fender produced two versions of a Gilmour signature Strat based on his black 1969 model. Also in 2006, Gilmour released a live version of Pink Floyd's first single, "Arnold Layne," as a tribute to Barrett, along with a solo album, *On an Island* (#6), followed by *Live in Gdansk* (#26) in 2008, both of which featured Wright.

While Waters continued with his solo career, Barrett died in 2006 at the age of 60, followed in 2008 by Wright's death at the age of 65. Meanwhile, Gilmour toured, and in 2010, released an album, *Metallic Spheres*, with the electronic music group the Orb, on which he played guitar, sang, co-wrote all tracks, and produced. He also appeared with Waters at a charity event in Oxfordshire, England, that seemed to signal an end to their feud. Waters announced that Gilmour had agreed to play the guitar solo on "Comfortably Numb" on the bassist's forthcoming The Wall Live tour in 2011, with Nick Mason also joining in at the end of the show. To date, Waters seems to still hold out hope for a full reconciliation of the remaining three Pink Floyd members, though Gilmour appears to remain adamant.

In 2012, Gilmour and Mason conspired to create a final Pink Floyd album as a tribute to Richard Wright by revisiting songs cut with the late keyboardist during the *Division Bell* recordings that were originally slated for a disc to be called *The Big Spliff*. Studio musicians were brought in to help create an album of "mainly ambient" and instrumental music with Waters nowhere to be seen or heard. The resulting *Endless River* (#3, 2014, gold), the 15th and last Pink Floyd album, became the largest selling pre-order album on Amazon UK.

Meanwhile, it had been reported in 2013 that Gilmour was at work on his fourth solo album. In the spring of 2015, he announced plans for a tour of the UK and Europe in the fall to support the as yet unreleased album. Like his fellow classic rock Brits, the Stones and the Who, he clearly has no interest in sitting at home and becoming "comfortably numb."

THE GUITAR STYLE OF DAVID GILMOUR

Coming up through the age of heavy blues-rock virtuosity, David Gilmour eschewed the pursuit of chops in favor of taste and melody, while still including a noticeable degree of bluesy phrasing. Clearly, it has been a logical and intelligent choice, as Pink Floyd compositions, as well as his own, tend to be drawn from diatonic progressions begging for melody. Add a dose of folk music to the mix, and the harmonic results are appealing chord sequences propelled by steady, gently propulsive strumming.

Performance Tip: Experiment with a combination of downstrokes and upstrokes until a natural-sounding rhythmic flow occurs.

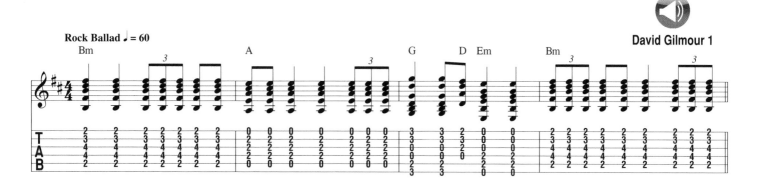

Carefully chosen G major bass-string licks embellish and gracefully connect the following chord voicings, providing a memorable melodic hook.

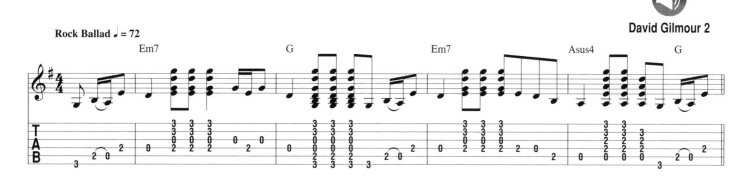

A useful and tasty musical tool for the improvising guitarist is double stops, or dyads. Observe how Gilmour creates a rich harmonic and melodic flow over the chord changes with sliding 4ths and G major scale licks.

Performance Tip: Execute both bends with the ring finger, backed by the middle and index.

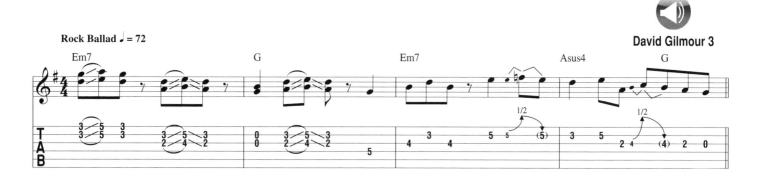

Gilmour once admitted that he sometimes sped up his solos to make them sound faster. Ascertaining *which* solos is likely an exercise in futility and is beside the point, as he arguably gets more from less than any of his esteemed peers. Check out how, in the short span of four measures, he employs a slippery double-string bend, dyads relative to the B Aeolian mode, regular emphasis on the root (B) note, generous musical space, and a long, languid bend from the 4th (E) to the 5th (F#) to produce anticipation of the next chord change.

Performance Tip: Play the double-string bend by pulling *down* with the index finger.

Bluesy string bending is always a welcome dynamic to—or even a substitution for—fast riffing. The fluid, undulating series of bends in measures 2–4 is a striking display of creative virtuosity over the iv (Em) chord from a B minor progression.

Performance Tip: Utilize the ring finger for all bends, relocating to the appropriate fret where necessary.

RITCHIE BLACKMORE
(1945–)

As the volcanic force behind the greatest rocking hits of Deep Purple, as well as his subsequent musical projects, Blackmore holds a unique place among classic rock guitarists in that he was the first to successfully combine classical influences with heavy blues rock. The results opened the door for others with a similar bent to walk through, along with producing a template for music that stimulates the mind and body.

Richard Hugh Blackmore was born on April 14, 1945, in Weston-super-Mare, Somerset, England, to a Welsh father and English mother. As a young schoolboy, he joined the 21s Coffee Bar Junior Skiffle Group on washboard and then, at age 11, asked his parents for a guitar. His father agreed and a Framus acoustic was purchased with the following admonition: "He said if I was going to play this thing, he was either going to have someone teach it to me properly, or he was going to smash me across the head with it. So, I actually took the lessons for a year—classical lessons—and it got me on to the right footing, using all the fingers and the right strokes of the plectrum and the nonsense that goes with it." The discipline and technique would serve him well, even as he would come to be influenced by the British instrumental guitar star Hank B. Marvin of the Shadows, after other decidedly non-classical musicians such as Scotty Moore, Buddy Holly, Cliff Gallup, Duane Eddy, and Chet Atkins. After quitting school at 15, Blackmore formed the Dominators with his school chum, drummer Mick Underwood, and the two would go on to join the Satellites. Blackmore would then leave to play with Mick Dee and the Jaywalkers, all the while hewing to a rigorous practice routine. He bought a Gibson ES-335 and began to study with the late session guitarist and British legend Big Jim Sullivan. A great mentor to countless British guitarists, Sullivan had the first Les Paul guitar in the U.K.—a 1955 Goldtop previously owned by the legendary gospel and blues musician Sister Rosetta Tharpe.

In 1962, Blackmore joined the infamous and outrageous Screaming Lord Sutch and his Savages. By early 1963, Blackmore and Underwood were playing with the instrumental group the Outlaws, and his rapidly improving skills brought him to the attention of British pioneering producer Joe Meek, the man responsible for the Tornadoes' instrumental hit "Telstar" and a disturbed, paranoid rival to Phil Spector. Meek provided him with lucrative session work while producing records for the Outlaws and, during the next three years, Blackmore would back a long list of aspiring English acts, from Heinz Burt to Tom Jones. In addition, he and the Outlaws would get the opportunity to open for American rockabilly cats Jerry Lee Lewis and Gene Vincent. The experience with Meek would also lead to Blackmore meeting engineer Derek Lawrence, the eventual producer of the first three Deep Purple albums. In 1964, he left the Outlaws for Heinz & the Wild Boys. In 1965, he recorded the Yardbirds-inspired "The Train Kept A-Rollin'" b/w "Honey Hush" with Lord Sutch, and "The Getaway" b/w "Little Brown Jag" as the Ritchie Blackmore Orchestra. He then rejoined Lord Sutch for a tour of Germany and ended up moving to Hamburg. The year 1965 would prove to be a busy one, as he formed the short-lived Three Musketeers, joined Neil Christian's Crusaders, and played in Italy with the Trip. In 1966, he again returned to Lord Sutch and his Roman Empire, followed by convening Mandrake Root in Hamburg in 1967. Blackmore was then contacted by manager Tony Edwards to come back to the U.K. to help put a "supergroup" together with organist Jon Lord and ex-Searchers drummer Chris Curtis as lead singer/frontman.

In Hertford, England, Blackmore and Lord formed the rocking Roundabout with Chris Curtis (vocals), Dave Curtis (bass), and Bobbie Woodman (drums). When the erratic behavior of Chris Curtis revealed itself, the personnel would change to Rod Evans (vocals), Nick Simper (bass), and Ian Paice (drums) and has come to be known by fans as the "Mk I" version. At that point, their name was changed by Blackmore to "Deep Purple" in honor of the pop standard recorded by Nino Tempo and April Stevens (1963) and a favorite of his grandmother, before their 1968 debut album, *Shades of Deep Purple* (#24). The album contained a progressive rock version of Joe South's "Hush" (#4), while the follow-up, *The Book of Taliesyn* (#54), released in 1969, featured Neil Diamond's "Kentucky Woman" (#38) along with other covers, including Ike & Tina Turner's "River Deep, Mountain High," done in the over-wrought "baroque" style espoused by Vanilla Fudge. Their self-titled third release featured the classical influence of organist Lord, and Evans and Simper were replaced by Ian Gillan and Roger Glover, respectively, to create the beloved, classic Mk II lineup of Deep Purple.

The grandiose *Concerto for Group and Orchestra* (1969), a live collaboration with the Royal Philharmonic Orchestra, bombed, convincing Blackmore to take the wheel from Lord and steer the band in a snarling rock guitar direction. The result was the million-selling *Deep Purple in Rock* (1970), which pounded long and hard. Though it did not break the Top 100, the album, along with *Fireball* (#32) the following year, set the pace for the Purp's rule as rock titans in the early '70s. The benchmark was *Machine Head* (#7) in 1972, followed by the incendiary *Live in Japan* (#6), which put them in the company of Led Zeppelin and Black Sabbath courtesy of "Highway Star," "Space Truckin'," and especially, "Smoke on the Water" (#4). Based on a true story, "Smoke on the Water" documented the burning of the historic Montreux casino in Switzerland and the extraordinary effort necessary to complete the song and album. Adding to their legacy, Deep Purple has been cited by the *Guinness Book of World Records* for being the world's "loudest rock band" and for having the most guitarists play their "Smoke on the Water" riff.

Ritchie Blackmore performing with Deep Purple in 1973.

(Photo by Ian Dickson/MediaPunch)

Though *Who Do We Think We Are* (#15, 1973), with the classic "Woman from Tokyo" (#60), maintained their momentum, the wheels started to come off. Gillan left after a long-simmering conflict with Blackmore, and Glover soon followed. Singer David Coverdale and bassist/singer Glenn Hughes (Mk III) were brought in for *Burn* (#9, 1974), which benefitted from the alternating lead vocals of the new recruits. While not the smash of the previous release, *Stormbringer* (#20, 1974) nonetheless showed that the fans were warming up to the two new vocalists. Alas, the good times were not to last as Blackmore found the soul and R&B influences of Coverdale and Hughes, which he derogatorily called "shoeshine music," not to his liking and the live *Made in Europe* (#148, 1975) would be his last. In 1974, he split and moved to Los Angeles for tax reasons, forming Ritchie Blackmore's Rainbow with American vocalist Ronnie James Dio and his band Elf (minus their guitarist), but the new heavy metal aggregation never played a gig. Ex-James Gang guitar ace Tommy Bolin was summarily recruited to replace Blackmore in Deep Purple and played his heart out on *Come Taste the Band* (#43) in 1975 (Mk IV), but after a farewell tour, the band pulled the plug in 1976.

Blackmore took up the cello in private in order to put a classical spin on his compositions, and the hit debut album, *Ritchie Blackmore's R-A-I-N-B-O-W* (#30), was released in 1975 with the classic "Man on the Silver Mountain." However, both Blackmore and Dio were unhappy with the sound and shortly thereafter Blackmore fired the band and assembled a new lineup, including former Jeff Beck Group drummer Cozy Powell. The team of Blackmore and Dio would create their acknowledged high point: the lauded, neo-classical metal masterpiece *Rising* (#48) in 1976, along with the live double-disc set *Onstage* (#65) in 1977, after which the band was just known as "Rainbow." The release of *Long Live Rock 'n' Roll* (#89) in 1978 debuted yet another new lineup, and "Hire and Fire" Blackmore sprang into action as the strength of the single "Long Live Rock 'n' Roll" convinced him, to the dismay of Dio, to alter the direction of the band towards hard rock.

For *Down to Earth* (#66, 1979), Deep Purple bassist Roger Glover was brought in to play and produce, but Dio left during the recording due to a clash of egos, or the euphemistic "creative differences," with Blackmore, who grew to dislike Dio's signature gothic fantasy lyric style. Dio would go on to join Tony Iommi in a retooled Black Sabbath, replacing the departed Ozzy Osbourne, while Blackmore found R&B-inflected singer Graham Bonnet as his replacement. The album showed a marked commercialization towards hard rock, and though sales were disappointing in comparison to past efforts, it contained Rainbow's first chart successes: the cover single "Since You Been Gone" (#57) and "All Night Long." Bonnet, however, was no comparison to Dio onstage, and after a singularly drunken performance at a rock festival, was sacked in conjunction with Powell quitting and moved on to join the Michael Schenker Group for a short stint.

The next album, *Difficult to Cure* (#50, 1981), introduced the toned-down American vocalist Joe Lynn Turner and a new drummer. The instrumental title track was an arrangement of Beethoven's *Ninth Symphony* and a personal favorite of Blackmore's. The album revealed yet a further attempt at crossing over, with the goal being to conquer the U.S. audience, as evidenced by the highest-charting Rainbow single, "I Surrender" (#19). Blackmore tellingly described his affinity for the popular arena rock band Foreigner, but older fans thought the vocals were too pop and melodic compared to previous releases, as the music was deliberately aimed at AOR. The next release, *Straight Between the Eyes* (#30, 1982), featuring the hit singles "Stone Cold" (#40, #1 Mainstream Rock) and "Power" (#35 Mainstream Rock), was deemed an improvement and was justly rewarded by the fans. It would be followed a year later with the even better received *Bent Out of Shape* (#34), which sported the single "Street of Dreams" (#60, #2 Mainstream Rock), received a Grammy nomination for the classically influenced instrumental "Anybody There," and featured two new band members. However, despite the chart success, it was apparent that after seven years, numerous personnel changes, and a major change of artistic direction, the ride "over the rainbow" was finished, and Blackmore called it quits in 1984 after their last performance with a full orchestra in Japan. *Finyl Vinyl*, patched together from live tracks and B-sides of various singles, was released in 1986.

A reunion of Deep Purple's classic Mk II line-up, including Blackmore, occurred in 1984 for the platinum *Perfect Strangers* (#17), *The House of Blue Light* (#34, 1987), and the live double-disc *Nobody's Perfect* (#105, 1988). From there on, the band became the proverbial revolving door, with Gillan and Blackmore quitting at regular intervals. Rainbow vocalist Joe Lynn Turner (Mk V) appeared on *Slaves and Masters* (#87, 1990), while Gillan (Mk II) replaced Turner for *The Battle Rages on...* (#192, 1993). Blackmore remained for the live *Come Hell or High Water* in 1993 before becoming disenchanted with Gillan and quitting midway through a European tour to revive Rainbow briefly, with Joe Satriani finishing out the tour in Japan prior to Steve Morse signing on in 1994. In 1993, Blackmore moved to Long Island from Connecticut, where he had lived since 1978. The new Ritchie Blackmore's Rainbow recorded *Stranger in Us All* in 1995, followed by a hugely successful European tour, before "the man in black" started to turn his attention elsewhere.

Following his appearance on Pat Boone's *In a Metal Mood* in 1996 at the conservative singer's request, a Rainbow tour of South America, recording a version of "Apache" for a Hank B. Marvin tribute album, receiving a display at the Rock and Roll Hall of Fame in Cleveland, and being inducted on the Rock Walk in Hollywood, Blackmore recorded the original, acoustic, Renaissance-based Blackmore's Night with his fiancé, Candice Night, who sings and plays a variety of medieval instruments. The two had met in 1989 when Deep Purple played a soccer match against the employees of a radio station on "Lon-giland" where Night worked, and they began living together in 1991. Consequently, she contributed lyrics to four tracks on *Stranger in Us All,* resulting in Blackmore being reluctant to deem it a Rainbow project, but his record company prevailed. During a U.S. tour in support of the album, *Shadow of the Moon* debuted in Japan as the first official release of Blackmore's Night. Avoiding large rock concert venues for smaller rooms and even castles, the duo regularly appeared decked out in medieval costumes to complete the effect. Under Candice Night's sweet, ethereal vocals, Blackmore slipped in some electric guitar, acoustic guitar, bass, mandolin, and drums, as well as the contributions of a cast of backing musicians, including Ian Anderson. In 1998, *Shadow of the Moon* was released in the U.S., followed in 1999 by *Under a Violet Moon*. Released in Japan and the U.S., the album contained acoustic "shredding" and was more upbeat than its predecessor in anticipation of a tour. In 2001, *Fires at Midnight*, featuring English folk, 16th century melodies, and a larger dose of progressive rock, came out in Japan and Europe, followed by the live double-album *Past Times with Good Company* in 2002, and *Ghost of a Rose* in 2003, as the duo and their retinue of session musicians continued to be received with great enthusiasm, particularly in Japan and Europe.

Beyond the Sunset (#3 New Age), the "romantic album," was released in 2004 in the U.S. and Europe. In 2005, Blackmore's Night finally cracked the U.S. pop market with their holiday single "Christmas Eve," hitting #38 on the *Billboard* Adult Contemporary chart. It was a long way from the days of *Machine Head*. *Village Lanterne* (European Top 100) was released in Japan, Europe, and the U.S. in 2006 and showed Blackmore and Night expanding their vision with vigor and progressive inventiveness, followed by *Winter Carols*, which harkened back to "olde tyme" Christmas sounds and classic carols. After a brief respite, *Secret Voyage* (#1 New Age) was released in 2008 and combined Renaissance and contemporary music, as did *Autumn Sky* (#1 New Age), which followed in 2010. In 2011, Night was featured on her solo album, *Reflections*, which showcased her pop/rock vocal stylings and instrumental prowess while being backed by a large orchestra.

Despite his fearsome image over the years as the "Dark Knight" of rock, Blackmore, along with Candice, has contributed an impressive amount of time to charitable projects on Long Island, as well as around the world. With Blackmore's Night, his approach to making music has also mellowed, allowing him to grow by incorporating his classical chops and indulging his and Candice's Renaissance fantasies.

THE GUITAR STYLE OF RITCHIE BLACKMORE

Ritchie Blackmore is a virtuoso rock guitarist conversant in a variety of styles, from blues rock to proto-heavy metal and classical rock, as well as his current focus: Renaissance music. However, he will always be known for simple classic rock riff in 4ths, like the one below.

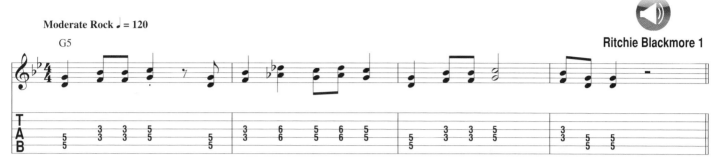

As the possessor of one of the strongest right hands in rock, Blackmore can blister 16th notes at will. The descending chromatic run below begins with octave Es on string 1, interspersed with the open E string, and ends on F♯ (6th) before reversing direction and producing great musical tension and anticipation. Be aware that this figure can also be applied to the keys of E and B.

Showing his respect for blues technique, in the figure below, Blackmore reins in his speed chops and executes a gradually released bend, moving from the 5th (D) to the 4th (C) before arriving at his bluesy destination: the ♭7th (F). Roy Buchanan was a master of this technique, as it produces tremendous tension while creating the dynamic illusion of musical time slowing down.

Performance Tip: Use the ring finger, backed by the middle and index, for the bend.

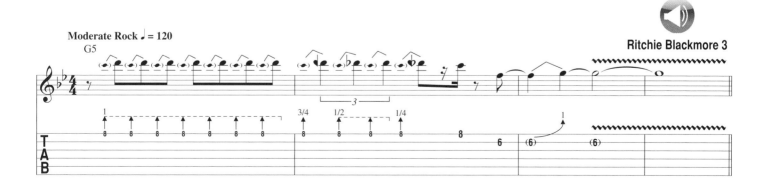

Though occasionally guilty of excess like some of his metal peers, Blackmore was more likely to craft tasty forms that have stood the test of time. Notice the effectiveness and utter simplicity of this classic riff:

Ritchie Blackmore 4

In this next figure, fast, serpentine bends embellish basic E minor pentatonic licks at the root-octave position with a blues hue and dynamics. Of particular importance is the sharp musical tension created by the bends from A (4th) to B (5th) and from G (♭3rd) to A. However, resolution to the root (E) occurs in each measure most dynamically by way of D (♭7th) bent to E (measures 2–4).

Performance Tip: Bend the A note on string 3 with the ring finger backed up by the middle and index fingers. Bend the D note on string 2 and the G note on string 1 with the pinky backed up by the ring, middle, and index fingers.

Ritchie Blackmore 5

CARLOS SANTANA
(1947–)

Starting in the late '60s in the San Francisco scene as a Mexican immigrant who fused exuberant, syncopated salsa and African rhythms with rock, blues, and jazz to produce a virtually new category of popular music, Carlos Santana confounded every popular stereotype. Still active, vital, and winning awards and accolades over 45 years later, his virtuosity, creativity, and spirituality propel him ever forward as a vaunted instrumental virtuoso who "sings" magnificently through his guitar.

Born July 20, 1947, in Jalisco, Mexico, Carlos Augusto Santana Alves began playing the violin at the age of 5, like his Mariachi musician father. At around 8 years old, he came to the guitar through the blues of B.B. King and John Lee Hooker, and later, the Hungarian jazz guitarist Gabor Szabo, at a time when there were few Latino rock guitarists outside of the late Ritchie Valens. When he was a teenager, Santana's family moved to Tijuana and he began playing in clubs, where he would meet Javier Batiz, the legendary Mexican blues pioneer and rock guitarist, who claims to have given the aspiring guitarist lessons in return for playing bass in his band. It appears that in addition to instruction, Batiz offered other tips, both musically and sartorially, to Santana and drummer Fito de la Parra (later of Canned Heat). When his family moved on to San Francisco, Santana stayed behind in Tijuana through the late '50s, cutting his teeth in the notorious, freewheeling destination for tourists seeking gambling and other vices.

In the early '60s, Santana followed his family to San Francisco, where he played on the street and washed dishes for several years before deciding to go for it and become a full-time blues musician. In 1965, he became a naturalized American citizen and the music of and a meeting with Michael Bloomfield would have a profound effect on him. Frequent visits to the Fillmore East afforded him the opportunity to see his idol B.B. King in person, while the hallowed counterculture venue would also prove to be the scene of his "discovery." He was looking forward to seeing Paul Butterfield at the Fillmore in 1966, but the Chicago harp star cancelled and impresario Bill Graham assembled a pickup band from the Butterfield band, the Grateful Dead, and the Jefferson Airplane. Santana was also recommended as one of the guitarists and his exceptional talent and passion was exposed to the audience, as well as to Graham, who would become a loyal booster.

Santana would go on to form the Santana Blues Band. Featuring Gregg Rolie (keys and vocals), David Brown (bass), Mike Carabello (congas), who was on board only briefly, Bob "Doc" Livingston (drums), and Marcus Malone (percussion), the group debuted at the Fillmore in the summer of 1968. In the early fall, Santana was one of the San Francisco musicians called upon to fill in for the ailing Mike Bloomfield at the Fillmore, playing a powerful blues solo on Jack Bruce's "Sonny Boy Williamson," which was recorded for the famous *The Live Adventures of Michael Bloomfield and Al Kooper*. Late in the year, the band, now known simply as "Santana," with the guitarist rising to be the unquestioned leader and featured soloist, signed with Columbia Records. Livingston and Malone split in 1969 and were replaced by Mike Shrieve and Carabello, respectively. In addition, Jose "Chepito" Areas joined as a second percussionist to complete the sextet. Bill Graham arranged their appearance at Woodstock in August of 1969 and the subsequent movie and soundtrack album, highlighted by their orgasmic "Soul Sacrifice," came just prior to the release of their self-titled, platinum debut album (#4), which contained the Willie Bobo song "Evil Ways" (#9), suggested by Graham, and "Jingo" (#56), based on an Olatunji composition.

In an era of revolutionary musical evolution, the paradigm had changed in rock music. Unfortunately, schisms erupted early within the band, as Rolie and others wanted to continue in the heavy Latin rock vein while Santana desired to follow his growing interest in spirituality and jazz via John Coltrane and Miles Davis.

In addition, Areas suffered a serious illness, necessitating a leave of absence, and some band members felt it inappropriate to continue on before he could return. The seeds of dissension were sown. In a story all too common to the era and the music business, drug abuse would also plague the band for years.

The epochal, sensational, and platinum *Abraxas* followed in 1970, reaching #1 with the early Fleetwood Mac/Peter Green composition and classic rock staple "Black Magic Woman" (#4), a stunning version of Tito Puente's salsa classic "Oye Como Va" (#20), the original "Samba Pa Ti," and the dramatic and ambitious Latin/rock/jazz landmark "Incident at Neshabur." Most significantly, extended instrumental passages boldly revealed Santana's evolving guitar skills and progressive musical direction, establishing him as a major "voice" on the guitar to be considered in the same company as other contemporary rock guitar heroes like Eric Clapton, Jimmy Page, and Jeff Beck. By the end of the year, 15-year-old blues guitar wiz Neal Schon was added to the lineup, Thomas "Coke" Escovedo temporarily replaced Areas, and the equally spectacular *Santana III* earned the group another #1, going double platinum in 1971. Highlighted by "Everybody's Everything" (#12), featuring the Tower of Power horn section, "No One to Depend On" (#36), and a rare Carlos vocal, "Everything's Coming Our Way," the album marked the end of the original Santana lineup and its democratic philosophy. Carlos would eventually gain legal rights to the band name and henceforth record and perform with various sidemen over the years, including several original members. Coke Escovedo and his brother Pete went and formed Azteca, a big, multi-instrument Latin orchestra that would briefly include Schon. In the meantime, in early 1972, Santana, Schon, and Escovedo toured with former Electric Flag and Jimi Hendrix/Band of Gypsys drummer Buddy Miles, recording the million-selling, live double-disc *Carlos Santana & Buddy Miles! Live!* (#8), which featured "Evil Ways" (#84) and "Them Changes" (#84).

Caravanserai (#8), released in 1972, contained holdovers Rolie, Schon, Shrieve, and Areas, as well as keyboard wiz Tom Coster, bassist/guitarist Douglas Rauch, and percussionists James Mingo Lewis, Armando Peraza, and Rico Reyes. A major departure from his previous releases in that individual musician credits appeared on each track, the album, a mostly instrumental release, resulted in the guitarist moving firmly in a more introspective, jazz fusion direction. It was nominated for a Grammy for Best Pop Instrumental Performance with Vocal Coloring and eventually hit platinum status. Rolie would leave the rock scene to become a restaurant partner before he and Schon formed Journey with singer Steve Perry, while Santana would become an acolyte of guru Sri Chinmoy, adopting the name "Devadip" (the "eye, the lamp, the light of God"). That same year, Carlos Santana recorded *Love, Devotion, Surrender* (#14) with fellow Chinmoy follower and Mahavishnu Orchestra firebrand John McLaughlin. Inspired by tenor saxophone giant John Coltrane, the wildly improvisational and deeply spiritual jazz collaboration alienated hardcore Santana fans who hoped it was an aberration, but it served to expand his audience, as well as provide a measure of credibility in the jazz community.

The hopefully titled *Welcome* (#25, 1973) only further baffled his fans, as Santana fully embraced jazz fusion, with the emphasis on jazz. His core lineup of Shrieve, Rauch, Coster, Areas, and Peraza was augmented by a large group of guest artists, including singers Leon Thomas, Wendy Haas, and Flora Purim, soprano saxophonist Jules Broussard, and McLaughlin. The progressive and ground-breaking gold record only further burnished his growing reputation as a visionary guitarist who was fearless in the pursuit of his art. *Lotus*, a three-LP set of the same band playing live in Japan in 1974, was originally available outside the U.S. only, as CBS objected to the length of the tunes. In 1991, the collection finally saw stateside release. Continuing his quest, Santana next recorded *Illuminations* (#79) with Alice Coltrane, the widow of the jazz legend, in the process producing the first of his albums not to go gold. Meanwhile, in response to the shrinking popularity of the band, Columbia Records helped fill their coffers by putting out the slim, 10-track *Santana's Greatest Hits* (#17), which would reach double platinum. Closing out a busy and productive year for Santana, *Barboletta* (#20) was an attempt at returning to the classic Latin rock sound that Bill Graham, now involved with management of the band, strongly encouraged, even as

Carlos Santana, circa late 1960s – early 1970s.

(Photo Courtesy CEA/Cache Agency)

bassist David Brown returned to the fold. Still, a feeling existed that the band was marking time, and the record slipped down the charts rather quickly, after which Shrieve would exit for a solo career, replaced by Leon "Ndugu" Chancler.

Determined to reclaim his share of the pop audience with a comeback, Santana released the gold *Amigos* (#10), featuring the track "Let It Shine" (#77), in 1976. The R&B and funk outing was produced by his original producer, David Rubinson, and contained Brown as the only original band member in the trimmed-down sextet. The gold *Festival* (#27), released in 1977, edged back towards Latin rock and was likewise produced by Rubinson. With Brown gone, the concept of a band with a leader and a group of backup musicians was complete, as no original members from the '60s remained. Though more than respectable, *Festival* is the lowest-charting Santana band album to date. After almost a decade, Santana finally released a live Santana "band" album, the platinum *Moonflower* (#10), in late 1977. In reality, it is only partially live, as the Zombies' classic "She's Not There" (#27) single was a studio track, along with others. By any yardstick, the disc sent a welcome, positive signal. *Inner Secrets* (#27), released in 1978 and featuring "One Chain (Don't Make No Prison)" (#59) and a cover of the Classics IV's "Stormy" (#32), as well as Buddy Holly's "It's Alright" (#69), saw long-time keyboardist/cowriter/co-producer Tom Coster leave after admirably filling Gregg Rolie's shoes for years. Even with its lower chart position (compared to the previous release), *Inner Secrets* still went gold with yet another revamped lineup.

At the same time, Santana was also playing as Devadip and continuing to delve into jazz and fusion. In 1979, he put out his first true "solo" album, the largely instrumental and contemplative *Oneness/Silver Dreams Golden Reality* (#87), with Coster and current members of his band, quickly following it with *The Swing of Delight* (#65, 1980), featuring members of the latest incarnation of the Miles Davis band, including Herbie Hancock, as well as his own. In between, the Santana band, with singer Alex Ligertwood, released *Marathon* (#25), which contained "You Know That I Love You" (#5), as well as other original tracks in his tried-and-true rocking R&B style that was a hit in the mid-'70s. Despite the credible chart position, *Marathon* became the first studio album not to go gold. Showing resilience, in 1981, he bobbed back up with *Zebop!* (#9), selling one million copies, with "Winning" (#17) and "The Sensitive Kind" (#56) exhibiting a more commercial rock sound at the expense of his pioneering Latin rock. *Shango* (#22), released in 1982, saw Gregg Rolie return to co-produce and co-write. "Hold On" (#15), with its popular MTV video, and "Nowhere to Run" (#66), could not spin the album into gold, however, and it would be almost 20 years before the Santana band achieved a higher chart position. In 1983, Santana released a solo album that was a surprising departure from his Devadip musings. *Havana Moon* (#31), with its Chuck Berry title track and Bo Diddley's "Who Do You Love," as well as original material, was a look back at '50s rock 'n' roll and Tex-Mex music. Produced by Jerry Wexler and Barry Beckett, it was graced by Booker T. Jones, the Fabulous Thunderbirds, Willie Nelson, and members of the Santana band among its long list of sidemen.

Over two years passed before the next band release, *Beyond Appearances* (#50, 1985), an album that was clearly in the slick '80s pop mode, boasting synthesizers and drum machines. With singer Greg Walker back in the group, "Say It Again" (#46) achieved moderate success, but loyal fans did not embrace the album as illustrated by its chart position. It would be almost 15 years before Santana would have another single in the Top 100. More encouraging that year was their high-powered appearance at Live Aid courtesy of Bill Graham, who stepped in and convinced festival organizers to let them play. In 1986, Santana convened a reunion concert in Mountain View, California, with virtually all the former band members from *Santana III*, including Neal Schon. If the YouTube videos from the show are any indication, the band was as fiery and explosive as ever, with Schon pushing the "boss" to the limit. *Freedom* (#95), from 1987, benefitted artistically from yet another return to Latin rock and a reunion with several former Santana musicians, including Tom Coster and Gregg Rolie, as the ensemble swelled to nine members, with Buddy Miles reenacting his role of lead singer from 15 years earlier. Commercially though, it seemed for naught, as sales and the popularity of the band eroded further. A bright "note" followed, however, when

Santana won his first Grammy for Best Rock Instrumental Performance, for the title track of his "solo" release, *Blues for Salvador* (#195), despite the poor showing of the album on the charts. A collection of mostly outtakes from previous releases, it is remembered for "'Trane," which featured drummer Tony Williams. In 1988, Santana organized a tour with former band members and the addition of tenor saxophonist Wayne Shorter in recognition of the 20th anniversary of the Santana band official debut. In conjunction with the celebration, a 30-track retrospective album exuberantly titled *Viva Santana!* (#142) was released, with the re-release of "Black Magic Woman" (#4) proving the ageless vitality of the classic early '70s recordings.

After 22 years and 15 albums, Santana closed out his association with Columbia Records in 1990 with *Spirits Dancing in the Flesh* (#85), featuring guest artists Bobby Womack, Wayne Shorter, and Vernon Reid. The wide-ranging array of covers included "Gypsy Woman" (Curtis Mayfield), "Third Stone from the Sun" (Hendrix), "Who's That Lady" (Isley Brothers), and "Jin-Go-La-Ba" (Olatunji), from which "Jingo" was originally derived, with the accent heavily on guitar. In 1991, Santana signed with Polydor Records and released *Milagro* (#102) the following year. The album was dedicated to the late Bill Graham and Miles Davis. Besides including songs by Bob Marley and John Coltrane, it also contained solos from the tenor sax legend and Miles Davis, as well as an excerpt from a speech by Dr. Martin Luther King. *Sacred Fire: Live in South America* (#181), released in 1993 and featuring the usual selection of past hits, added to the Santana "in concert" catalog, but contributed little to the coffers or his legacy, as it spent one week on the charts and is the low-water mark of his career. A period of further recording decline for Santana followed, including *Santana Brothers* (#191), featuring his brother Jorge (guitar) and nephew Carlos (drums, percussion, producer), in 1994. That same year, former original band members Rolie, Shrieve, Areas, and Carabello joined forces in Abraxas, but the resultant album failed to chart.

Santana broke with Polydor, had a brief fling with EMI, and was without a label for a few years before hooking back up with Clive Davis, his champion from the early, "heady" days at Columbia Records and the founder of Arista Records, in 1997. The signing would eventually and effectively end his hiatus from recording that had consumed the better part of five years. Before his sensational comeback, in 1998, a stone-cold lock guaranteed Santana and his original band induction into the Rock and Roll Hall of Fame, where they shared honors and the stage with Peter Green on "Black Magic Woman." But it was the presciently named and 15 times platinum *Supernatural* (#1) in 1999, containing the mega-hit singles "Smooth" (#1) and "Maria, Maria" (#1), that brought Santana renewed fame and fortune in an unexpected second act for the veteran axeman. A guest-laden affair conceived by Davis, featuring artists from Eric Clapton to Lauryn Hill, Dave Matthews, and Eagle-Eye Cherry, *Supernatural* intelligently minimized Santana's guitar presence from a commercial point of view, selling 27 million copies worldwide and earning eight Grammys, including Album of the Year. "Smooth," featuring Matchbox 20 singer Rob Thomas, won Record of the Year, Best Pop Collaboration with Vocals, and Song of the Year/New Song of the Year. "Calling," with Clapton, won Best Rock Instrumental Performance. "El Farol" garnered Best Pop Instrumental Performance, while "Maria, Maria" and "Put Your Lights On" (#8 Mainstream Rock) both snared Best Pop Performance by a Duo or Group with Vocal awards.

Released in 2002, the double-platinum *Shaman* (#1) won a Best Pop Collaboration with Vocals Grammy for "The Game of Love" (#5), a song featuring pop artist Michelle Branch. The winning follow-up to *Supernatural*, the album utilized the same successful, star-spangled template as its predecessor, including guests Me'Shell Ndegeocello, Macy Gray, Seal, Musiq, and Placido Domingo (!). In what must have galled his long-time fans, the album displayed even less of the sensuous, vocal-like guitar upon which Santana had built his awesome reputation. Taking a breather but not changing the money-making formula, the even shinier pop pastiche *All That I Am* (#2) arrived three years later, spotlighting Steven Tyler, the returning Michelle Branch, Joss Stone, Mary J. Blige, and will.i.am from the Black-Eyed Peas. "I'm Feeling You" (#55), featuring Branch gamely trying to repeat the magic of "Game of Love," and "Just Feel

Better" (#99), sung by Tyler, paced the singles. Though his guitar prowess is featured more prominently, Santana still ends up sounding like a hired gun on his own project for the third straight release, and it took longer than usual to go gold.

The year 2005 continued to be a busy one for Santana, as he was honored as a BMI icon at the 12th annual BMI Latin Awards, was invited to collaborate with Herbie Hancock on *Possibilities* (#22), and soloed on Shakira's light rock ballad "Illegal" (#1 Hot Dance Club Song). In 2006, he toured Europe with his son Salvador as his opening act.

Loyal Santana fans who may have thought *Guitar Heaven* (#5, 2010) would be a welcome return to the passionate, inventive improvising he does best may have been shocked to hear pop cover versions of classic guitar-rock hits like "Whole Lotta Love" (Led Zeppelin), "Sunshine of Your Love" (Cream), "While My Guitar Gently Weeps" (The Beatles), "Back in Black" (AC/DC), "Smoke on the Water" (Deep Purple), and "Little Wing" (Hendrix). With a passel of eclectic guest singers, again including Rob Thomas, along with Joe Cocker, Chris Cornell, Scott Weiland, India.Arie, and Nas, it rewarded Santana and Arista Records handsomely, though the Beatles track reaching #13 on the Smooth Jazz Songs chart perhaps said it all.

In the spring of 2012, the mostly instrumental *Shape Shifter* (Starfaith Records) was released, his 36th album to date, as Santana headed out on a summer tour while taking a hiatus from his Las Vegas House of Blues residency. Dedicated to Native Americans, the 13 tracks feature father and son, on piano, as soloists, as well as select members of the current Santana band, including Benny Rietveld (bass), Dennis Chambers (drums), Karl Perazzo (percussion), Tony Lindsay (vocals), Andy Vargas (vocals), Chester Thompson (keyboards), and Salvador Santana (keyboards). The mix of originals and covers collects song ideas from the past 15 years and is clearly the alternative to the post-1999 Santana Band albums for those who want to hear the now-legendary guitarist blow his horn.

THE GUITAR STYLE OF CARLOS SANTANA

Exhibiting his unique, signature Latin rock style, in the following example, Santana riffs with idiomatic syncopation and phrasing over a classic i–IV (Am–D) vamp. Indicative of his signature style are the vibrato, hammer-ons and pull-offs, and notes sensually sustaining across the bar lines.

Carlos Santana 1

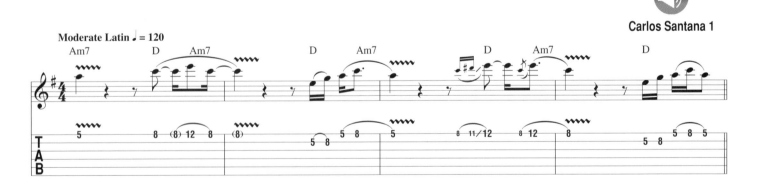

In contrast to his long, fluid lines, Santana is also known for his jack-hammer, staccato phrases. Utilizing the A Dorian mode, one of his favorites, along with the Aeolian mode, he rips 16th notes with precision. Repetition, particularly in measures 3–4, builds tremendous musical tension with A, E, and F♯ notes functioning as the root, 5th, and 6th over Am7, and the ♭7th, 4th, and 5th over Bm7, respectively.

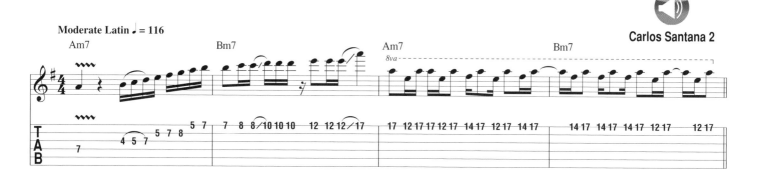

Motifs are prominently featured in Santana's music. Employing the "blue collar" minor pentatonic scale, he fashions memorable riffs emphasizing the 5th (A), ♭3rd (F), and resolution to the root (D). Observe the microtonal bends of the root in measures 1 and 3, which contribute a hint of bluesy dissonance, as well as the dynamic contrast between the staccato notes and the smooth gliss in measures 2 and 4.

Performance Tip: Play the glisses with the index finger.

Perhaps above his other characteristics is his finely tuned ear for melodies. The C major scale provides him with the proper palette of scale tones to not only create beautiful melodies, but to gracefully navigate the IV (F)–I (C) chord changes. Check out his striking emphasis of the major 7th respective to the chords in measures 1 and 2, complementing the major 7th harmonies, and the way the bent 3rd (E) "sings" over the Cmaj7 chord in measure 4.

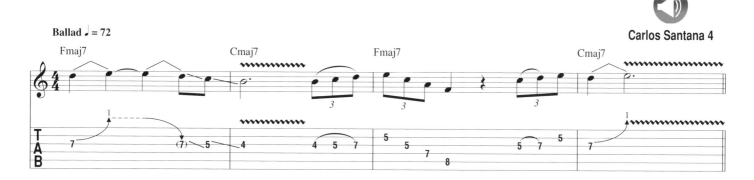

This next phrase demonstrates Santana's mastery of the C Aeolian mode within the context of a smooth, jazzy ballad. His use of the ♭7th, B♭, and A♭ in measures 1 and 2, respectively, produces anticipation to the chord changes that follow. As in the previous example, Santana opts to complete the four-measure sequence with the sweet major 3rd (G).

Performance Tip: Vibrato with the middle finger backed by the index in measure 2 and the ring finger backed by the middle and index in measure 4.

Carlos Santana 5

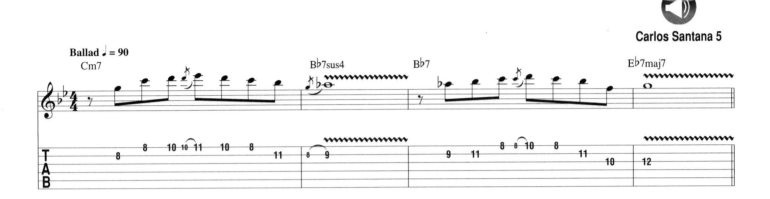

RICK DERRINGER
(1947–)

Rick Derringer enjoyed the distinction of heading the McCoys, one of the few American blues-based bands to briefly hold the line against the oncoming British Invasion in 1965 with their #1 hit "Hang on Sloopy," now the official rock song of the state of Ohio and Ohio State University. Derringer would move forward to play with and produce a wide range of famous artists, as well as foster an ongoing solo career. An exceptionally versatile blues-rock guitarist and producer, Derringer has continued to evolve in his own way while having weathered the vicissitudes of rock stardom at a young age, as rumored to be referenced by Steely Dan in "Rikki Don't Lose That Number."

Born Richard Zehringer on August 5, 1947, in Celina, Ohio, he and his younger brother Randy (drums), Randy Jo Hobbs (bass), Sean Michaels (saxophone), and Ronnie Brandon (keyboards) went from being called the McCoys to the Rick Z Combo and then Rick and the Raiders. "Hang on Sloopy" was written by Wes Farrell and Bert Berns and named for jazz singer Dorothy Sloop Heflick, who used the name "Sloopy" on stage. It was first played in concert in 1965 by the Strangeloves, a trio who claimed to be from Australia, but in fact were three successful writer/producers from Brooklyn, New York. They planned to eventually make it the follow-up to their hit single at the time, "I Want Candy." However, not wanting to compete with themselves, and after finding out that the Dave Clark Five were going to record the Strangeloves arrangement, they quickly enlisted Rick and the Raiders to record the song instead. With their name changed back to the McCoys to avoid confusion with Paul Revere and the Raiders, the Zehringer brothers added Rick's lead vocal, stinging guitar solo, and band background vocals to the completed Strangeloves track. The single was released on Bang Records in October, beating the Dave Clark Five to the punch.

Rick changed his name to "Derringer" after seeing a Derringer pistol pictured on the Bang Records logo. In 1966, the McCoys opened for the Rolling Stones on their American tour before relocating to New York City, but never duplicated the success of "Hang on Sloopy," even though they gamely shed their early "bubblegum" sound to become a psychedelic rock band in the late '60s.

In 1970, Derringer, brother Randy, and bassist Hobbs backed Johnny Winter, becoming the raunchy blues-rocking group Johnny Winter And (also the name of the Winter album). The recording featured Derringer's production, guitar, and "Rock and Roll Hoochie Koo," which he penned especially for Winter. Derringer also played on and produced *Edgar Winter's White Trash* (#111, 1971), featuring "Keep Playin' That Rock and Roll" (#70)*,* and the live, two-disc *Roadwork* (#23), featuring "I Can't Turn You Loose" (#81, 1972).

In 1973, Derringer released his solo debut, *All American Boy* (#25). An appealing combination of teeny-bopper rock, blues rock, and pop rock, it features his classic version of "Rock and Roll Hoochie Koo" (#23) along with "Teenage Love Affair" (#80). Though an impressive first outing, he was not yet ready to make a go of it alone and continued producing records for the Winter brothers. Finally, in 1975, he assembled "Derringer" with guitarist Danny Johnson, bassist Kenny Aaronson, and drummer Vinny Appice and proceeded to gig to cheers, opening for Aerosmith and Led Zeppelin, among others. Following the release of the disappointing *Spring Fever* (#141, 1975), featuring a fey cover photo, as well as a handful of live discs including *Derringer Live* (#123), which conclusively proved he could blaze in concert, Derringer had his road band back him on *Derringer* (#154, 1976), containing "Let Me In" (#88), and on *Sweet Evil* (#169, 1977).

His band deserted him in 1978 and a downturn began in Derringer's recording career, including the forgettable *If I Weren't So Romantic I'd Shoot You*. There were artistic if not commercial exceptions like the Todd Rundgren-produced *Guitars and Women* (1979), however, and his excellent soloing is almost

Rick Derringer performing 1991.

(Ian Dickson/MediaPunch)

always in evidence, though *Face to Face* (1980) was a bust, as was *Good Dirty Fun* (1983). He went on to employ his extensive experience as a producer and guitarist for artists as varied as Meatloaf, Bette Midler, KISS, Barbra Streisand, and Alice Cooper. In addition, he was Cyndi Lauper's tour guitarist for six years and spent five years with Weird Al Yankovic. Derringer and Yankovic won a Grammy in 1984 for Best Comedy Album, *Weird Al Yankovic in 3-D*, on which Derringer uncannily imitated Eddie Van Halen's "Beat It" solo for Weird Al's Michael Jackson parody "Eat It."

Back to the Blues (1993), *Electra Blues* (1994), *Blues Deluxe* (1998), and *Jackhammer Blues* (2000) provided unencumbered opportunities for him to wail among his uninspired releases of the era. The one bright spot was *Rick Derringer & Friends* on the King Biscuit Flower Hour, released in 1998. A benefit show from the Palladium in 1983, organized by Lorna Luft to raise money for the band after all their gear was stolen on a Greenwich Village street, it featured Dr. John, Edgar Winter, and Ian Hunter, as well as Luft. Derringer next joined Tim Bogert and Carmine Appice in DBA for the ill-fated *Doin' Business As…* in 2001. He also took an unsuccessful stab at pop jazz with the mostly instrumental *Free Ride* in 2002.

By 2004, he and his wife, Jenda, were producing Christian rock records featuring their children. Derringer has since changed the lyrics to some of his old hits to reflect his religious beliefs. For example, "Rock and Roll Hoochie Koo" was altered to "Read the Word, Live It Too." In 2008, he and Edgar Winter jammed with Johnny Winter for the first time in many years. Again reminding his fans that he used to deliver the great high-powered blues rock they craved, in 2009, *Live at the Ritz, New York—1982* appeared in record bins. Unfortunately, the hits had long ago dried up, though he has doggedly released product virtually every year. Also in 2009, he put out *Knighted by the Blues*, which featured the Jenda-penned "Sometimes," and the DBA album *The Sky Is Falling*. *Rock and Roll Hoochie Koo Spectacular* and *The Three Kings of the Blues* followed in 2010. That same year, Derringer toured alongside Edgar Winter in Ringo Starr's 11th All-Starr Band.

THE GUITAR STYLE OF RICK DERRINGER

Derringer can play authentic blues, as was especially displayed when he was with Johnny Winter in the '70s. Besides being a tasty soloist, he knows how to accompany with empathy and expression. Measures 9–12 of a slow 12-bar blues show his sense of dynamics and propulsion as he blends the hip 7#9 chord (V), the major pentatonic scale relative to E♭ (IV), and the B♭ blues scale to logically connect the turnaround to a walk up to the V chord.

Rick Derringer 1

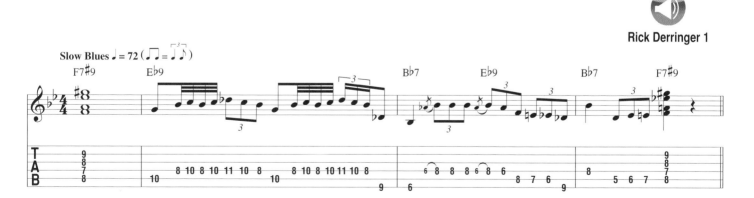

Derringer is an expert at creating bluesy pop tunes out of basic forms and progressions. Utilizing a classic I–♭III–IV–♭III (A–C–D–C) chord sequence, he employs a variety of voicings and licks to propel the punchy vamp forward to measure 4, where a run up the A minor pentatonic scale culminates in a bend from the root (D) to the 9th (E) in order to create anticipation to the next measure.

Aggressive blues-rock soloing helps drive this vamp. Derringer has chops to burn but uses his reliable intuition to keep them in the service of the song. Ever the bluesman, dig his insertion of the gritty ♭5th (E♭) from the A blues scale on beat 3 of measure 2.

Performance Tip: In measure 1, bend the D note on string 3 with the ring finger, backed by the middle and index, while holding down the G note on string 2 with the pinky.

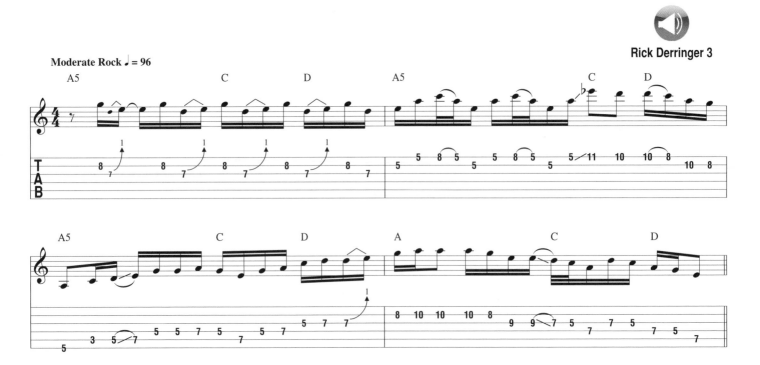

Derringer could get dark and introspective as well as exuberantly bluesy when it comes to a minor key ballad. The elegance of the four-measure melody below, derived from the D minor pentatonic scale, is predicated on the sheer simplicity of the sparse notes. The two-note (C–D) motif functions as ♭7th–root in measure 1 over the Dm chord and as 2nd–3rd in measures 2 and 4 over the B♭ chord. Amongst the smooth and mellow expression of the other measures, the jagged line in measure 3 produces a degree of musical tension that is released in measure 4.

Rick Derringer 4

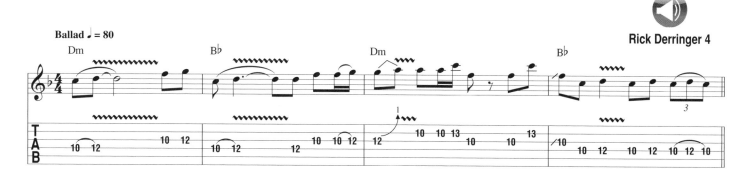

This next example, a powerful diatonic progression that also contains a couple of non-diatonic cords—vii (G♯m), ♭III (C), and ♭VII (G)—is typical of R&B and classic rock and shows the propulsive acoustic rhythm guitar of a complete rock guitarist.

Performance Tip: Utilize a combination of downtrokes and upstrokes for the eighth- and 16th-note strums.

Rick Derringer 5

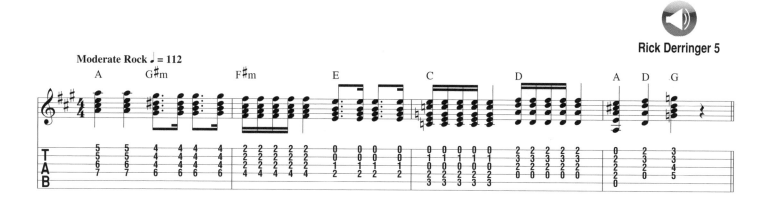

Joe Perry of Aerosmith performs July 23, 1978 at the "Bill Graham Day on the Green" concert in Oakland, California.

(Photo by Jon Sievart/Cache Agency)

JOE PERRY
(1950–)

Along with his Aerosmith image of playing "Keith Richards" to Steven Tyler's "Mick Jagger," Joe Perry has influenced a generation of aspiring, crunching, string-manglers. His muscular yet funky style, based on the blues via the Bluesbreakers and his hero, Jeff Beck (circa Yardbirds), has been the firm foundation keeping his outrageous lead singer from taking off into the wild, blue yonder.

Anthony Joseph Perry was born on September 10, 1950, in Lawrence, Massachusetts, to a Portuguese father and an Italian mother. His paternal grandfather, from Madeira, had changed the family name from Pereira to "Perry" upon immigrating to the U.S. At the age of 6, during the early days of rock 'n' roll, he heard primal music such as "Rock Around the Clock" by Bill Haley & the Comets and Little Richard's "Tutti Frutti" from his neighbors. When the British Invasion came ashore to conquer America in the early '60, the young teen was inspired by the Beatles and Rolling Stones to begin playing guitar. He was in a series of local bands, including Flash, Just Us, Plastic Glass, and Joe Perry's Jam Band, in Sunapee, New Hampshire, where he met future Aerosmith bassist Tom Hamilton in 1969. Perry and Hamilton would relocate to Boston and meet drummer Joey Kramer, a Berklee College of Music student from Yonkers, New York, who opted to drop out of school to form a power trio. Coincidentally, drummer and singer Steven Tyler (née Tallarico), also from Yonkers, knew Kramer and had been in New Hampshire since 1964 with the Strangeurs (later changed to Chain Reaction) with Ray "Crazy Raymond" Tabano on bass. In another coincidence that would seem fateful in retrospect, Tyler previously met Perry in Sunapee, where the singer had worked at an ice cream parlor one summer. In 1970, the Jam Band and Chain Reaction played a gig together and Tyler was so impressed with the "Jammers" that he wanted to combine forces, with the demand that he be the lead singer. It was agreed and Kramer suggested the name "Aerosmith," inspired by Harry Nilsson's album *Aerial Ballet*, which featured a biplane on the cover. Ray Tabano was enlisted to play rhythm guitar, but in 1971, was replaced by Brad Whitford, another Berklee student, and the band was ready for lift-off.

Local Boston- and New York-area engagements allowed Aerosmith to build a reputation as "rough boys" bashing out unrefined blues rock while they went through a succession of booking agents. When they found the management who would later call them "the closest thing I've ever seen to the Rolling Stones," they had the clout to convince Columbia Records producer Clive Davis to come and see them at Max's Kansas City in Manhattan, where the members literally had to pay in order to get on the bill. It turned out to be worth the effort, as Aerosmith signed with Columbia in 1972 for $125,000. Their self-titled debut (#21), released in 1973, contained the Tyler-penned "Dream On," a pioneering power ballad and minor hit at the time that would eventually become an AOR classic. Though uneven, the album hinted at what they would become: aggressive hard rockers with a rebellious attitude and a charismatic, outrageous frontman, not reverential blues scholars.

Get Your Wings (#74), from 1974, may not have suffered the sophomore jinx, but it did not fare nearly as well on the charts. Nonetheless, the mold for "raunch 'n' roll" was cast for their greatest triumphs, thanks in part to Tyler's obsession with sleaze and sex pushing forward on "Lord of the Thighs" and "Same Old Song and Dance," while Perry and Whitford proudly display their lessons learned from the Yardbirds with a sensational, over-the-top cover version of the classic "The Train Kept A-Rollin'." Only years later would it be revealed that the blistering solos were actually played by session greats Steve Hunter and Dick Wagner.

Following a schedule of non-stop touring, the breakthrough came with their third release, *Toys in the Attic* (#11, 1975). A hard rock tour de force, it contained their signature compositions, "Walk This Way" (#10) and "Sweet Emotion" (#36), and was so stripped down with bashing riffs that it seemed to coexist with the emerging punk rock of the era. Based on the band's newfound success, "Dream On" was re-released in 1976 and promptly shot to #6. The platinum *Rocks* (#3), released in 1976, was an even greater smash, thanks to songs such as "Home Tonight" (#71), "Last Child" (#21), and "Back in the Saddle" (#38). The band continued to play increasingly harder, with words like "brutal" routinely applied to their music. Unfortunately, they were playing just as hard away from the music, with serious drug use in the band escalating as their rocketing commercial success and creative energy blinded them to the dangers of sudden stardom.

Perhaps as either a reaction to their punishing performance and recording schedule, with the former marred by increasing violence on the concert circuit, including a cherry bomb that was thrown onstage at the Spectrum in Philadelphia injuring Perry and Tyler, or as the result of substance abuse, Aerosmith took a break for the better part of 1977. Nonetheless, they released the more adventurous *Draw the Line* (#11), containing the title-track single (#42) and "Kings and Queens" (#70), later in the year. Also featured was Perry playing screaming slide on the title cut and his first lead vocal, "Bright Light Fright." Though a continuation of their recent successes, the group would look at this time as when the music became "cloudy" as the result of their growing dependence on hard drugs, along with the clash of egos that was almost inevitable, given the outsized personalities of Tyler and Perry, now known as the "Toxic Twins." Unforeseen at the time, the album would be their last true studio release with the original lineup for almost 10 years.

The year 1978 signaled another exhausting tour and an appearance in the critically slogged film version of *Sgt. Pepper's Lonely Hearts Club Band*, where they performed the Beatles' "Come Together." The double-album *Live! Bootleg* (#13), released at the end of the year, maintained their status as premier American rockers and enabled their audience, known as the "Blue Army" due to their blue denim clothing, to relive the concert experience. A selection of their most popular tracks, including their cover of "Come Together" (#23) and "Chip Away the Stone" (#77), along with a couple of rare gems, would trump the various illegal bootlegs cropping up. With a punning title, *Night in the Ruts* (#14), released in 1979, would reach gold status despite being their least successful release in the '70s and containing the Shangri-Las' "golden oldie" hit "Remember (Walking in the Sand)" (#67). Nonetheless, Aerosmith managed to return to their taut, no-nonsense, basic hard rock style despite the drug-fueled conflict between Tyler and Perry. While headlining a tour with Van Halen, Ted Nugent, AC/DC, and Foreigner, Perry's wife got into a "cat fight" with Tom Hamilton's wife. Having had enough, Perry quit during the recording of *Night in the Ruts*, purportedly taking unreleased songs with him that would find their way onto his Joe Perry Project album.

Guitarist Jimmy Crespo was brought in to finish some tracks and would accompany Tyler on the subsequent tour, which suffered from the singer's growing erratic behavior. Alarmed, Joey Kramer and Tom Hamilton formed Renegade on the side with Crespo and singer Marge Raymond, whom Crespo had previously worked with in Flame. To the dismay of long-time fans, the resultant album was never released. In 1980, Brad Whitford left to form Whitford-St. Holmes with former Ted Nugent guitarist Derek St. Holmes, and Tyler brought Rick Dufay on board to complete the guitar section.

Perry went off and convened the Joe Perry Project with a group of excellent sidemen and produced an underappreciated debut album, *Let the Music Do the Talking* (#47), in 1980. Clearly wanting to show his former bandmates, and particularly Tyler, that he could succeed without them, he shared lead vocal duties equally with Ralph Morman and wrote or co-wrote a passel of rocking numbers that would have made a great Aerosmith album. *I've Got the Rock 'n' Rolls Again* (#100), containing the moderately successful "Listen to the Rock" (#48 Mainstream Rock), was released the next year and featured a different singer, yet contained songs of lesser quality and the concomitant lack of energy, as drugs would again bedevil Perry. Two years would pass before the swan song of the Joe Perry Project, *Once a Rocker, Always a Rocker*, saw the light of day. A new backing band and yet another lead singer was the tip-off that the solo career was not panning out even before the music was heard, and its lack of acceptance would compel Perry to reconsider his relationship with Tyler and Aerosmith.

Concurrently, Tyler spurned CBS for Geffen Records and *Aerosmith's Greatest Hits* (#53) was issued in 1980, eventually topping six million in sales. In addition, Tyler was hurt in a serious motorcycle accident that kept him off the road for most of the year. Two years later, the "ersatz" Aerosmith, with Crespo writing songs with Tyler, did its best to move on with *Rock in a Hard Place* (#32), which featured "Lightning Strikes" (#21 Mainstream Rock) and made a more than respectable showing. Strikingly, it achieved its success with an approach counter to classic Aerosmith of the '70s: incorporating trendy vocoders, synthesizers, and "spacey" effects, though punchy hard rock was also in evidence. Alas, *Rock in a Hard Place* only served to point up the absence of Perry and Whitford, who returned in 1984, reportedly at Tyler's invitation, and to everyone's relief. A "reunion" tour dubbed "Back in the Saddle" ensued, but was marred by Tyler passing out onstage after getting high with Perry before a show, confirming that drugs were still a serious issue in the group. In 1985, *Done with Mirrors* (#36) came out on Geffen Records, heralding the "comeback" of Aerosmith with yet another return to their patented brand of sleazy hard rock featuring Tyler's sassy lyrics and powered by the grinding guitars of Perry and Whitford. The ironic "Let the Music Do the Talking" (#18 Mainstream Rock) and "Sheila" (#20 Mainstream Rock) had them back on the radio again as fans rejoiced. However, Tyler's continued heroin addiction and its resultant effects compelled the band to stage an intervention to get him into rehab, followed by Perry, and eventually the entire band.

A career break from a surprising source came their way in 1986, when they were asked to appear with rappers Run-D.M.C. on their hit cover and MTV video of "Walk This Way" (#4). The boost in momentum coincided with the release of *Permanent Vacation* (#11) in 1987, confirming the "permanence" of their comeback and producing the classics "Dude (Looks Like a Lady)" (#14), "Ragdoll" (#17), and "Angel" (#3), thanks in part to the services of commercial rock songwriters Holly Knight and Desmond Child. The "train kept a-rollin'" in 1989 with the release of *Pump* (#5), which featured the Grammy-winning "Janie's Got a Gun" (#4), "Love in an Elevator" (#5), and "What It Takes" (#9), with the songwriting chores firmly back in the hands of the band. However, for *Get a Grip*, released in April of 1993, the pro songwriters were hired again. Despite critics "cryin'" foul for its pop leanings, the album reach #1 on the *Billboard 200*, making it difficult to argue with success. "Livin' on the Edge" (#18) won the Grammy for Best Rock Performance by a Duo or Group with Vocal and several other singles achieved significant radio success, including "Cryin'" (#12), "Amazing" (#24), "Crazy" (#17), "Eat the Rich" (#5 Mainstream Rock), and "Fever" (#5 Mainstream Rock). With "Crazy," Aerosmith would also win the Grammy for Best Rock Performance by a Duo or Group with Vocal in 1994. A collection of their Geffen hits, *Big Ones* (#6), was also issued in 1994, featuring the hits "Blind Man" (#48), "Deuces Are Wild" (#1 Mainstream Rock), and "Walk on Water" (#16 Mainstream Rock). It promptly went double platinum and most of their contractual obligation with the label was fulfilled.

Though Aerosmith had resigned with Columbia in the early '90s, it took until 1995 before they were free to begin recording for their original label. After the band members had taken time off to be with their families, *Nine Lives* (#1) finally arrived in 1997, and it delivered the goods, with hired hands contributing to the writing of virtually every track. With "Pink" (#27), Aerosmith once again won the Grammy for Best Rock Performance by a Duo or Group with Vocal, and several other songs were well-received on radio as well, including "Falling in Love (Is Hard on the Knees)" (#1 Mainstream Rock), "Hole in My Soul" (#4 Mainstream Rock), "Nine Lives" (#37 Mainstream Rock), and "Taste of India" (#3 Mainstream Rock). The recording process survived a period of great turmoil involving producers and songwriters, and the band was almost torn asunder again. Most troubling was the sacking of their manager, Tim Collins, who had been instrumental in saving them from addiction while engineering their comeback, and he took a parting shot by accusing Tyler of being back on the hard stuff. During the tour to support *Nine Lives,* Aerosmith, with an uncredited Perry, recorded "I Don't Want to Miss a Thing," the love theme for the movie *Armageddon*, which starred Liv Tyler, Steven's daughter. Ironically, it would be their only #1 single.

Marking time, in 1998, Aerosmith released the live double-dip *A Little South of Sanity* (#12) as their final album for Geffen Records. After a three-year layoff, the "bad boys from Boston" returned to the limelight with *Just Push Play* (#2), which contained the singles "Fly Away from Here" (#34), "Jaded" (#7),

"Just Push Play" (#10 Mainstream Rock), and "Sunshine" (#23 Mainstream Rock). Hot on the heels of their appearance at Super Bowl XXXVI in 2001 (coincidentally won by the New England Patriots), the album confirmed the loyalty of their fans and their evergreen status as classic hard rockers. With Tyler and Perry back in charge as the "Boneyard Boys," some of the old fire and attitude was evident, along with a slicker style that appeared to resonate with their audience, if not the critics. As if further validation was needed, Aerosmith was inducted into the Rock and Roll Hall of Fame in the spring of 2001.

In 2004, Aerosmith followed in the footsteps of past blues-rockers and recorded their "blues album," *Honkin' on Bobo* (#5, #1 Blues Album), featuring "Baby Please Don't Go" (#7 Mainstream Rock) and other classic and lesser-known blues covers by Jimmy Reed, Sonny Boy Williamson II, Mississippi Fred McDowell, and Willie Dixon, along with one original—the appropriately titled "The Grind." As a sincere if unauthentic blues tribute to their "roots," it could be rightly slagged; however, as a spirited, rude rock album matched only by its vulgar title, it succeeds unapologetically. A year later, they trotted out their first DVD/CD, *You Gotta Move*, which contained concert performances from the tour and documentary footage of the making of *Honkin' on Bobo,* and a live disc, *Rockin' the Joint* (#24), recorded at the Hard Rock Café in, of all places, Las Vegas in 2002. Perhaps they saw the latter as a goof, but whatever their motives, they turned in a tight, professional set. However, the latter dates on the "Rockin' the Joint Tour" had to be canceled when it was revealed that Tyler required throat surgery from the years of abuse to which he subjected his vocal cords.

In 2005, Joe Perry released his debut solo album, the self-titled *Joe Perry* (#110), which featured the Grammy-nominated single "Mercy" (ironically, he lost out to Les Paul). In 2006, it was announced that Tom Hamilton had throat cancer and he was replaced for a tour by the bassist from the Joe Perry Project. Released in 2006, *Devil's Got a New Disguise* (#33) was another Aerosmith greatest hits compilation purportedly spanning their entire career, but mostly focused on the Geffen years, with the title track (#15 Mainstream Rock) released as a single as part of an obligation to Sony in lieu of a new studio album.

In 2007, Aerosmith kicked off a huge world tour, the first in a decade, and also began work on their long-anticipated new album. The same announcement was made in 2008, when Perry finally had knee-replacement surgery to fix an injury that dates back to a fall he took in 1986. In 2009, with the album still on hold, another tour was slated with ZZ Top as the opening act. Alas, in the fine Aerosmith tradition, all would not go well with any of the "drama queens'" plans. In order: Perry had emergency surgery on his artificial knee after he developed an infection; Tyler injured his leg and then fell off a stage, resulting in serious injuries; Tyler pulled out of a South American tour to pursue solo projects; Perry announced that Tyler was going to quit the band and that a new singer would be found; Tyler appeared with the Joe Perry Project at Irving Plaza in New York City and tells the crowd that he is not quitting, and entered rehab for his addiction to painkillers related to his many injuries. Tired of waiting to begin recording the next Aerosmith album, at the end of the year, Perry released the experimental *Have Guitar, Will Travel*, playing most of the instruments and recording quickly in his home studio, the Boneyard, with very little polish and the rough edges showing.

In 2010: Perry announced that the band was looking for a replacement singer for the convalescing Tyler, and Tyler responded with a "cease and desist letter"; Aerosmith planned and played a "Cocked, Locked, Ready to Rock Tour" in South and Central America, Europe, and North America; Tyler accidentally hit Perry in the head with a mic stand and Perry accidentally pushed Tyler off a stage; Perry was incensed that Tyler planned to become a judge on *American Idol* without telling the band first; Perry wished Tyler "luck" and announced that he will pursue other projects; and Joey Kramer stated that the band intends to finish the long-delayed new album in 2011.

In the spring of 2011, yet one more Aerosmith greatest hits album, *Tough Love: Best of the Ballads*, was released. In the summer, Perry declared that the band will meet soon to work on the new album with their former '70s producer, Jack Douglas. In the fall, the band initiated a tour, but Tyler fell in a shower after contracting food poisoning, losing two teeth and sustaining facial injuries due to dizziness. In the spring of 2012, Aerosmith announced a planned summer "Global Warming Tour" with Cheap Trick, and Tyler, the "Screamin' Demon," promised their 15th studio album would be released in early summer. Perry revealed that *Honkin' on Bobo* should have been the new album, but the energy was not right and it ended up being their blues record, and that one riff on the record "has to be 20 years old." On November 6, 2012, Aerosmith finally released *Music from Another Dimension!* (#5), which contained the singles "Legendary Child" (#17), Lover Alot" (#47), "What Could Have Been Love" (#48), and "Can't Stop Lovin' You," a song featuring country artist Carrie Underwood.

With Tyler enjoying his new-found celebrity on *American Idol,* it remained to be seen what would transpire with the band following the release of the new album. Perry lives on a farm in Vermont and raises horses and has created a line of hot sauces, Joe Perry's Rock Your World Hot Sauces. A quesadilla featuring a flavor of the namesake hot sauce is available as an appetizer at the Hard Rock Café. On top of that, in 2008, Perry was featured in a television episode of Rachael Ray's "Inside Dish," where he prepared a meal, displayed his passion for knives, discussed his hot sauce brand and cooking, and gave insight into what goes into meal preparation on Aerosmith tours. In 2013, the live concert DVD *Rock for the Rising Sun* (#1), featuring footage from their 2011 tour of Japan, was released. Then, in July of 2014, Aerosmith embarked on the "Let Rock Rule Tour" of North America with Slash (with Myles Kennedy and the Conspirators) as the opening act.

THE GUITAR STYLE OF JOE PERRY

Early on in Aerosmith, Perry utilized streamlined classical guitar technique to produce a serious, somber, minor key mood in a manner unique to the band.

Performance Tip: For the C note (string 3) in measures 1–3, use (in order) your middle, ring, ring, pinky, middle, and index fingers. In measure 4, employ the index finger.

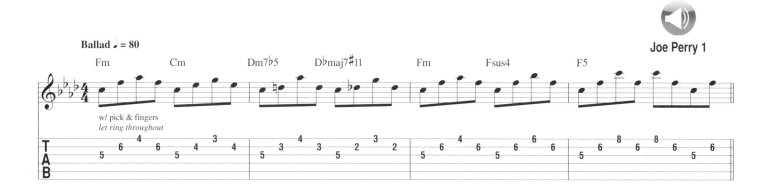

In this next example, Perry quickly establishes the major tonality via the root (C) and the 3rd (E) within beats 1–3 of measure 1 before heading off to phrase, with palpable energy, in the C minor pentatonic scale. Observe his frequent emphasis of the blues-approved ♭3rd (E♭), adding spicy seasoning to the rock mix.

Performance Tip: For the bends on beat 4 of measure 2, use the ring, backed by the middle and index, followed posthaste by the pinky, backed by the ring, middle, and index.

When not abusing the minor pentatonic scale, Perry is sometimes known to inject fat double stops and triads into his solos for harmony. Check out how he builds intensity with his increasingly rhythmic phrasing in measures 1–3 before releasing it in the root-octave position of the E minor pentatonic scale in measure 4, with resolution to the root (E) note.

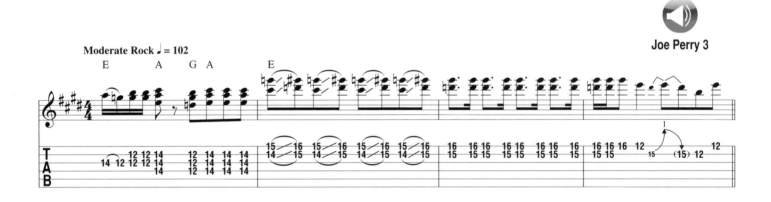

Perry transitions smoothly from raw country blues licks in the root-open position of the E blues scale in measure 1 to the open E Mixolydian mode in measure 2. He follows that phrase with a dynamic leap up to the ninth-position E major pentatonic scale in measure 3 and ultimately, the root-octave position of the composite blues scale (blues scale plus Mixolydian mode). His virtuosic display features fluid combinations of hammer-ons and pull-offs, along with numerous sinewy bends, including the mellifluous half-step variety from the 6th (C♯) to the ♭7th (D) in measure 4.

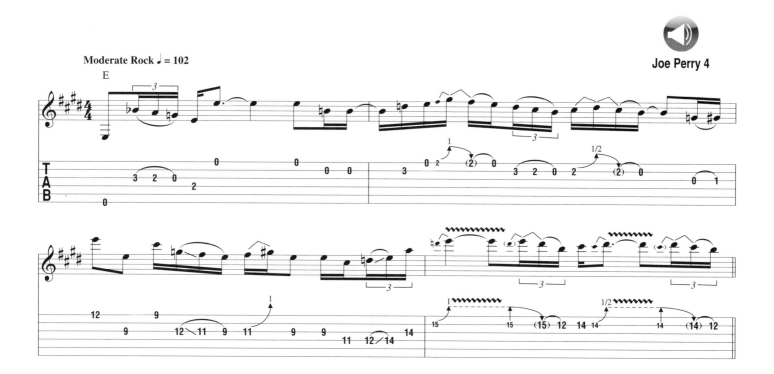

Joe Perry 4

Over a rocking boogie pattern, Perry proves his blues credibility by creating a classic two-measure riff as a motif in the open and root positions of the G minor pentatonic scale. Be sure to note the subtle quarter-step bends of the ♭3rd (B♭) to the "true blue note," located in between the minor 3rd and major 3rd (B), in measures 1 and 3, along with the half-step bend of the 2nd (A) to the ♭3rd in measures 2 and 4.

Performance Tip: In measure 4, bend the A to B♭ with the index finger while holding the middle finger on the D note (string 2). After quickly accessing the root (G) note on string 6 with the thumb, bend the 4th (C) on string 3 with the ring finger, backed by the middle and index, while simultaneously playing the ♭7th (F) with the pinky.

Joe Perry 5

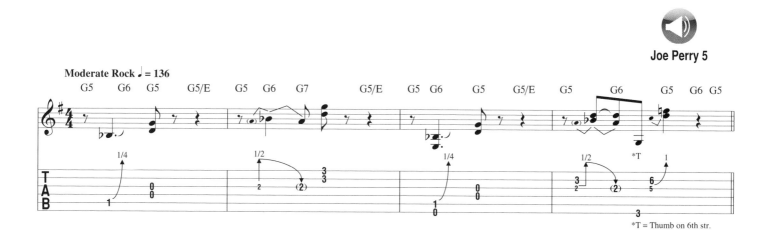

Angus Young of AC/DC, in concert, 1991.

(Photo: by Ian Dickson/MediaPunch)

ANGUS YOUNG
(1955–)

Like Lynyrd Skynyrd and some other bands in the U.S., AC/DC, as powered by lead guitarist Angus Young, thumbed their collective noses at the sensitive singer/songwriter music of the early '70s and let their loud electric guitars run rampant. Ignoring impotent critics who disdained carnal, blues-based rock and carped about "self-indulgent guitar solos," Young and his brother Malcolm play unremittingly bruising three-chord rock with testosterone-fueled riffs and solos that hit like a punch in the ear. Though wrongfully classed as "heavy metal," AC/DC were—and remain—an unrepentant classic hard rock band.

Angus McKinnon Young was born to Margaret and William on March 31, 1955, in Glasgow, Scotland. The youngest of eight, in 1963, he moved to Sydney, Australia with his parents, older brothers Malcolm and George, and sister Margaret. George became the first to play guitar and was a member of the Easybeats, who scored the huge international hit "Friday on My Mind" in 1966 and were the first significant rock band to come out from "down under." Angus initially began playing banjo, restrung like a guitar, until 1970, when his mother bought a 1967 Gibson SG with a very slim neck, which appealed to the slight-framed, aspiring rocker. Malcolm had actually begun playing first and was in a band called the Velvet Underground, where he played covers of T. Rex and Stones songs, while Angus was in Kantuckee, which evolved into Tantrum. In late 1973, Malcolm founded AC/DC and soon brought in Angus to share guitar chores. According to band lore, "AC/DC" stands for "Alternating Current/Direct Current," an acronym the brothers saw on the side of their mother's sewing machine.

In their early years, AC/DC would undergo several personnel changes. Their first single was "Can I Sit Next to You, Girl" b/w "Rockin' in the Parlour," featuring Dave Evans on vocals, Larry Van Kriedt on bass, and Colin Burgess on drums. Conscious of stage image, the band had experimented with various glam-rock styles until Angus, at the suggestion of his sister Margaret, adopted his iconic English schoolboy look and five years were shaved off his birth year to help validate the effect. Consequently, the satin and spangles were tossed out for being derivative of another Australian group and dissatisfaction grew with Evans, who was unflatteringly likened to glam rocker Gary Glitter. Though criticized from the beginning for being too loud, AC/DC, with support from Australia's biggest rock radio station, began building a rabid following. By early fall of 1974, the seriously sleazy Ronald Belford "Bon" Scott, a friend of George Young, had replaced Evans and the band had a contract with the Albert Productions label, which had a distribution deal with EMI in Australia and New Zealand.

In November of 1974, *High Voltage* (#7 in Australia) was recorded with the Young brothers on guitar, Scott on vocals, Rob Bailey on bass, and Tony Currenti on drums, among others in the rhythm section who were performing live with the band. Included on the album were the Big Joe Williams blues classic "Baby, Please Don't Go" and the original "She's Got Balls," which candidly declared where they were going lyrically. In 1975, *T.N.T.* (#1 in Australia) was released as the follow-up and likewise released only in Australia and New Zealand. The album featured "High Voltage," written and recorded after the debut album of the same name, and "It's a Long Way to the Top (If You Wanna Rock 'n' Roll)," which contained a snatch of bagpipes played by Scott, and along with "The Jack" and the title track, would go on to become a concert staple. On the album, Angus (lead) and Malcolm (rhythm) no longer shared guitar duties and were joined by Mark Evans (bass) and Paul Rudd (drums), who was now a solid band member.

With regular appearances on Australia's top pop music TV show, AC/DC saw their popularity and success grow exponentially through to 1977. However, the first significant turning point in their career would occur in 1976, when they signed an international deal with Atlantic Records. A compilation of tracks from their first two albums, *High Voltage*, was put out in conjunction with their first European tour, where they supported Aerosmith, Black Sabbath, Blue Öyster Cult, Cheap Trick, KISS, and UFO. Also included was a concurrent tour of the U.K., the appropriately titled "Lock up Your Daughters Summer Tour," where AC/DC were surprisingly welcomed with open tattooed arms by the punk rockers. *Dirty Deeds Done Dirt Cheap* (1976) would go platinum six times, with the title track (#4) and the salacious "Big Balls" (#26) further plating their reputation as dangerous bad boys, even if the album concept was inspired by Humphrey Bogart movies. In line with the convoluted release schedule of their early records, *Dirty Deeds* would not be officially available in the U.S. until 1981, following the immense success of *Highway to Hell* (1979) and *Back in Black* (1980). Meanwhile, their live shows had evolved into a high-energy, raucous rock 'n' roll spectacle, with Angus riding on the shoulders of Scott while soloing and dropping his drawers and mooning the audience.

The platinum *Let There Be Rock* (#154, 1977) was the last album with bassist Mark Evans, who was reportedly fired for his differences with Angus and for being "too much of a nice guy." The album was a step forward in terms of heavier, harder riffs from the Young brothers and also featured Scott in all his sleazebag rock star glory, particularly on "Whole Lotta Rosie" (about a groupie), "Hell Ain't a Bad Place To Be," and "Crabsody in Blue" (about venereal disease), the latter of which being pulled by Atlantic Records from release in the U.S. and Japan, as well as the international album. The likewise platinum *Powerage* (#133, 1978) was the first album to be released simultaneously in all markets and the first with new bassist Cliff Williams. It gained particular popularity with musicians, as both Keith Richards and Eddie Van Halen named it their favorite AC/DC album and Joe Perry singled out "Sin City" for praise. In a sense, *Powerage* would signal the beginning of the end of the first era of AC/DC, as it was the last to be produced by George Young. *Powerage* was followed in 1979 by *Highway to Hell* (#17), their top charting release to date. The album would go on to reach platinum status seven times and move the band ever upward as one of the reigning hard rock bands of the day. Originally, it was to be produced by Eddie Kramer (of Jimi Hendrix fame), but he was fired and replaced by Robert John "Mutt" Lange. The title track (#47) and "If You Want Blood (You Got It)" have become band classics, but "Night Prowler" would later embroil them in controversy. In 1985, several brutal murders were committed in Los Angeles by a criminal nicknamed the "Night Stalker," who was a fan of AC/DC and especially that track. He was seen wearing one of their T-shirts and left a "devil's horns" hat with their logo at one of his crime scenes, resulting in protests against the group by parents in the L.A. area. AC/DC would later reveal that the song was about a boy sneaking into his girlfriend's bedroom at night while her mother and father slept, and how their music was moving farther away from their extremely casual interest in Satanism anyway.

Just when they were poised for their greatest commercial and artistic triumph, tragedy struck AC/DC. As they were beginning to get to work on their next album, on February 19, 1980, after a night of heavy drinking at a club in London, Scott passed out drunk in the car of a friend, who could neither rouse him nor move him inside his house. Scott, who had asthma, was left in the freezing car overnight and discovered dead the next morning from pulmonary aspiration of vomit, with the official cause of death listed as "acute alcohol poisoning." He was 33 years old. Coming to the same conclusion as Led Zeppelin upon the death of their drummer, John Bonham, AC/DC mulled quitting, but with the support of Scott's parents, they soldiered on. Several replacements were considered, with Brian Johnson eventually getting the nod. Ironically, Scott had alerted the band to Johnson after he saw him while in England prior to joining AC/DC, commenting that he was "a great rock 'n' roll singer in the style of Little Richard," whom Scott idolized.

With Johnson on board, the band went about finishing the songs and recording the album with Lange in Nassau, Bahamas, and at Electric Lady in New York. It would become the landmark *Back in Black* (#4, 1980). Though it could be seen as a tribute to Scott, with its dedication to randy sex, party drinking, and rowdy rock 'n' roll, it is not an elegy but a superb collection of rebellious anthems into which Johnson fits perfectly. It would go platinum 22 times, with sales of 50 million by 2011, second only to

Thriller worldwide, while sporting the hit singles "You Shook Me All Night Long" (#35), "Back in Black" (#37), "Hells Bells" (#52), and "Rock and Roll Ain't Noise Pollution" (#15 U.K.). Besides overflowing with memorable riffs, nut-busting grooves, and some of the greatest hard rock solos ever, the exceptional sound quality of the recording is still lauded down to the current day, and the disc is acknowledged as their masterpiece. The year 1980 also saw the theatrical release of *AC/DC: Let There Be Rock*, featuring band interviews, including ones with Scott, and a concert shot in Paris.

The quadruple-platinum *For Those About to Rock* (*We Salute You*) (#1, 1981) was the highly successful follow-up to *Back in Black* and the first AC/DC album to shoot to #1 in the U.S. The title track (#15) and the unsubtle "Let's Get It Up" (#13) again helped to prove their new commercial viability. The former was performed with theatrical cannons on stage during their first arena tour of North America (1981–82) and has since become their regular encore tune. *For Those About the Rock* would be the last AC/DC album produced by Lange. The self-produced *Flick of the Switch* (#15) went platinum in 1983 but was savaged by critics, and despite the Young brothers professing pride in their achievement of getting back to the "raw and simple" sound of their earlier albums, is considered a flop. During the recording sessions, long, simmering conflict between Malcolm and Phil Rudd was exacerbated by the drummer's alcohol and drug use to the point that their friendship was destroyed by a literal fist fight. Rudd was fired immediately and session drummer and former Procol Harum member B.J. Wilson was brought in to take his place, though his work was not needed as Rudd had already completed his parts. After conducting over 700 auditions in the U.S. and U.K., Simon Wright was selected to "permanently" fill the position in the summer of 1983.

There followed a period of perceived artistic and actual commercial drought for AC/DC, though the latter was relative. The platinum *Fly on the Wall* (#37, 1985) was seen in the same light as *Flick of the Switch*, and was the first with Wright and their last self-produced venture. In 1986, the five-times-platinum *Who Made Who* (#33) was the soundtrack to *Maximum Overdrive* by Stephen King. It contains a selection of songs from previous albums, along with three new originals: the title track and the instrumentals "D.T." and "Chase the Ace." Despite back-to-back substandard releases, *Fly on the Wall* and *Flick of the Switch*, *Who Made Who* proved that AC/DC still had a substantial fan base eager for their music.

With a title that was a knock on MTV, *Blow up Your Video* (#12, 1988) went platinum, initially selling more copies than the two previous studio releases combined, and saw the return of producers George Young and Harry Vanda. It would receive a Grammy nomination for Best Hard Rock/Metal Performance Vocal or Instrumental, but lost out, confoundingly, to Jethro Tull's *Crest of a Knave*, proving just how out of touch the Academy was with regard to contemporary rock music. A world tour followed, though Malcolm bowed out of the North America leg to "dry out" and was temporarily replaced by Stevie Young, the son of brother Alex. Apparently, many audience members were unaware of the switch, as there was a strong family resemblance. After the tour, Wright quit to play with Dio and was replaced by veteran blue-ribbon session drummer Chris Slade, who had first made a name with Tom Jones, and later in the Firm with Jimmy Page and Paul Rodgers, among many other notables. Brian Johnson went on hiatus to deal with his divorce and the Young brothers would avail themselves of the down time to write all the material for their next album, in what would become their *modus operandi*.

As often happens with bands staying around for decades and having a long history, AC/DC made a comeback in 1990 with the five-times-platinum *The Razor's Edge* (#2), featuring "Thunderstruck" (#5), "Moneytalks" (#23), and "Are You Ready" (#16). This time out the producer was Bruce Fairbairn, who had previously worked with Aerosmith and Bon Jovi. The tour that followed had several shows recorded and released in 1992, in what many believe is one of the greatest live CDs. Slade would remain on the drummer's throne until 1995, when an amicable split occurred. After several jams with the Young brothers in 1994, all was forgiven with Paul Rudd, and he was brought back in the fold. Released in September of

1995, *Ballbreaker* (#4), produced by American wunderkind Rick Rubin, who had produced the AC/DC single "Big Gun" (#1) for the soundtrack to *Last Action Hero* in 1993, went double platinum. "Hard as a Rock," "Hail Caesar," and "Cover You in Oil" were released as singles, while the critical reaction again tended to be negative and in the vein that they were "making the same album over and over."

In 2000, following a five-year recording break, brother George Young returned to the helm for the platinum *Stiff Upper Lip* (#7). Featuring the title track (#1), "Satellite Blues" (#7), "Meltdown" (#22), and "Safe in New York City" (#21), it confirmed their unstoppable resurgence and popularity, despite the usual critical carping and a growing economic downturn in the record industry. A massive world tour ensued, but with an unfortunate downside, as a fan was killed in a fall in Belgium and another was injured in Nashville after being pushed from behind. An even longer recording layoff followed, even as AC/DC was inducted into the Rock and Roll Hall of Fame in 2003 with introduction and guest vocals by Steven Tyler of Aerosmith. That same year, they appeared in front of half a million fans with the Stones and Rush in Toronto, which still stands as a North American record for a "paid" concert.

In 2008, in an event watched with great anticipation, the double-platinum *Black Ice* (#1) was released with 15 songs and sold exclusively at Wal-Mart and Sam's Club in the U.S., debuting at #1 in nine countries. To call it a triumphant comeback for the ageless nasty boys of hard rock would be an understatement, and it was nominated for a Grammy for Best Rock Album. With compositions that dated back to 2003, and delayed due to an injury to bassist Cliff Williams, *Black Ice* included the singles "Rock 'n' Roll Train" (#1), nominated for a Grammy for Best Rock Performance by a Duo or Group with Vocal, "Big Jack" (#10), "Anything Goes" (#34), and the political "War Machine," which won a Grammy for Best Hard Rock Performance. Noticeable was an emphasis on more melodic songs with hooks, as suggested by producer Brendan O'Brien at a time of changing tastes, described as "the year that songs overtook albums." Appropriately, another huge world tour with a spectacular stage presentation supported the record. It lasted from late 2008 to early summer 2010 and was the third-highest grossing tour of all time.

The AC/DC soundtrack to *Iron Man 2* was released during the tour in the spring of 2010 and reached gold status. A year later, Angus announced that the band was contemplating another world tour to support their next studio album, in "a couple of years" and possibly to coincide with their 40th anniversary in 2013. However, Brian Johnson revealed in early 2012 that an unnamed "band member," later revealed to be Malcolm, was very ill and plans to begin recording the new album were on hold until he makes an expected recovery. In addition, Johnson had to cancel his own solo tour to promote his book due to surgery for a wrist injury. In the fall of 2012, *Live at River Plate*, recorded in Buenos Aires, Argentina, on the Black Ice World Tour, was released in conjunction with the DVD. It was the first live AC/DC album in 20 years and debuted at #1 in 17 countries. In June of 2014, Johnson announced that the band was "very likely" to hit the road before the end of the year. A month later, the band confirmed that they had finished recording their next album, with Stevie Young replacing the ailing Malcolm in the studio.

If you called AC/DC rock fossils from the age of dinosaurs, they would probably laugh it off with a sneer and an expletive. Boisterous legions of loyal fans of their bare-knuckled, profane music, with the willingness to put their money where their mouths are, would likewise dismiss the comment. Heading into their fifth decade without let up, it would only be fitting to acknowledge AC/DC with "For Those About to Rock, We Salute You."

THE GUITAR STYLE OF ANGUS YOUNG

Blues rock channeled through the Stones and stripped down to the basics has been the hallmark of AC/DC and Angus Young. His balls-out lead guitar style owes a debt of thanks to Eric Clapton and other British guitar heroes while evolving into his own signature sound. Though capable of multi-note assaults, his classic work depends more on fat, natural amp distortion and dynamic phrasing. Chuck Berry-derived double-string bends of 3rds and 4ths, also favored by Clapton in Cream, add additional heft and contrast in combination with single-note minor pentatonic lines. The half-step double-bend of F#/D (6th/4th) is a favorite of many and produces a howling siren effect.

Performance Tip: Chuck Berry executes the F#/D bend by pulling down with his ring finger, but others may find it more efficient to push up with the middle and ring fingers, low to high.

Angus Young 1

Young creates tremendous musical tension with an onslaught of bends centered around the gritty ♭3rd (C) before resolving to the root (A) in measure 4. The 10th position of the A minor pentatonic scale, though not as popular with rock and blues guitarists as the root position at fret 5, offers many options beyond the typical clichés.

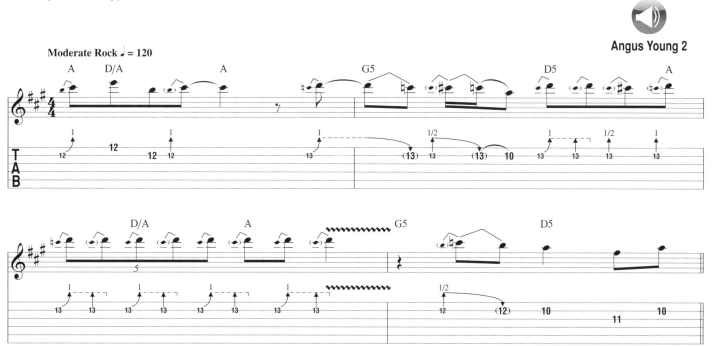

Angus Young 2

By including the major tonality-defining major 3rd (D♯) in the root position of the B minor pentatonic scale in measures 2–4, Young adds a welcome dollop of diatonic melody to contrast the majority of blues rock, emphasizing the overused ♭3rd (D). The minimal selection of notes, played in similar repetitive phrases, compresses the energy and tension before releasing it later in the solo.

Angus Young 3

Occasionally, Young opts to play horizontally instead of vertically for fluid, diatonic phrasing, with the inclusion of the open third (G) string as a pedal tone to hammer home the G major key. Observe the choice of notes on string 2 from the G major scale, which produce a smooth, consonant sound.

Angus Young 4

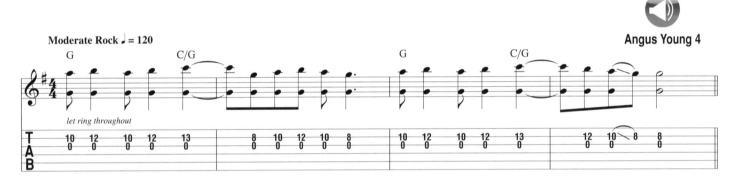

Clapton learned the composite blues scale (blues scale plus Mixolydian mode) from B.B. King and "passed it on" to Young, as well as countless other rock and blues guitarists. From a practical standpoint, it also could be seen as including the major pentatonic scale and easily accessed by moving the root position of the minor pentatonic scale, relative to the key of the song or progression, down the fingerboard three frets. Hence, what looks like F♯ minor pentatonic at fret 2 (see measure 1), actually relates to A major pentatonic. Measures 2–3 contain strict minor pentatonic licks, while measure 4 features the composite blues scale.

Angus Young 5

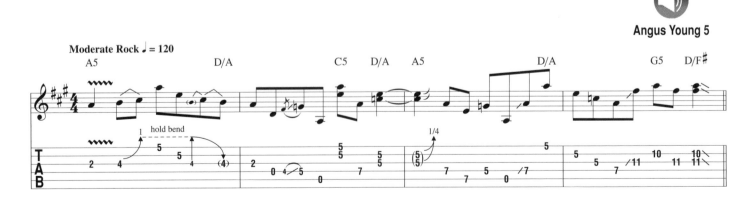

EDDIE VAN HALEN
(1955–)

In the late '70s, Eddie Van Halen and his band arrived on the scene with a wildly original hard rock style based on volume, athletic licks, and eclectic melodies, not to mention the showmanship and randy humor of lead singer David Lee Roth, or simply "Diamond Dave." The fans agreed and through 2007, the band sold more than 80 million records worldwide. More than most, they have endured especially egregious squabbles that have resulted in the popular Roth being fired and rehired several times, only to return triumphantly, while original bassist Michael Anthony quit and was replaced by Wolfgang Van Halen, the son of Eddie and actress Valerie Bertinelli.

Edward Lodewijk Van Halen was born on January 26, 1955, in Nijmegen, Netherlands, to Jan (a clarinetist, saxophonist, and pianist) and Eugenia. Lodewijk, Dutch for "Ludwig," was in honor of Beethoven. In 1962, the family immigrated to Pasadena, California, where Eddie and his older brother, Alex, were compelled by their disciplinarian mother to take classical piano lessons. Eddie never learned to read music and instead learned by ear, resulting in inaccurate performances that he deemed correct. Both brothers grew bored, however, and when Alex began playing the guitar, Eddie took up the drums. They switched instruments after it became clear that Alex was advancing faster on the drums and Eddie threw himself into practicing the guitar to the point of obsession. While in elementary school around 1964, Eddie and Alex formed their first band, the Broken Combs, displaying early on the Van Halen penchant for offbeat humor.

As Eddie progressed, he became enthralled with Eric Clapton in Cream and learned many solos note for note, including the famous and challenging live version of Robert Johnson's "Crossroads" from *Wheels of Fire* (1968). By the early '70s, he was singing lead and playing guitar with Alex and bassist Mark Stone in a band named Genesis, changing it to "Mammoth" after becoming aware of the British group with the same name. The band had no P.A. system and were forced to rent one from David Lee Roth, who charged by the night. The mounting financial drain on their meager resources, combined with Eddie's growing dissatisfaction with singing, led to the band bringing Roth in as lead singer along with his coveted P.A. system. Bassist and singer Michael Anthony from the band Snake replaced Stone and the name of the band was changed to "Van Halen" at Roth's shrewd suggestion, though Rat Salade was also considered and discarded.

By 1974, they were gigging incessantly in Pasadena and Hollywood, including Gazzari's and the Whisky A Go Go, playing a range of cover material gleaned from the current Top 40, from pop to R&B. In 1976, Gene Simmons of KISS caught one of their shows and was so impressed that he produced a demo and took it to KISS management, who infamously declared that "they would never make it." In the summer of 1977, however, Mo Ostin and Ted Templeman of Warner Bros. Records saw the band at the Starwood in Hollywood, and within a week, signed them to a contract. In the fall, Van Halen recorded their debut in three weeks with minimal overdubs or double-tracking, while minor "clams" were left in for the desired live feel. Meanwhile, they continued to play around the Los Angeles area, building a buzz that included guitarists coming to gigs to check out Eddie and his revolutionary finger-tapping technique. Going hand in hand with his innovative and unorthodox style, Eddie had built a "Frankenstrat" guitar from parts, personalized with angled racing stripes.

Eddie Van Halen, September 15, 1982.

(Photo by Jon Sievart/Cache Agency)

Released in 1978, *Van Halen* (#19), containing "Runnin' with the Devil" (#84), along with the Kinks cover "You Really Got Me" (#36) segueing from the epochal solo-guitar cadenza "Eruption," spawned legions of imitators. A snarky version of John Brim's "Ice Cream Man" showed a bluesy side of Eddie rarely seen, while the album, one of the most popular debuts in rock history, achieved diamond sales. The following year, *Van Halen II* (#6) sported their first hit single, "Dance the Night Away" (#15), in addition to "Beautiful Girls" (#84), and a version of "You're No Good," which would signal future inventive covers. The instrumental "Spanish Fly," with its naughty name, was performed on a classical guitar in a stupendous bit of virtuosity, while the black-and-yellow Charvel pictured on the album cover (but not used on the recording) was buried with Dimebag Darrell in 2004 at Eddie's behest. The all-original *Women and Children First* (#6, 1980) contained "And the Cradle Will Rock…" (#55), which was certainly true if taken literally as the band amped up the heavy-rock quotient, though conversely, Eddie played a significant amount of keyboards, including on the single, in addition to guitar. *Fair Warning* (#5, 1981) reflected their growing popularity, though it sold a relatively paltry two million copies. The growing ego battles and conflicting artistic visions between Roth and Eddie were heating up, resulting in a dark, cynical album lacking Roth's sense of wry, winking humor. *Diver Down* (#3, 1982), featuring "Dancing in the Street" (#38) and "Oh, Pretty Woman" (#12), was a mashup of covers and originals, though it did score platinum sales. The band earned a citation in the *Guinness Book of World Records* for their set at the 1983 US Festival, where they were paid a then-record $1.5 million for their headlining performance. However, friction in the band continued to mount, with bass virtuoso Billy Sheehan rumored to have been approached by Eddie to replace Anthony.

Van Halen's next album, *1984*, reached #2, finishing just behind Michael Jackson's mega-hit *Thriller*, on which Eddie had lent an iconic solo to "Beat It." It boasted their first and only #1 single, "Jump," while also featuring "Panama" (#13), "I'll Wait" (#13), and "Hot for Teacher" (#56), and is one of their commercial high points, with sales of over 10 million copies, even though driven by Eddie's current obsession with keyboards rather than his brawny guitar style. Roundly praised in the rock press, it generated several popular MTV videos as well. Nonetheless, when Roth reportedly delayed the follow-up in order to do his own successful solo album in 1985, he was fired, though he claims his leaving was precipitated by Eddie playing on projects outside of the band, as well as his suspected drug use hampering rehearsals. Also figuring into the equation was Eddie's loss of patience with Roth's upstaging antics. Loyal fans of the band howled in protest. After Scandal's Patty Smyth turned down the invitation to sing in the band, Sammy Hagar, who was enjoying a successful solo career after having fronted Montrose, was brought in for *5150* in 1986. Featuring "Why Can't This Be Love" (#3), "Love Walks In" (#22), and "Dreams" (#22), *5150*, to the surprise of many, became their first #1 album, as the Hagar era would produce Van Halen's biggest hits. Released in 1988, *OU812* ("Oh, You Ate One, Too") repeated at #1 and featured more variety in the songwriting, as heard on "Black and Blue" (#37), "Finish What Ya Started" (#13), "When It's Love" (#5), and "Feels So Good" (#35), with Eddie's virtuosity again coming to the fore as it rang up four million in sales. Winning the Grammy for Best Hard Rock Performance, *For Unlawful Carnal Knowledge* ("F.U.C.K.") was the band's third straight #1 with Hager and contained the hit singles "Poundcake" (#1 Mainstream Rock), "Runaround" (#1 Mainstream Rock), "Top of the World" (#27), and "Right Now" (#55), with Eddie riffing madly on pounding rockers that were seemingly designed with Hagar's vocal chops in mind.

Following the double-disc *Van Halen Live: Right Here, Right Now* (#5) in 1993, the band released *Balance* (#1) in 1995. Featuring "Can't Stop Lovin' You" (#30) and "Not Enough" (#97), amazingly, *Balance* was their fourth consecutive studio chart topper with Hagar. Eddie's recent sobriety clashed with the lead singer's boozing, however, and after Roth was brought in surreptitiously to record, Hagar either quit or was fired (depending on whose version is accepted) in 1996. However, after recording two new tracks for *Best of: Volume 1*, including "Me Wise Magic," which materialized at #1 on the Mainstream Rock chart, a reunion with Roth fell through and former Extreme singer Gary Cherone was subsequently hired for *Van Halen III* (#4, 1998), containing "Without You" (#1), "Fire in the Hole" (#6), and "One I Want" (#27). The title referred to it being the third incarnation of the group, as well as the first two Van Halen albums being named *I* and *II*. *Van Halen III* would be the last album with Michael Anthony, who later stated that Eddie not only dictated his bass lines, but played most of them as well as many of the drum parts (along with guitar), thereby creating a de facto "solo album." It was their poorest selling album, reaching "only" gold status, and would be their last until 2012. Even though a follow-up was planned and some demos recorded, Cherone left amicably while Eddie had hip replacement surgery in 1999. In 2001, rumors about another Roth/Van Halen reunion surfaced when the flashy frontman described new recorded tracks, but news of Eddie's battle with oral cancer quashed them, and the band stated that they had not yet decided on their next singer.

The next few years were unsettled, as both Roth and Hager joined the Heavyweight Champs of Rock 'n' Roll Tour. In 2004, Hagar returned to Van Halen for an American tour, but he and Anthony went back to the Waboritas in 2005. In 2007, the band was inducted into the Rock and Roll Hall of Fame, once again fueling rumors of a reunion with Roth, which proved true when a financially successful tour, interrupted by Eddie's lack of sobriety, was launched in the fall with his son, Wolfgang, on bass. With health problems becoming a regular issue with Eddie, in 2009, he had surgery on his left hand to treat arthritis that he had been experiencing since 2007. In 2011, another tour with Roth was announced and *A Different Kind of Truth* was released in conjunction with a tour of North America in 2012. It was their first full album of new material in 14 years and the first with Roth since *1984*.

By any yardstick, the album and subsequent tour with fan favorite "Diamond Dave" back out front were unqualified successes. The first single, "Tattoo," hit #1 on the Hard Rock Tracks chart and the album locked into #2 on the *Billboard 200*, being kept out of the top spot by Adele's Grammy-winning *21*. With the emphasis on the unrelenting heavy guitar rock that made the band a hit and Eddie a guitar hero, critical and commercial response to the record was positive. Both "Stay Frosty" and "You and Your Blues" share form and content with the blues and seven of the 13 tracks have a genesis that goes all the way back to demos from the '70s, with the overall vibe being that of Eddie and Roth simultaneously pushing each other to the limit while competing for attention. In other words: classic Van Halen. The tour was almost universally sold out, despite inordinately high ticket prices. Many in the rock world saw it as positive economic news in a declining market. However, in the spring of 2012, the last 32 dates of the tour were abruptly cancelled, though the band insisted that they were all in good health, getting along famously, and just needing a breather after an extended period of performing and recording. Meanwhile, Eddie underwent emergency surgery for diverticulitis, putting off plans for a resumption of touring until 2013.

There is no denying the game-changing effect Eddie Van Halen had on rock guitar after 1978. Like Buddy Guy in the world of blues and beyond, Eddie's technique and lack of inhibition has touched virtually all who have entered his deceptively "goofy" aura. And though he was "honored" in 2007 with a silly "Eddie Van Halen Award" in the Xbox 360 version of *Guitar Hero II*, when a player hit 500 or more notes in succession, it is his unique creativity and sensitivity to the endless potential of the electric guitar that places him in the pantheon of the all-time greats.

THE GUITAR STYLE OF EDDIE VAN HALEN

Playing horizontally, as opposed to just vertically like many rock guitarists, Van Halen emphasized his extraordinarily fast, fluid chops. In the example below, he includes the open first (E) string to fatten up the A minor pentatonic line and the rapid hammer-ons contribute to its fluidity. However, in typical "Edward the V" fashion, he ends his four-measure romp with an anarchistic, dynamic dive bomb on string 6, arriving at a low, rumbling A before sliding off the ♭6th (F).

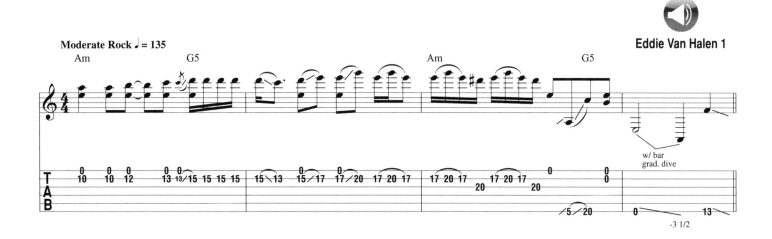

Though he did not invent the technique of tapping, Van Halen popularized the improvisational tool via his epic "Eruption," from the band's debut album. The results are large, legato interval leaps that are virtually impossible to execute with conventional fingerings, producing a sound similar to an organ or synthesizer. Note that extreme volume and/or distortion/sustain contributes to the effect.

Performance Tip: Van Halen is known for his wide left-hand finger stretches, particularly between his index and ring fingers. However, employing your index and pinky fingers, especially for the stretches from fret 7 (E) to fret 3 (C), is recommended.

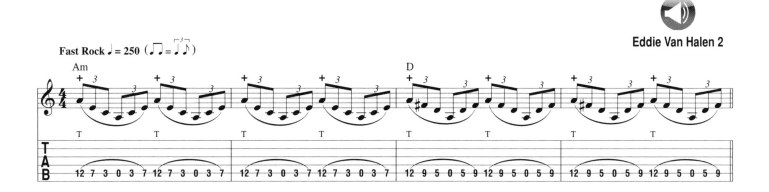

Blazingly fast runs with extreme bends and whammy-bar manipulation are hallmarks of his style, revealing a guitarist totally immersed in the electric instrument. Check out his creative move on beat 1 of measure 1, where string 3 is picked open (G, the 4th) while the whammy bar is depressed to slack, followed by hammering onto the D note (root) at fret 7 and releasing the bar. In measure 2, he repeats a similar lick. However, after slacking the picked D note (2nd), he releases it to A (6th) on the way back to D, which is subsequently bent a soaring two steps to F# (#4th)! If that is not enough, he completes his dizzying musical statement with lightning hammers and pulls in the fifth-position pattern of the D minor pentatonic scale, resolving to the root (C).

Eddie Van Halen 3

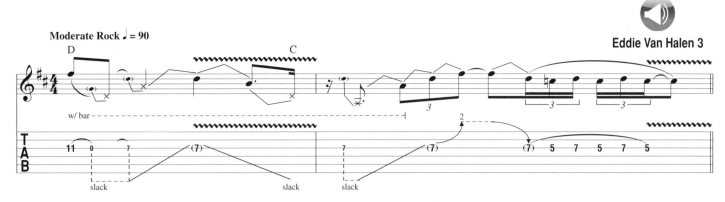

Rightly revered as a virtuoso lead guitarist, Van Halen is likewise a consummate rhythm guitarist in what essentially has been a trio situation throughout his career. Notice how, for rich musical variation, he defines each chord change with a different approach, even as he makes seamless connections between each. Measure 1 is a mini-lesson in intelligent note choices, as he moves brilliantly from Am to F and G, while measures 3–4 spice things up with hip harmonics relative to G major.

Eddie Van Halen 4

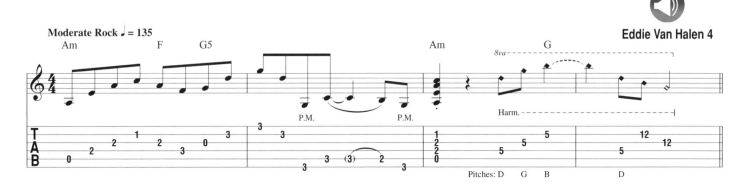

After establishing the C#sus2 harmony in measure 1 with a strummed barre chord and descending arpeggio, Van Halen walks up string 3 with select notes from the C# minor scale, phrased with string-melting tremolo picking for yet another example of his expansive technique. In measure 4, the hefty two-step bend to the major 3rd (E#) is a sweet way to conclude the relative dissonance of the phrase.

Eddie Van Halen 5

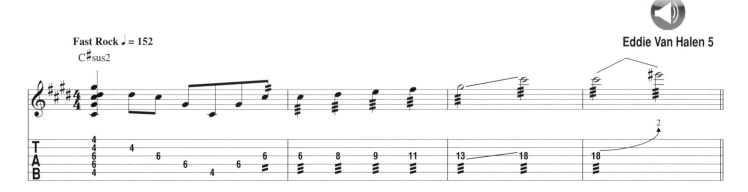

ANDY SUMMERS
(1942–)

England's the Police were often erroneously lumped in with the punk and new wave retro rock of the late '70 and '80s due more to their hairstyle than music style. Combining reggae and rock in a smooth, accessible manner palatable to the pop audience, they nonetheless brought sophisticated rhythms, dynamic, angular arrangements, and hip instrumental harmony to the fore. Most responsible for the latter was their guitarist, Andy Summers, who boasted classical, jazz, and rock influences in his playing and used them to dish up a tasty bouillabaisse of many flavors, adding substance to the soufflé lyrics of lead singer and songwriter Sting. He was honored by the readers of *Guitar Player* magazine by winning the Best Pop Guitarist award from 1984–89, resulting in him being named to their Gallery of the Greats.

Andrew James Somers was born on December 31, 1942, in Poulton-le-Fylde, Lancashire, England, to Jean and Maurice. He would later change his name to "Summers" for professional reasons, as it made it easier for others to remember the spelling. In 1944, his father moved the family of five to Bournemouth, a resort town on the south coast of England where he opened a restaurant. Summers was drawn to music at an early age and took years of piano lessons before starting to play guitar on a battered Spanish acoustic, handed down from an uncle in 1956. Without instruction, he progressed slowly until a border, taken in by his mother, showed him how to tune his guitar to the piano. In the watershed years of 1957–59, after being introduced to the world of jazz—specifically Django Reinhardt and Wes Montgomery—through the records of his older brother Tony, he began to develop more quickly. With money raised from a paper route, he bought a brand new Hofner President guitar and joined a few different skiffle groups while laboriously learning jazz guitar solos from records. Seeing Thelonious Monk in a jazz club in London was a transcendent experience and sparked a love for the eccentric piano master that continues unabated. Though there was an active flamenco community in Bournemouth and he had a good friend who played classical guitar, many years would pass before he would take a serious interest in the music.

Concurrently, Summers also had the taste of a teenager in the late '50s and was a big fan of French rock 'n' roll singer Cliff Richards and guitarist Hank Marvin of the Shadows, even going so far as to chase down Marvin on a city street for an autograph. His first pro gigs were playing "society" jobs with local hotel bands in Bournemouth, and in 1959, he quit school to work in a local music shop during the day. In 1961, while performing at the Blue Note jazz club in Bournemouth, he was heard by Hammond organist Zoot Money, and the two renewed a schoolboy friendship, as well as beginning a new musical relationship. When Money went to London in 1963 to play with pioneering British blues avatar Alexis Korner, Summers stayed behind, but soon joined him, as his friend Robert Fripp assumed his hotel gig.

Having a more ambitious and progressive take on R&B than the traditionalist Korner, Money and Summers formed Zoot Money's Big Roll Band and settled in for an extended engagement at the Flamingo, where they took the place of Georgie Fame and the Blue Flames. In the spring of 1966, they recorded the live album *The All Happening Zoot Money's Big Roll Band Live at Klook's Kleek*. They also had a hit single, "Big Time Operator," and opened for James Brown in France. After seeing Jimi Hendrix perform at one of his first London gigs, and rubbing slim shoulders with Eric Clapton and Jimmy Page, Summers was soon enmeshed in the burgeoning blues and R&B scene. In a cherished gear story from the annals of rock guitar, around 1965, Summers bought a '59 Les Paul that Clapton, who was playing a Tele at the time, lusted after. Summers told Clapton that the music shop had another one and Clapton went and purchased what became the LP used and pictured on the Bluesbreakers' *Beano* album. However, it was stolen shortly thereafter and Clapton pestered Summers into selling his sunburst, getting it hand-delivered to the studio where "Slowhand" was finishing up *Fresh Cream* in 1966.

Coming under the pervasive psychedelic influence surging through the British music scene in the late '60s, Money and his band altered their approach to try and fit the times, changing their name to "Dantalion's Chariot" in 1967 and making their debut at the Windsor National Blues Festival alongside Peter Green's Fleetwood Mac. They became infamous for their elaborate light shows and produced one recording of note, "Madman Running Through the Fields." When they disbanded in 1968 after their tour bus crashed, Money went with Eric Burden and the Animals and Summers joined the progressive Soft Machine for approximately six months, including a tour of the U.S. He was fired and back in London, however, before they opened some shows for Jimi Hendrix and recorded their debut album. Summers would join Money in the Animals for a short stint, playing on the double album *Love Is*, which contained a side of Dantalion's Chariot songs and featured Summers' extended solo on Traffic's "Coloured Rain." While in L.A. during a tour with his band, Burden broke up the Animals to pursue an acting career.

Remaining in Southern California and deciding he needed to take time out to formally learn, from 1969–74, Summers studied classical guitar, including composition, harmony, Renaissance music, and Baroque counterpoint, as well as ethnic music, at Cal State University in Northridge, California. He also acted in local theater troupes, roomed with *Starsky & Hutch* TV star Paul Michael Glaser, married singer Robin Lane from Neil Young's band in 1968, gave guitar lessons, and worked in a guitar shop with chord master Ted Greene to scrape out an existence while acquiring his iconic, hot-rodded '63 Tele from a student for $200 and playing in a Latin rock band. In 1970, after his marriage to Lane ended badly and left him in a funk, Summers took sitar lessons and tried to form a band with Tim Rose, who wrote "Morning Dew" and arranged the version of "Hey Joe" appropriated by Hendrix. Summers would get a chance to jam with Hendrix in the studio, with the "voodoo child" ironically playing bass.

In 1973, Summers married Kate Lunken and returned with her to London. Although penniless, he had a new resolve to get his rock music career re-energized. He recorded and toured with a selection of artists, including Jon Lord, Neil Sedaka, David Essex, and Kevin Ayers from the Soft Machine. His old pal Robert Fripp made the introduction to Sedaka, who graciously lent him money to buy an amp before even hearing him play. Always open to whatever was available to earn a living, in 1975, Summers played in an orchestral presentation of *Tubular Bells* by Mike Oldfield of *The Exorcist* soundtrack fame. Coincidentally, Sting (nee Gordon Sumner) and his band Last Exit opened the show. Always somewhere in the mix on the music scene in England, rock legend has Summers being offered the opportunity to replace Mick Taylor in the Stones in 1976. Late in the year, at a Christmas party, Summers was invited by singer/bassist Mike Howlett to check out his band Strontium 90, which featured Sting and American expatriate Stewart Copeland.

The year 1977 proved to be the turnaround year for his career, as Summers again met Sting and Copeland, this time at a recording session booked by Howlett, and the rhythm section invited him to stop by the famed Marquee Club to jam with their punk band, the Police. Copeland, late of the progressive band Curved Air, formed the punk band in the early part of the year and they recorded a number of tracks with guitarist Henry Padovani. Though not shy about publicly stating his desire to be in a trio format, Summers played two gigs with the quartet and enthusiastically joined them following an abortive recording session produced by John Cale, formerly of the Velvet Underground. The session exposed the limits of Padovani and he was summarily sacked, to Summers' delight. In August of 1977, the new and improved Police trio, destined for greatness, made their debut in Birmingham, England. The year 1978 would be a whirlwind for the band of innovative musicians with distinctly individual personalities, though they would struggle at first. Sorely in need of cash, they agreed to dye their hair blond for a Wrigley's gum commercial. Though it was never shown, the look proved to be fortuitous in a pop music industry so enamored with image.

Miles Copeland III, brother of Stewart, was heavily involved in the British punk movement as a producer, promoter, and record company owner and wanted to help the Police, but was initially leery of their credibility now that the jazzy Summers was on board. Reluctantly, he agreed to finance their debut, *Outlandos d'Amour* (roughly French for "outlaws of love"), which was created with a meager budget and

The Police with Andy Summers in 1983.

(© Pictorial Press/Alamy)

no manager or record deal. However, when he heard Sting's "Roxanne," which was inspired by a visit to the red light district in Paris, Copeland immediately had a change of heart and scored a contract for the single with A&M Records. The radical mix on the album—mostly punk but with reggae, new wave, and pop influences—including the frantic "Next to You," featuring a rare Summers slide solo, was poorly received initially by the record company and the general public. The former was more confident in the singles "Roxanne" (#32 in 1979, #28 in 1982) and "Can't Stand Losing You" (#42 and #2 in the U.K.), though the lyrics about prostitution and suicide, respectively, were controversial in Great Britain. Encouraged by their charting, in the late fall of 1978, A&M released the album, which reached #23 in 1979. Additionally, "So Lonely" (#6) was plucked out as a single in 1979.

Regatta de Blanc (loosely French for "white reggae") followed at #25 in 1979, with the singles "Message in a Bottle" and "Walking on the Moon" reaching #1 in the U.K. and Australia. The title track won a Grammy for Best Rock Instrumental Performance. The songwriting and recording were approached far more casually by the band, with many pre-Police compositions being cannibalized for material and the title track coming from an onstage jam. Even with less pressure than its predecessor, *Regatta de Blanc* saw the band step away from punk and closer to the seamless synthesis of styles for which the Police are lauded.

Sensing their march towards stardom, A&M pressured the Police for a new album. The result was *Zenyatta Mondatta* (#5, 1980), which was quickly recorded during their second tour and contained a title that was invented more for its sound than any literal meaning. Sting's "Don't Stand So Close to Me" (#10) won the Grammy for Best Vocal Performance by a Duo or Group with Vocal and, along with "De Do Do Do, De Da Da Da" (#10), kept them on Top 40 radio. "Behind My Camel" won the 1982 Grammy for Best Rock Instrumental Performance and was Summers' first totally self-penned song. Sting refused to play on the track, as he had done in the past on most compositions written by Summers or Copeland, among his other divisive behavior, and Summers ended up playing the bass part. Despite its commercial success and critical praise, *Zenyatta Mondatta* remains the lowest regarded of the Police's five albums and would be the last to feature their basic trio sound. However, Jerry Moss, the "M" in A&M, did name one of his champion thoroughbred racehorses "Zenyatta," after the album.

Ghost in the Machine (#2, 1981), containing "Every Little Thing She Does Is Magic" (#1), "Spirits in the Material World" (#7), and "Secret Journey" (#29), went platinum initially, eventually reaching triple-platinum status. The title refers to a book on philosophical psychology written by Arthur Koestler in 1967 and was their first album to expand beyond the basic trio format to include substantial use of horns, keyboards, and synthesizers, including the Roland Guitar Synthesizer played by Summers. Serious seeds of dissent were sown, however, as Summers felt the dynamic interaction of the trio was lost and he and Copeland were now backing a singer and his pop songs. Additionally, Summers wanted to release his composition "Omegaman" as the debut single, but Sting nixed the idea. Following a tour, the band took a break as each member pursued outside projects. Copeland composed film scores and Summers recorded *I Advance Masked* with his old friend Robert Fripp, who had achieved cult fame in King Crimson. Increasing the strain, particularly with Copeland, was the growing acting career and burgeoning success of Sting. Complicating matters was the dissolution of both Sting's and Summer's marriages, though the guitarist would remarry his ex-wife in 1991.

Released in 1983, *Synchronicity* (#1) was the last studio album from the Police, and they went out with a bang. The title was derived from an Arthur Koestler book about parapsychology, *The Roots of Coincidence* (1972), again showing Sting's literary interests. Along with the mega-hit "Every Breath You Take" (#1), "Wrapped Around Your Finger" (#8), "King of Pain" (#3), and "Synchronicity II" (#16), the Police stayed on the charts and before the public for months. However, tensions within the band erupted to the point where Sting and Copeland had a fist fight during the recording of "Every Breath You Take" and the producer threatened to quit the project. The reggae influences that had been so much a part of their unique sound were mostly absent in the face of more elaborate pop productions. The album lost the

Grammy for Album of the Year to *Thriller*, though "Every Breath You Take" won for Song of the Year and "Synchronicity II" grabbed Best Pop Performance by a Duo or Group with Vocal. The former single also took other industry honors. The world tour supporting the record was their largest to date, featuring additional musical gear and backup singers and highlighted by a show at Shea Stadium in New York City before 70,000 fans. When the tour ended in 1984, Sting decided to pursue a solo career and the band went on hiatus. Copeland continued with film scoring and Summers recorded his second album with Fripp, *Bewitched*. In the summer of 1986, the Police regrouped to play three concerts for Amnesty International, followed closely by an ill-fated Police session date. The night before, Copeland broke his collarbone while horseback riding, thereby curtailing his drumming. Using a drum machine, the brief reunion produced nothing of value, Sting and Copeland argued over the choice of drum machines, and the band was essentially finished after seven years and 80 million in sales.

Summers embarked on a solo career that included movie soundtracks and guest appearances on other albums. In 1987, he released his first solo album, *XYZ*, the only vocal record in his post-Police career, though singers would sometimes appear on selected cuts. His brief and commercially unsuccessful foray into pop music compelled him to pursue a more artistic, jazz, and progressive instrumental direction in the future, starting with the gentle new-age loops and effects of *Mysterious Barricades* (1988) and followed by *The Golden Wire* (1989). The latter has more of a world music flavor and more in common with his textural playing in the Police. Ironically, Sting had called on Summers to play on his *Nothing Like the Sun* (#9) album, which reached double platinum in 1987, and the singer/bassist returned the favor on the guitarist's *Charming Snakes* (1990) and *Green Chimneys: The Music of Thelonious Monk* (1999). The former is a muscular jazz-rock workout showcasing the full range of Summers' extensive skills, while the latter is an ambitious project with some moments of authentic jazz. *World Gone Strange* (1991) likewise continued in the fusion vein, as Summers indulged his best instincts as a soloist of style and taste. Following the similar *Invisible Threads* (1993), Summers took a surprising turn towards rock with *Synaesthesia* (1996), featuring former Cream drummer Ginger Baker supporting power chords and Summers' always lyrical if more aggressive and adventurous guitar. *The Last Dance of Mr. X* (1997) found Summers exploring a wider range of styles, from jazz classics to Latin, polka, and even surf music!

A duo with Brazilian guitar virtuoso Victor Biglione resulted in the acoustic *Strings of Desire* (1998), spotlighting bossa nova covers with "lite" jazz stylings. *Peggy's Blue Skylight* (2000) is a tribute to Charles Mingus and very much like *Green Chimneys*, including a vocal track by Blondie's Deborah Harry. *Earth + Sky* (2004) saw Summers returning to his eclectic mix of jazz, pop, rock, and progressive influences, with his guitar providing the harmonic and melodic foundation of the compositions. However, he recorded *Splendid Brazil* (2005), another duo album of Brazilian classics with Victor Biglione, and also appeared at Carnegie Hall with classical guitarist Benjamin Verdery for the premier of *Dark Fluorescence*, a 20-minute, genre-bending concerto for acoustic and electric guitars. In 2006, Summers released his autobiography, *One Train Later*, to acclaim and awards. There followed the highly regarded *First You Build a Cloud* (2007) with Verdery, containing duets on mostly original Summers songs for acoustic and electric guitars. Concurrently, to the great joy of their many fans, the Police reunited for a year-long world tour following an announcement at the 49th Annual Grammy Awards in 2007. It would be the third-highest grossing tour ever. That same year, Summers saw his second book, *I'll Be Watching You*, published. A memoir of his years with the Police, the book features 600 of his personal photographs.

A true renaissance man with interests in photography, literature, beat poetry, art films, and Zen philosophy, Andy Summers forges onward with the soul and spirit of a true artist, always expanding and improving in search of the "lost chord." In the early fall of 2012, he went on a Brazilian tour with Brazilian singer Fernanda Takai from the band Pato Fu in support of their Japanese import album *Fundamental*. In the late fall, a documentary titled *Can't Stand Losing You*, based on *One Train Later*, premiered at the DOC NYC Film Festival in New York City.

THE GUITAR STYLE OF ANDY SUMMERS

Summers' assignment in the Police was to back Sting, accompany his tunes, and fill the sonic space between the bass and drums. Rather than playing a virtuosic combination of lead licks, chords, and bass riffs as other guitar heroes did in a power trio situation, he made the brilliant decision to mainly create diaphanous, shimmering chordal forms, enhanced by deep delay and other effects. He discovered that suspended and "add" chords, particularly, would produce musical tension, making them seem "bigger" and more prominent. Rhythmically, he would often apply syncopated strums on the rock reggae songs and arpeggios or broken chords on others.

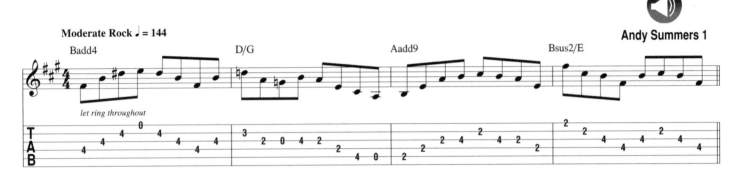

An exception to his "less is more" credo occurs with a fat F#m7 barre chord, embellished with a subtle pull-off from the 4th (B) to the tonality-defining ♭3rd (A).

Performance Tip: Barre across fret 9 with the index finger, utilizing the pinky for the pull-off on string 2.

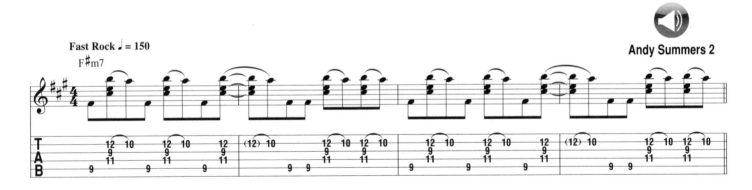

Going hand in hand with his deliberate minimalist approach, Summers tended to play tasty, melodic lead lines shorn of excess or flash. An elegant melody derived from the A major scale says all he needs over the tonic chord.

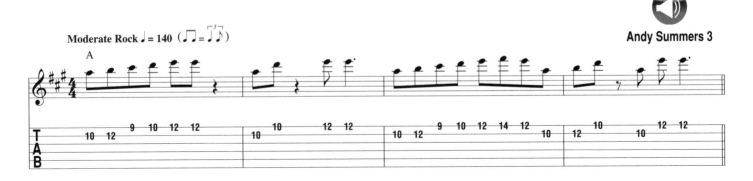

This next example is similar to his signature broken-chord pattern, proving the expressive power of "add9" and "sus2" voicings.

Performance Tip: In measure 1, barre across all six strings and form an A major chord. However, use the pinky for the B note at fret 9 of string 4, rather than for the root note at fret 7. In measure 2, barre as if accessing an F#m7 chord, but utilize the pinky to play the G# at fret 6 of string 4 (alternatively, Summers eschews the barre, instead moving the index back and forth from the low F# to the A, while keeping the other fingers planted). In measure 3, hold down the root (D) at fret 5 of string 5 with the index finger while barring strings 4–3 at fret 7 with the ring finger to from a D5 power chord. However, employ the pinky to access the E note at fret 9 of string 3, removing it for the D note on beat 3, which is handled by the ring-finger barre. In measure 4, use the same fingerings as in measure 3, but two frets higher on the fingerboard.

Andy Summers 4

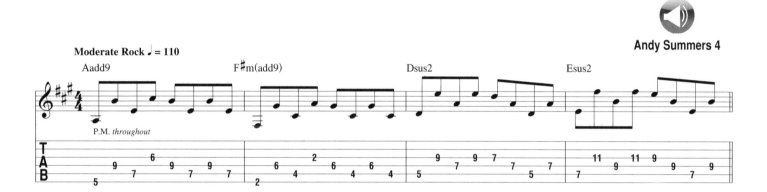

In this next example, an exotic ambience is created with a short, graceful ascending line that moves straight up the C minor pentatonic scale, from the root (C) to the 5th (G), in measure 1. In measure 2, the line is coupled with a dynamic descending leap from the first-string D (root) to fourth- and sixth-string Ds, respectively, creating a memorable motif.

Andy Summers 5

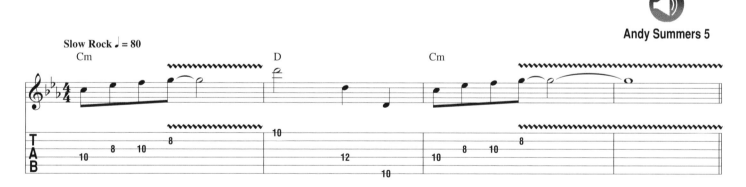

MARK KNOPFLER
(1949–)

Sometimes one band, or literally one song, signals and affects a sea change in the music world. When Dire Straits' instant classic "Sultans of Swing" hit the airwaves in late 1978, back when commercial radio actually broke songs, it not only was the proverbial "breath of fresh air" in the dog days of disco and nihilistic punk, but proved the vitality of classic rock forms, confirming that there was an audience for well-crafted rock music featuring impeccable technique, emotional expression, and intelligent, thoughtful lyrics. Introducing Mark Knopfler, who appeared to sing like Dylan and play like Clapton, Dire Straits also heralded the emergence of a new guitar hero with exemplary taste, passion, and a sound all his own. In the narrowly defined age of "new wave," his roots extended beyond the blues of B.B. King to the great fingerstylist Chet Atkins, rockabilly pioneers Scotty Moore and James Burton, jazz legend Django Reinhardt, American cult favorite J.J. Cale, and British instrumentalist Hank Marvin.

Mark Freuder Knopfler comes from a background as diverse as his music. He was born on August 12, 1949, in Glasgow, Scotland, to an English mother and a Jewish-Hungarian father who had fled the Nazis in 1939. In 1956, the family, including younger brother David, settled in their mother's home town of Blyth, Northumberland, in North East England. As an adolescent, Knopfler became fascinated with the boogie-woogie piano and harmonica playing of an uncle, and in the early '60s, his desire to play guitar turned into an obsession with having a custom color (Fiesta Red) Strat like Hank Marvin of the Shadows. However, he would have to wait for that prize and instead be satisfied with a Hofner Super Solid. In the early '60s, he played in a number of bands with his schoolmates, and in 1965, appeared on local TV in a duo with Sue Hercombe.

Following high school, Knopfler, one of the most literate rock writers outside of Dylan, initially pursued a career path as a writer. In 1967, he took a year of undergraduate journalism studies at Harlow Technical College, and in 1968, worked as a reporter at the *Yorkshire Evening Post* in Leeds, where he attended the University of Leeds in 1970. During the latter, he played in Silverheels and recorded a demo of his first original composition with blues guitarist and singer Steve Phillips, who would mentor him on how to play country blues, including the style of Lonnie Johnson, in a critical and generous gesture. They would play together off and on for five years and Knopfler would guest on Phillips' *Just Pickin'* album in 1996.

Knopfler graduated with a degree in English in 1973 and promptly moved to London to play music, joining the blues band Brewers Droop, featuring drummer Pick Withers, who appeared on *The Booze Brothers* album. In a tale that would likewise figure prominently in his back story, one night, Knopfler tried to play a friend's badly warped acoustic with extra light-gauge strings and found it impossible to do with a flat pick. Using bare fingers instead, he had a "eureka" moment, later claiming it was when he "found his voice" as a fingerpicker on the instrument, though he would later admit to using a flat pick in the studio for rhythm parts. Knopfler's fingerpicking technique has been compared to the idiosyncratic, legendary Oklahoma guitarist and songwriter J.J. Cale.

To make ends meet, for the next three years, Knopfler took a position as a lecturer at Loughton College in Essex while forming the Café Racers with friends and playing in a duo, the Duolian String Pickers, with Steve Phillips. His brother David would move to London and by 1977, the Knopflers were sharing a flat with bassist John Illsley and rehearsing and gigging with drummer Pick Withers in a revamped version of the Café Racers. A friend of Withers suggested the new name "Dire Straits" as reflective of their "dire" financial situation at the time, though it has since been refuted by David Knopfler, who pointed out that they all had day gigs. As it became abundantly clear, Mark Knopfler was not only a uniquely expressive guitarist and singer, but also a talented songwriter. Starting in the summer, they commenced recording demos of "Wild West End," "Sultans of Swing," "Down to the Waterline," "Sacred Loving," "Water of Love,"

Mark Knopfler performs with Dire Straits at the Oakland Coliseum on February 2, 1992.

(© Clayton Call/Retna Ltd.)

"Southbound Again," "In the Gallery," "Six Blade Knife," "Setting Me Up," "Eastbound Train," and "Real Girl." At the end of the year, the tapes were given to author, rock historian, and DJ Charlie Gillette, who excitedly secured a contract for the band with the Phonogram subsidiary Vertigo, and they were put on a tour with Talking Heads through the auspice of Ed Bicknell, who became their manager.

In 1978, *Dire Straits* (#2) garnered little attention upon its debut in the U.K., but the subsequent release months later of "Sultans of Swing" (#8) in Europe, and then the U.S. and Canada, broke the band as a major rock act and the album went gold. Dark, melancholy, often in minor keys, and autobiographical, with moody blues riffs and solos gracing a variety of syncopated rhythm tracks, the album revealed an artist of uncommon intelligence and lyricism. The fact that relatively low volume, nuanced electric music could have such depth and power was a revelation. The effect on guitarists would be immediate and substantial, as the sweet, unfiltered sound of a Strat straight into the amp became ubiquitous on pop and rock recordings. The gold *Communiqué* (#11), produced by the American team of Jerry Wexler and Barry Beckett in the Bahamas, followed a year later. The single "Lady Writer" (#45), a minor key song about British journalist Marina Warner, rocked harder than "Sultans of Swing" while also hinting at where Knopfler might follow his muse. The album would be the last to feature the original Dire Straits lineup. Likewise, in an event that would definitely forecast the future for Knopfler, both he and Withers guested on Bob Dylan's *Slow Train Coming* in 1979, with the "Bard" effusing that the Englishman was the "best guitarist he had heard since Mike Bloomfield and Robbie Robertson."

In 1980, *Making Movies* (#19) also went gold and was released minus David Knopfler, who had left in the summer after virtually all his tracks had been recorded, only to have them replaced. The stress of recording and touring apparently took its toll on the younger Knopfler, though he would go on to have a long if undistinguished solo career, with big brother and Illsley playing on his debut, *Release*, in 1983. Sid McGinnis and R.B. Brown contributed guitar tracks to *Making Movies* and Roy Bittan was added on keyboards, which would become a new and increasingly important element in the evolving sound of the band. Not coincidentally, the songs and arrangements became more expansive, involved, and sophisticated. Concurrently, the album produced a greater number of viable singles, including "Skateaway" (#58), "Expresso Love" (#39), "Solid Rock" (#56), "Tunnel of Love," and "Romeo and Juliet." Going "hand in hand" (another album track) with Knopfler's growing ambition and unchallenged leadership was his willingness to write more personally in lengthier songs, with the epic "Tunnel of Love" clocking in at 8:11 and two others at six-plus minutes.

The gold *Love over Gold* (#19) followed two years later and featured only five tracks, though longer and more epic and progressive than previous works, with extended instrumental passages. "Industrial Disease" (#75) and "Private Investigations" comprised the singles, though, in a commercial snafu, the latter was the lead single in Europe and was a huge hit, while the former performed poorly in the U.S. Of more critical importance was the recording of "Private Dancer," with Dire Straits stopping after finishing the instrumental tracks. Knopfler decided it needed a woman's touch and graciously passed it off to Tina Turner, who used it to great advantage on her comeback album of the same name. *Love over Gold* would be the last album with drummer Withers, and Alan Clark and Hal Lindes supplied keyboards and rhythm guitar, respectively.

In a burst of continued creativity, however, in late 1983, Dire Straits released a three-song EP, *ExtendedanceEPlay* (#53), containing "Twisting by the Pool" (#12) and featuring the debut of new drummer Terry Williams, formerly of Rockpile. With Williams, Clark, Lindes, and original bassist Illsley comprising the next edition of Dire Straits, Knopfler opted to take a break from the self-imposed heavy composing load and released the double-disc *Alchemy: Dire Straits Live* (#46) in 1984, which likewise achieved Gold status. During the same era, Knopfler wrote film scores for *Local Hero*, *Cal*, and *Comfort and Joy*, as well as producing *Infidels* for Bob Dylan and *Knife* for Aztec Camera.

The year 1985 was pivotal for Dire Straits, as they performed to acclaim at Live Aid and released the blockbuster *Brothers in Arms*, their only #1 album, a position it maintained for nine weeks. The spectacular array of more concise, melancholy tracks included "Money for Nothing" (#1), "Walk of Life" (#4), "So Far Away" (#3), "One World" (#8), "Ride Across the River" (#21), and the title track (#29). *Brothers in Arms* won an album Grammy for Best Engineered Recording, Non-Classical, as well as Best Rock Performance by a Duo or Group with Vocal for "Money for Nothing," co-written by Sting. Keyboardist Guy Fletcher was added to the band in addition to Clark, thereby making the instrument a significant element in the sound, and a large number of session players appear on the album as well. Jazzy drummer Omar Hakim was deemed more appropriate for the material and, consequently, replaced Williams on all tracks save for the intro to "Money for Nothing." Controversy surrounded the hit single due to the use of the word "faggot," though it was obviously used satirically in a composition lambasting the material world, particularly MTV, which had recently debuted on cable TV. The album was one of the first aimed at the CD market and the increased capacity of the disc allowed longer, complete versions of the songs, which wasn't possible on the vinyl format. Along with "old school" cassettes (!), the three formats would combine for sales of nine million in the U.S. and over 30 million worldwide to date.

Knopfler led Dire Straits on a massive world tour in 1985–86, after which he took time away from the band to work on film soundtracks, including *The Princess Bride* in 1987. He would not reconvene the group until the summer of 1988, when they were part of a 70th birthday celebration for Nelson Mandela in Wembley Stadium, where they headlined and were joined onstage by Eric Clapton. However, in early fall, Knopfler announced that he was pulling the plug on Dire Straits, citing that he "needed a rest" and revealing an aspect of his personality that would always be uncomfortable with rock stardom. Besides providing the soundtrack for *Last Exit to Brooklyn* in 1989, he turned his attention to an area of roots music that would receive his attention down to the present day.

Knopfler formed the Notting Hillbillies, named for the London neighborhood of Notting Hill, where their one album, *Missing… Presumed Having a Good Time* (#52), was recorded. The album was released in 1990 and contained the original "Your Own Sweet Way" (#20), in addition to a selection of country classics by the Louvin Brothers, Charlie Rich, and the Delmore Brothers. Knopfler brought in old mate Steve Phillips, perhaps repaying a musical debt as well as gaining an experienced folk musician, and Dire Straits band members Guy Fletcher (keyboards), Brendan Croker (guitar), manager Ed Bicknell (drums), Marcus Cliffe (bass), Paul Franklin (steel guitar), and Chris White (sax). The band members had all returned to other gigs by the release of the record, but embarked on a modest tour of the U.K. and would be brought 'round to play many times in the ensuing years. That same year, Knopfler realized a long-held dream when he recorded the wryly titled *Neck and Neck* (#127, #27 Country) with his idol, Chet Atkins. An undeniable triumph, it features a rich set of country classics and one Knopfler original, "The Next Time I'm in Town." Along with the always reliable Fletcher (bass, drums, keyboards) as Knopfler's right-hand man, an all-star selection of country greats supported the historic project, including Floyd Cramer (piano), Vince Gill (vocals), Steve Wariner (guitar), and Mark O'Connor (fiddle, mandolin). Critics hailed it as one of Atkins' best recordings, bringing him back to his roots (from jazz fusion), as "Poor Boy Blues" won a Grammy for Best Country Collaboration with Vocals, and "So Soft, Your Goodbye" garnered Best Country Instrumental Performance.

The year 1990 was a busy one for Knopfler, as he, Illsley, Clark, and Williams were joined by Eric Clapton and his band members Phil Palmer (guitar) and Ray Cooper (percussion) to perform at Knebworth as Dire Straits, though Williams would depart shortly afterwards. Perhaps inspired by the show and re-energized after the hiatus, Knopfler, Illsley, and manager Ed Bicknell agreed to reform Dire Straits with Clark, Fletcher, and select session musicians, including Jeff Porcaro (drums) from Toto. The result was the platinum *On Every Street* (#12, #1 in the U.K.), which was released in 1991 and featured "Heavy Fuel" (#1), "Calling Elvis" (#3), and "The Bug" (#8). Had it not followed *Brothers in Arms,* albeit by six years, *On Every Street* would have been considered a rousing commercial and critical success. An extensive and punishing world tour, lasting well into 1992, was initiated and likewise not as successful as the previous one. It would ultimately prove to ignominiously signal the end of the line for the "Sultans of Swing." In 1993, Knopfler took another extended break from the business of making music on a large, sprawling scale, while *Screenplaying*, a compilation of his soundtracks, was released to the public. In the meantime, he received an honorary doctorate of music degree from the University of Newcastle-upon-Tyne and oversaw the release of two live Dire Straits albums, *On the Night* (1993) and *Live at the BBC* (1995). Shortly thereafter, he announced his desire to no longer continue with his signature band.

In 1996, the release of *Golden Heart* (#105) would signal the beginning of his ongoing solo career. The album was met with a degree of indifference, especially in the U.S., due to the similarity to previous Dire Straits material and Knopfler's historical references, which many found obscure. His backing band, the "96ers," was anchored by Fletcher and Danny Cummings (percussion), in addition to a large supporting cast of session and guest musicians. The following year, he contributed the soundtrack to *Wag the Dog*, followed by *Metroland* in 1999, continuing his success with providing film scores, while also receiving an Order of the British Empire (OBE) medal. *Sailing to Philadelphia* (#60, 2000) went gold and righted the ship of his listing solo career, and it remains the high point so far. Inspired by a book by Thomas Pynchon about colonial America surveyors Charles Mason and Jeremiah Dixon, Knopfler created another literate record very much in the musical mold of Dire Straits, while employing the talents of James Taylor (who co-wrote and sings on the title track), Van Morrison, and Glenn Tilbrook and Chris Difford from Squeeze. He contributed the soundtrack to *A Shot at Glory* in 2001, while in the most unusual of many acknowledgments in his career, British scientists named a newly-discovered dinosaur *Masiakasaurus Knopfleri* in his honor.

In 2002, he surprised and tantalized his loyal fans by playing Dire Straits songs at four charity concerts in the U.K. with John Illsley, Guy Fletcher, Danny Cummings, and Chris White. Revisiting the best of his early years, he likewise performed as the Notting Hillbillies with Steve Phillips and Brendan Coker. That same year, he released *The Ragpicker's Dream* (#38) with his core group of Fletcher, Richard Bennett (guitar), Glenn Worf (bass), and Chad Cromwell (drums) playing a selection of American folk-inspired ballads, blues, and country about the downtrodden that hew close to the spirit, if not the letter, of unplugged music. An artistic and commercial triumph for him by any yardstick, *The Ragpicker's Dream* validated Knopfler and his vision of championing the traditional lower classes. However, the optimism generated by the reception to the recording was blunted in the spring of 2003, when he was involved in a serious motorbike accident too similar to the one suffered by Bob Dylan in 1966. Though he would fully recover with no apparent residual damage, particularly to his valuable hands, the accident did derail plans for a supporting tour. Fortunately, by 2004, he was able to resume performing and *Shangri-La* (#66) was recorded in Malibu, California, with basically the same group as the previous album. At the time, Knopfler lauded his current band by declaring that they "play Dire Straits songs better than Dire Straits." Breaking with his tradition of referencing historical events or characters, he now composed tracks about Elvis, Ray Croc (the founder of McDonald's), the troubled boxer Sonny Liston, and Lonnie Donegan, the influential Scottish folk musician. From the winter of 2004 to the summer of 2005, Knopfler and his group toured the world to great acclaim while playing a mix of his solo repertoire and a selection of Dire Straits classics.

Indulging his deep desire to soak up and perform authentic American roots music, in 2006, Knopfler engaged in a duo performance with country music sweetheart Emmylou Harris on *All the Roadrunning* (#17), which was actually recorded over a span of seven years. It contains, among his other original compositions, "If This Is Goodbye," a poignant track about 9/11, and the inspired collaboration was well-received, as was their brief tour of North America and Europe. Finding comfort and artistic satisfaction in his solo career, Knopfler released *Kill to Get Crimson* (#26) in 2007, containing the singles "True Love Will Never Fade" and "Punish the Monkey," the latter title derived from a line in his song "Let It All Go," also included on the CD. If anything, his lengthy musical involvement with Harris mellowed out his approach even further, as he maintained his folky focus. His sixth solo album, *Get Lucky* (#17), was begun in the fall of 2008 and released in the fall of 2009, keeping the steady stream of recordings flowing smoothly, and in fact, matching his output of studio albums with Dire Straits. Like his previous solo work, *Get Lucky* mainly continued to mine the Anglo-Americana he admires, with tales of the rural working class and including Celtic music to which he can personally lay claim due to his Scottish background. Knopfler began work on his next solo album in 2010, taking a break in late 2011 to tour Europe with Bob Dylan.

In 2012, Knopfler released *Privateering*, an ambitious, expansive, 20-song double-disc set that seems to sum up his enduring fascination with various classic folk styles, from Celtic to American country music, with a larger dose of gritty blues, blues rock, and rock than previously heard. As he has sometimes done in the past, there are different formats available, with Deluxe and Super Deluxe Editions containing bonus material. Fletcher, Bennett, and Worf still anchor the band, with Ian Thomas (drums), Paul Franklin (pedal steel), and bluesman Kim Wilson (harp) from the Fabulous Thunderbirds guesting.

After reaching the pinnacle of rock stardom in the '80s, Mark Knopfler decided to turn away and pursue the American and British roots music closest to his heart. The results have not only brought him personal satisfaction, but have burnished his reputation as an artist with almost unlimited creativity, as well as the utmost integrity.

THE GUITAR STYLE OF MARK KNOPFLER

Knopfler is a master of the fill, along with his other superlative skills. Each measure contains root-position 3rds relative to the chord change. However, measures 2–3 also feature a Dm (F/D) dyad whose root functions as the 2nd degree of the C major scale in order to create musical tension before resolving to E/C (3rd/root). In addition, measure 4 utilizes an A/F dyad as a quick IV (F) chord "hit," which precedes resolution to a first-inversion C major (E/C) double stop.

Mark Knopfler 1

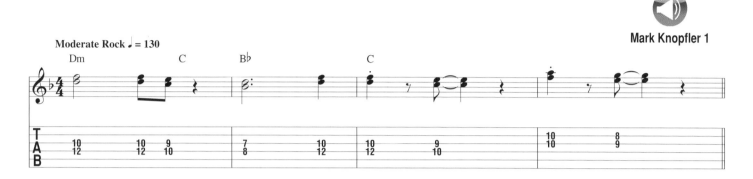

Though possessing exceptional chops, Knopfler tends to keep them in check. One of the few times when he chose to "air it out" resulted in a classic motif and dynamic musical tension. Observe how, in measures 1–2, he takes a rock guitar cliché relative to Dm and makes it memorably dramatic by moving it up a whole step in measures 3–4, where the notes relate directly to the C major scale.

Performance Tip: Barre strings 2–1 with the index finger and execute the pull-offs with the ring finger.

Mark Knopfler 2

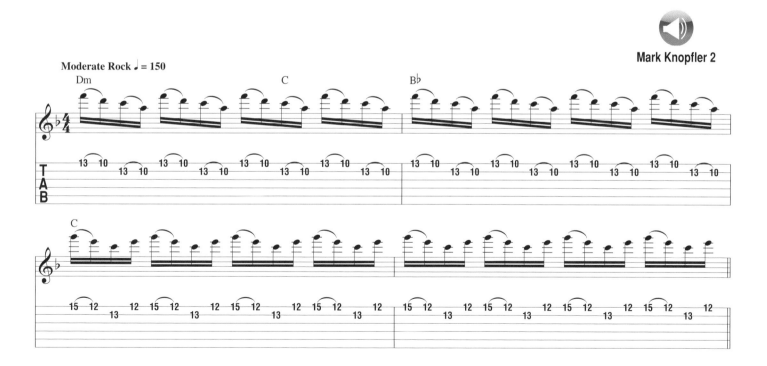

Knopfler favors minor key progressions in several of his most famous compositions where he employs the Aeolian mode, or natural minor scale, to expressive effect. In measures 1–2, check out his emphasis of the 2nd (D♯) to produce anticipation for the minor tonality-defining ♭3rd (E) that follows. Just as significant is his graceful, fluid phrasing in a rocking tune

In measures 2–3, the G♯ Aeolian mode is the basis for his improvisation. However, across the bar line of measures 1 and 2, he picks a slinky, pedal steel-type double-string bend relative to the C♯ harmony of measure 2. It not only emphasizes the major tonality of the C♯, but also contributes melodic contrast to the minor tonality.

Performance Tip: Bend the double stop with the ring and pinky fingers, low to high, thereby putting the ring finger on the C♯ note on fret 6, where it can efficiently access the ascending line. The hand will also be in an advantageous position to access the half-step bend on beat 3 with the ring finger.

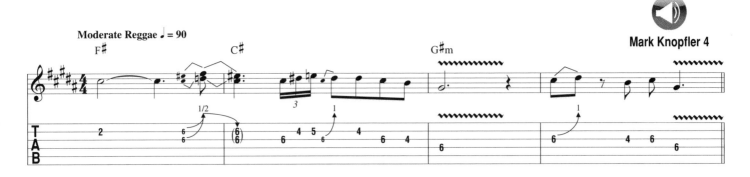

This classic hard rock riff is built upon a choice selection of 5ths (power chords) and 4ths. Though Knopfler has admitted to using a pick in the studio for rhythm parts, he is well-known for playing with bare fingers. Besides adding to his generally warm, smooth lead sound, bare fingers enable him to vary his phrasing, as well as to access more notes simultaneously.

Performance Tip: Pick with the index finger and thumb. In measure 1, barre across strings 4–2 with the index finger, voicing the D note on fret 7 with the ring finger and the F note on string 2 with the middle finger.

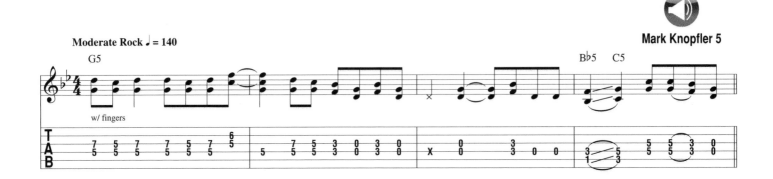

RANDY RHOADS
(1956—1982)

The world of rock guitar has a sad history filled with too many "shooting stars" who flamed out long before their time, a list that includes Jimi Hendrix, Terry Kath of Chicago, Paul Kossoff of Free, and Kurt Cobain. Like Buddy Holly and some others, including Steve Gaines of Lynyrd Skynyrd and Stevie Ray Vaughan, however, Randy Rhoads' tragic demise came through no fault of his own. Fortunately, though his many fans would have wished a much longer life for him to produce more great music, he left enough of a legacy to provide inspiration and instruction for many years to come.

Randall William Rhoads was born on December 6, 1956, in Santa Monica, California, as the youngest of three children raised by his mother, Delores. She and her husband, William, who deserted the family when his son was a baby, taught music at their Musonia School of Music in Burbank, where they lived. Delores had a little piano around for her son and taught him some theory, which Randy would later use while composing. However, Rhoads started playing guitar at the age of 6, after he received an old classical instrument that had belonged to his grandfather. He showed aptitude immediately, figuring out licks on his own and was soon taking lessons at the music school, including piano, music reading, and theory. By the time he was 8, he was playing electric guitar, an old f-hole Harmony, in a small ensemble that was created for him at the school by his mother. Everyone recognized his talent and dedication. Although he was precocious and had little patience for lessons, he had to learn to read in order to play in the group, as they worked from charts. The training would serve him well later on.

His mother hooked him up with a specific rock guitar teacher at the school who drilled him hard on scales that were derived from violin books. The musical discipline paid off, though his music reading would always remain limited. In a story beloved in Randy Rhoads lore, after a year of lessons, the excellent and experienced teacher told his incredulous mother that he had nothing left to teach her son. Around 14, Rhoads formed his first band, Violet Fox, named in honor of his mother's middle name, with his brother Kellie on drums. During that same period, he saw his first rock concert, Alice Cooper, and was literally dumbstruck by the allure of a rock 'n' roll career.

Rhoads was not only an exceptional guitar talent, but an intelligent young man in school, earning As and Bs in high school. In order to speed up the process so he could get out and play gigs, he enrolled in a special program and graduated at 16. His first "gig" was teaching at Musonia eight hours a day, six days a week. By all accounts, he was an extremely popular, effective teacher for whom his students had great affection. On account of their tight financial situation, the Rhoads children had grown up without a TV or record player. Therefore, the first time Randy was able to sit and learn other guitarists' licks was when his students requested them—after he had been playing for years! He would later credit it for the development of his unique style, along with the critical impact of the classical music that he heard around the house from his mother, who played and taught trumpet.

Rhoads taught his best friend, Kelly Garni, how to play bass in the early '70s and they played together in groups with the wildly eclectic names Mildred Pierce, the Katzenjammer Kids, Mammoth, and most memorably, the Whore. By this time, his main influences were "glam rockers" Glen Buxton from the Alice Cooper band and Mick Ronson, who backed David Bowie, and his rapidly expanding and innovative chops were already attracting attention and scaring other guitarists. In addition, his creativity and ambition to write were blossoming. The Whore rehearsed during the day in Rodney Bingenheimer's English Disco, an infamous glam rock hangout on the Sunset Strip. In 1975, Rhoads and Garni decided to get serious and formed a band originally called Mach 1 and then Little Women. They auditioned Kevin Dubrow and, after working with him for a number of months, finally decided he was the one to front the band. Drew Forsyth, who had previously played with Rhoads and Garni, was added on drums and the group began by playing bars in Hollywood and private parties in Burbank. With their local reputation growing, they soon graduated to the Whisky A Go Go, KROQ's Cabaret, and the Starwood in Santa Monica, where they would open for Van Halen before either band was signed. The eventual name for the group came about through a conversation with a member of the English band Status Quo, who said he would like to have a band named "Quite Right." Misunderstanding his thick, cockney accent, they thought he said "Quiet Riot."

As Quiet Riot, they now had hopes of landing a recording contract. Unfortunately, it was the disco era and no U.S. label was interested in a hard rock/heavy metal band, so they ended up signing with CBS/Sony in 1977 with the proviso that their records would only be released in Japan. The original albums, *Quiet Riot* (known affectionately as *QR I*), with "It's Not So Funny," and *Quiet Riot II* (*QR II*), were recorded in 1977 and 1978, respectively. In retrospect, *QR I* is amateurish garage rock that does not hold up and did little to nothing to show Rhoads at his best. *QR II*, on the other hand, was a step forward, with a glimmer of the revolutionary classical guitar influences Rhoads would incorporate later, though it would mostly be a boost for Dubrow's career. Nonetheless, the records sold respectably in Japan, but the lack of a contract with a U.S. company and the related inability to book a tour would prove to be a source of great frustration for the band. In 1979, Garni quit to become a paramedic and was replaced by bassist Rudy Sarzo, whose photo appears on the cover of *QR II*, though he does not play on either disc. Meanwhile, the band could not bust out of the rut as a popular but local L.A. band. Hoping that the signing of Van Halen would increase their chances, Quiet Riot was only further thwarted in their quest for greater success when record execs informed them that they didn't want "the second L.A. metal band." Meanwhile, Rhoads continued teaching guitar during the day, and in the process, inspiring countless students.

Rhoads would eventually leave Quiet Riot in 1980, but not before commissioning luthier Karl Sandoval to build what would become his iconic and signature polka-dot "Flying V" guitar. The young "guitar god in training" designed the instrument almost entirely by himself and the polka dots would be seized upon as a fashion statement by his growing legions of young fans, as the charismatic, androgynous-appearing Rhoads had become the focal point of the group.

Unbeknownst to Rhoads, in 1979, Black Sabbath frontman John Michael "Ozzy" Osbourne had left the pioneering metal band for the second time to form his own group and was searching around for a suitable guitarist. During an interview with *Raw Power* magazine, it was suggested he try Rhoads, who was summarily contacted before the guitarist's final show with Quiet Riot. Osbourne had auditioned and nixed many guitarists in New York and Los Angeles before Rhoads showed up at Osbourne's Malibu hotel room at 2 A.M., after teaching all his students that evening and having absolutely no hopes of landing the job. Another part of the Randy Rhoads legend has him showing up with his Les Paul and a small practice amp, tuning up, playing a few harmonics and licks, and having Osbourne respond, "You've got the gig." By November of 1979, Rhoads was in London tracking *Blizzard of Ozz*. Though they were complete opposites in personality and musical experience, Osbourne and Rhoads had tremendous rapport as songwriters and performers. Compared to his constant ego battles with Tony Iommi in Black Sabbath, the outrageous singer welcomed the collaboration with Rhoads, who gained a significant confidence boost from the relationship. Consequently, Osbourne apparently had no problem when his guitarist became so popular that fans were showing up at gigs to see and hear the angelic-looking young man, as well as the "star" of the show.

Blizzard of Ozz (#21) was released in the early fall of 1980 in the U.K. and in the spring of 1981 in the U.S., where it has been certified quadruple platinum. Hailed as a "masterpiece of neo-classical metal," the album, featuring the classic "Crazy Train" (#9) and "Mr. Crowley," was a commercial and critical success. Included in the set is the 49-second instrumental solo "Dee," a tribute to Randy's mother, Delores. A U.K. tour followed, after which the band returned to the studio to cut the appropriately titled *Diary of a Madman* (#16), which eventually reached triple-platinum status. The close chronology of the two albums and tour suggests a rush to record a follow-up album before an upcoming U.S. tour, and some reviewers fault it for not meeting the high standards of its predecessor. Nonetheless, Rhoads' playing had ascended to an even loftier plain on the best tracks and many fans prefer it. The singles "Flying High Again" (#2), "Over the Mountain" (#38), and "You Can't Kill Rock and Roll" (#41) attest to its popularity. Out on tour, Rhoads confided to his bandmates that he was thinking of taking a few years off from rock 'n' roll to study classical guitar and receive a degree at UCLA. Osbourne scoffed, asking him why he would want to do that instead of earning money in rock music. However, Rhoads was serious, and in every town they stopped in, he would look for classical guitar teachers and take lessons or attend seminars. Osbourne claims Rhoads applied himself to his studies, and within seven weeks, was playing at an amazingly high level. Ironically, during this time, Jackson guitars presented Rhoads with a prototype signature model guitar and were preparing to go into production. In addition, he was honored with *Guitar Player* magazine's award for Best New Talent.

Randy Rhoads, 1981

(© Everett Collection Inc./Alamy)

On March 18, 1982, the band played in Knoxville, Tennessee. The next day, they began the drive to a festival in Orlando, Florida. After traveling through the night, they stopped off in Leesburg, Florida, the home of Florida Coach and where their tour bus driver, Andrew Aycock, and his brother Calhoun lived. The compound included a small airstrip and Aycock, a licensed pilot, cajoled members of the crew to go up and take joy rides with him in a 1955 Beechcraft Bonanza. Rhoads had a fear of flying but went up with Rachel Youngblood, the band hairdresser and seamstress. He was then persuaded to go up a second time, convinced that nothing foolish would be tried, as the 58-year old Youngblood had a heart condition. In addition, Rhoads, a photography hobbyist, wanted to take some aerial photos. Inconceivably, Aycock decided to "buzz" the tour bus where the other band members were still sleeping. Not content to successfully execute the risky maneuver twice, he went for a third try and hit the bus, tearing off the roof and sending the plane spiraling, taking the top off a pine tree and crashing into the garage of a nearby house, where it burst into flames. All three occupants of the plane died instantly, their bodies burned beyond recognition. Dental records and Rhoads' jewelry were all that were available to confirm identification of the bodies. It was later revealed that Aycock had cocaine in his system, his medical certificate had expired, and his requisite biennial flight review was overdue.

Osbourne was bereft and went into a deep depression, even considering quitting rock 'n' roll, and a multitude of fans were devastated. In 1987, Osbourne released *Tribute,* the only authorized collection of their live performances. In 2004, Rhoads was posthumously given a plaque on Guitar Center Hollywood's Rock Walk, and in 2008, Marshall released an exact signature replica 1959RR Super Lead 100 amp. In 2010, the Gibson Custom Shop produced a signature cream-colored Les Paul Custom based on the 1974 model that Rhoads played with Osbourne, in addition to his Sandoval and Jackson RR guitars. In 2011, his name was submitted, for a second time, for consideration as a star on the Hollywood Walk of Fame.

To have any 25-year-old lose their life due to criminal negligence is a great tragedy. It is particularly so when the individual touched countless people with his talent, gentle nature, and generous spirit. Randy Rhoads lives on in the hearts and minds of his loyal fans through his expressive, innovative music.

THE GUITAR STYLE OF RANDY RHOADS

Rhoads had tremendous chops and employed them in the service of pumping energy and excitement into his solos, songs, and indeed, the bands whose presence he graced. Sixteenth notes flew effortlessly from his fingers in a rush of exuberance. In this example, he creates tension by moving a minor pentatonic lick up the fretboard chromatically, shifting from 14th to 18th position.

Randy Rhoads 1

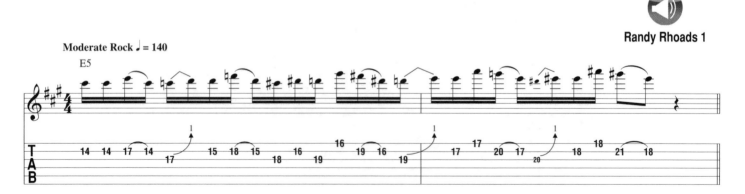

Using string manipulation techniques popularized by Eddie Van Halen and making them his own, Rhoads combined arpeggiated harmonics and whammy-bar dives for great dynamic effect.

Performance Tip: Play the F# note on string 4 with the index finger, followed by the ring finger for the fifth-fret harmonics.

Randy Rhoads 2

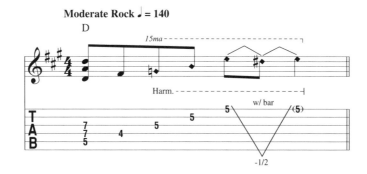

Rhoads could pack more musical information and expression into four measures than some of his contemporaries could in a whole extended solo. Utilizing the A major scale, fingered as the F# Aeolian mode with the addition of the spicy ♭3rd (C), in the breathtaking descending run in measure 2 and the D major scale ascending run in measure 3, he produces both consonance and dissonance in a seamless, fluid flow of notes.

Randy Rhoads 3

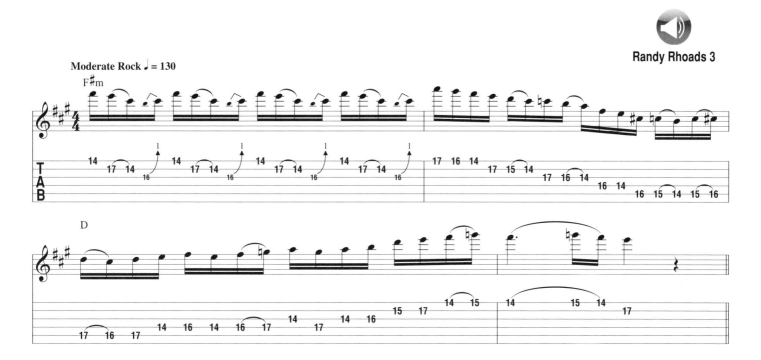

As would be expected of a bona fide guitar hero, Rhoads was the complete instrumentalist, totally in command of a variety of accompaniment techniques. Arpeggios, triads, bass lines, and a nimble run up the D major scale not only support the vocal, but contribute forward motion to the progression.

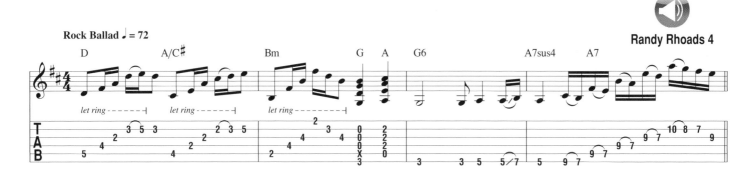

Like Van Halen, Rhoads was a master of tapping and employed the legato technique to add dynamic contrast to his rapid-fire, picked forays. Observe his emphasis of the 5th (D) and ♭7th (F) notes from the G minor pentatonic scale to produce riveting anticipation.

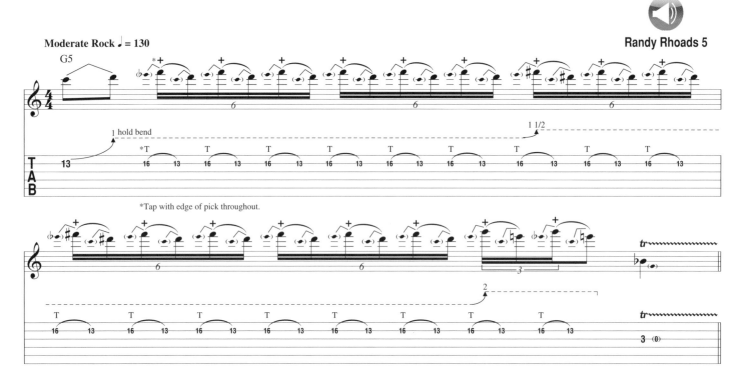

Rhoads was exceptionally skilled at creating musical tension via repetitive riffs. A favorite phrasing technique was to play pulse-racing, ascending, chromatic patterns. Check out how he begins his dizzying ascent with the 3rd (C#), root (A), and 6th (F#) notes from the A major scale and ends up including notes from the Aeolian and other minor modes along the way.

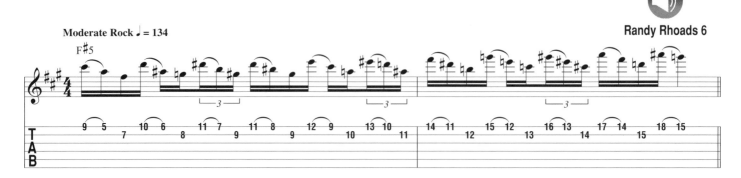

ALEX LIFESON
(1953–)

As the founder and guitarist of Rush, the Canadian virtuoso power trio, Alex Lifeson has contributed progressive licks, riffs, and solos to the sci-fi/fantasy rock for which the band is best known. Although famously dismissed by critics as pretentious, the "cult" group and Lifeson have garnered a large, loyal following down to the present day, with worldwide sales in excess of 40 million, including 24 gold, 14 platinum, and three multi-platinum albums. Moreover, they trail only the Beatles and Rolling Stones in consecutive gold or platinum studio albums by a rock band.

Aleksandar Zivojinovic was born August 27, 1953, in Fernie, British Columbia, to Serbian immigrants Nenad and Melanija. His professional name, "Lifeson," is an approximate English translation of Zivojinovic, Serbian for "son of life." He was encouraged to take viola lessons as a child, but gravitated to the guitar at 12 upon hearing his brother-in-law play flamenco music. Lifeson was given a Kent classical instrument by his father for Christmas, followed by a Japanese electric. Jeff Beck, Eric Clapton, Jimi Hendrix, and Jimmy Page were early inspirations, along with Steve Hackett and Allan Holdsworth at a later time. Clapton appeared to be the "easiest" from whom to cop licks, and Lifeson recalls learning "Spoonful" from a vinyl LP. In 1968, he formed a band called the Projection with his schoolmate, drummer John Rutsey, and two other members. In the summer of 1968, they decided to call themselves "Rush" at the suggestion of Rutsey's brother, who noted their "hurry" to come up with a new name, and they recruited Jeff Jones as lead singer and bassist. In the early fall, Jones was replaced by Lifeson's high school friend Gary Lee Weinrib, or "Geddy Lee," though after various personnel changes and additions over the next few years, Lee would be fired and form his own band. However, by 1971, Lee was back with Lifeson and Rutsey in a power trio in the mold of Cream.

In 1973, Rush saw their first single released, a cover of Buddy Holly's "Not Fade Away" b/w "You Can't Fight It." Dissatisfied with the issuing record company, they created Moon Records and put out a self-titled album that was panned by the critics for its obvious debt to Led Zeppelin. When a Cleveland DJ began playing their original "Working Man," however, fans responded and Mercury Records in the U.S. re-released the LP in 1974. Unfortunately, Rutsey, whose musical tastes were limited to the basic blues rock of Bad Company and was reluctant to tour, left the band due to health problems (and died in 2008). Auditions were held and Neil Peart was chosen as his replacement and has been with Lifeson and Lee ever since. He would not only become a rock virtuoso, but contributed the sci-fi/fantasy themes and lyrics for the instrumental-centric, platinum *Fly by Night* (#113) in 1975, featuring the epic "By-Tor and the Snow Dog," a preview of the "future" direction of Rush. Their first U.S. tour ensued, exposing them to a growing cadre of fans.

Caress of Steel (#148), a five-song set flirting with heavy metal and featuring two extended, complex compositions, "The Necromancer" and "The Fountain of Lamneth," followed quickly in 1975. Generally considered to be a misstep, Rush had counted on the project being their big breakthrough, but sales of the considerably less commercial album than the previous ones were disappointing, as was the resulting tour, dubbed the "Down the Tubes Tour." Lee has opined that both Lifeson and Peart were high during the recording sessions. However, the wider success and acceptance that Rush desired arrived the next year with their signature, triple-platinum *2112* (#61), despite the 20-minute title "suite" taking up an entire side of the vinyl LP. Nonetheless, the shorter songs were welcomed by the record company and fans. The supporting tour resulted in the release of the live album *All the World's a Stage*.

After the encouraging reaction to *2112*, Rush was determined to further pursue progressive rock in the manner of King Crimson, Yes, and Van der Graaf Generator. Released in 1977, *A Farewell to Kings* (#33) contained what was perceived as improved songwriting, including "Closer to the Heart" (#21 Mainstream

Rock) and "Xanadu." Notable was Lifeson incorporating classical guitar on the title track and Lee experimenting with synthesizers on "Xanadu" and writing the lyrics to "Cinderella Man," based on Frank Capra's *Mr. Deeds Goes to Town.* Meanwhile, Peart continued to expand his already estimable percussion chops and drum kit. Released a year later, *Hemispheres* (#47) harkened back to *Fly by Night* inasmuch as it featured the 18-minute "Cygnus X-1, Book II: Hemispheres," considered by many to be their best long composition, along with extensive use of complex rhythms and time signatures unusual for rock. In addition, the album also boasted the ironically titled, nine-and-a-half minute instrumental "La Villa Strangiato (An Exercise in Self-Indulgence)," while Lee continued to use bass pedal synthesizers and a Minimoog.

In 1980, a seismic shift in the rock of Rush occurred: the release of the platinum *Permanent Waves* (#4). Responding to the current popular music trends of new wave and reggae and pressure from their label, the band included radio friendly tracks like the Jamaican-influenced "The Spirit of Radio" (#51) and the anthemic "Freewill" and "Entre Nous," while the two epic compositions, "Jacob's Ladder" and "Natural Science," satisfied their evolving progressive rock tendencies. Concurrently, with Peart still the main lyricist, his content evolved away from fantasy and allegory to social and personal relationship topics. Building on the popularity of their new-found commercial direction, *Moving Pictures* (#3), released the following year, would prove to be even more successful and accepted as the paramount achievement of their career, reaching quadruple-platinum status and remaining their biggest seller to date. "Tom Sawyer" (#8 Mainstream Rock), their most popular song, was included alongside "Limelight" (#4 Mainstream Rock), "Vital Signs," "Red Barchetta," and the Grammy-nominated instrumental, "YYZ," which lost out to the Police's "Behind My Camel." "The Camera Eye," which referenced a work by American author John Dos Passos and dealt with the great world cities New York and London, was the last Rush composition longer than 10 minutes. The album featured synthesizers more prominently from Lee as the sound of things to come.

Indeed, the '80s are often referred to as the "synthesizer years," with Lifeson's melodic and driving guitar contributions basically minimized, again reflecting the trends in popular music. Released in 1982, *Signals* (#10) went platinum, employed Ben Mink on electric violin, and contained the singles "New World Man" (#1 Mainstream Rock), their only U.S. Top 40 pop hit, "Subdivisions" (#3 Mainstream Rock), and "The Analog Kid" (#19 Mainstream Rock). With reggae, funk, and ska influences, the album was a radical departure from previous releases. In 1983, Lifeson was voted Best Rock Talent by *Guitar for the Practicing Musician* magazine. *Grace Under a Pressure* (#10), named for an Ernest Hemingway saying, hit platinum in 1984 and featured the single "The Body Electric" (#105). It has been described by Lifeson as the "most satisfying of all our records," though he also admitted that "possibly, we lost our direction at times," while his guitar accompaniment was emphasized to a greater degree, even as he was utilizing extensive processed sounds at the same time Peart began playing synthesized drums. It is generally seen as their "darkest" recording, with songs referencing the Holocaust ("Red Sector A," #21 Mainstream Rock) and the threat of the Cold War ("Distant Early Warning," #3 Mainstream Rock), as well as personal loss and challenges ("Afterimage," "The Enemy Within"). In 1984, Lifeson was named Best Rock Guitarist in *Guitar Player* magazine.

Power Windows (#10) and *Hold Your Fire* (#13), released in 1985 and 1987, respectively, featured Lee's keyboard synthesizers, more accessible lyrics, pop song structures, and polished production, making them ripe for MTV. The former release featured several singles, including "The Big Money" (#4 Mainstream Rock), about the corrupting "power" of money, as well as "Marathon" (#6 Mainstream Rock), "Manhattan Project" (#10 Mainstream Rock), "Mystic Rhythms" (#21 Mainstream Rock), and "Territories" (#30 Mainstream Rock Tracks). The latter album eventually went gold, showed the influence of Chinese classical music (inspired by Peart's bicycle trip to China), and featured Aimee Mann singing on three tracks, including "Time Stand Still" (#3 Mainstream Rock). In 1989, the live *A Show of Hands* (#21) went gold in conjunction with a video, confirming their strong, loyal fan base. That same year, they changed labels, moving from Mercury to Atlantic, and promptly released a new studio album.

Three years elapsed before Rush was ready to release their next studio album, *Snakes & Arrows* (#3, 2007), which recalled their popular classics from the '70s, as reflected in its high chart position. Lifeson credited Pink Floyd's David Gilmour with encouraging him to compose on acoustic guitars, resulting in a "certain purity" maintained and a tough, live feel throughout. At the same time, Peart's lyrics dealt with faith and war, which he internalized after his motorcycle trip through the U.S. Appearing were three new instrumentals, the first since 1996, including "Malignant Narcissism," which referred satirically to Islamic terrorists and was nominated for a Grammy for Best Rock Instrumental Performance, losing to Bruce Springsteen's "Once Upon a Time in the West." The four singles released were "Far Cry" (#22 Mainstream Rock), "Spindrift," "The Larger Bowl (A Pantoum)," and "Workin' Them Angels" (#30 Mainstream Rock). Capitalizing on their resurgence as a force to be reckoned with in rock music, during the tour to support their hit album, they appeared on the *The Colbert Report* and in the movie *I Love You, Man.* In 2008, *Snakes & Arrows* was named Most Ferociously Brilliant Guitar Album and Lifeson was voted Best Rock Guitarist in *Guitar Player* magazine.

Rush was inducted into the Canadian Songwriter's Hall of Fame in the early spring of 2010 and commenced the "Time Machine Tour" shortly thereafter, performing the complete *Moving Pictures* album, followed by the release of the DVD/two-CD *Time Machine 2011: Live in Cleveland* (#54). They also received a star on the Hollywood Walk of Fame. Being back at the top of their game and genre afforded Rush the luxury of taking their time with *Clockwork Angels* (#1 Top Hard Rock Albums), as well as indulging their desire to produce a concept record, with the title track an epic, multi-section composition. Peart's lyrics deal with alchemy and steampunk sci-fi and are sung over an eclectic and impressive range of styles, including the obligatory prog rock, metal, jazz, and flamenco music. In addition, his drumming is featured and emphasized to a high degree throughout. Though released in 2012, the record was recorded in 2010–11, including the singles "Caravan" (#38 Mainstream Rock), "Headlong Flight" (#23 Mainstream Rock), "The Wreckers" (#5 Mainstream Rock), and "The Anarchist." Sci-fi novelist Kevin J. Anderson, who had become friends with Peart, would write a novelization based on the album. *Clockwork Angels Tour* (#33), a live album, was put out in 2013. As has become their *modus operandi*, all three musicians trigger various sampled instruments in real time in concert.

In the spring of 2013, Rush was belatedly inducted into the Rock and Roll Hall of Fame, though they had been eligible since 1998, leading Lifeson to comment: "I couldn't care less. Look who's up for induction; it's a joke." As often happens in rock music and the other arts, the opinions of fans and musicians outlast those of biased critics. Lifeson and Rush have been an inspiration to numerous bands, including Metallica, Rage Against the Machine, the Smashing Pumpkins, Anthrax, Primus, and Dream Theater, among others. Forty years into their career, Rush are still rocking to the beat of their own drum(mer), with Lifeson as ferocious as ever to the sheer joy of their fans.

THE GUITAR STYLE OF ALEX LIFESON

Lifeson has a signature guitar style that is recognizable due to his utilization of effects and signal processing. However, under the skillful electronic manipulation resides creative chord voicings, rhythms, lead lines, and melodies. One of the valuable tools that he employs as a trio guitarist is dynamic broken chords, implying a bigger sound than strummed voicings afford.

Alex Lifeson 1

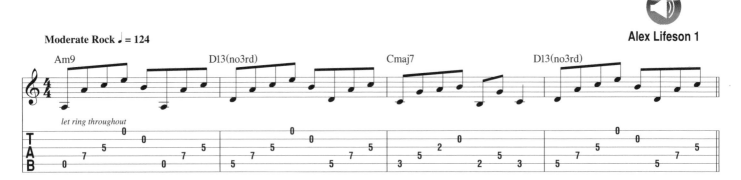

Dynamic contrast between bass and treble registers is another hallmark of the Lifeson approach to playing in a trio. Intervals of a 5th, or power chords, in conjunction with triads and triple stops, cover the sonic spectrum for a rich accompaniment. Observe how he varies the licks and riffs between the two similar measures (Bm and G–A).

Alex Lifeson 2

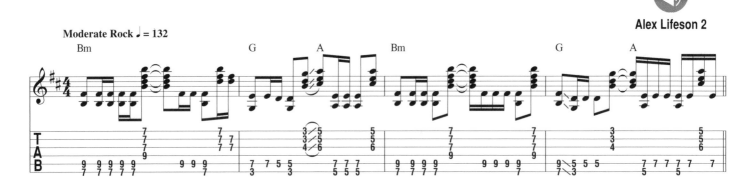

The unusual 7/4 time signature affords Lifeson the opportunity to give the impression that "time" is being stretched and extended. Though a simple, basic rock chord progression, notice his intelligent choice of voicings to smooth the way to the big open E chord and the E major bass line that follows.

Alex Lifeson 3

The Mixolydian mode provides both bluesy grit and diatonic melody in a hip, repetitive pattern that rings with open strings.

Alex Lifeson 4

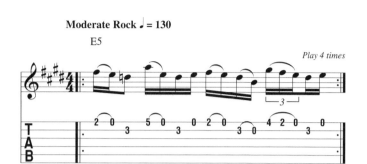

When Lifeson opts to play single-note lines, he often tends to create rapid shifts between taut repetition and bursts of forward motion. Check out his use of open strings as a way of expanding the dynamic sonic range of his scales without altering his left-hand position.

Alex Lifeson 5

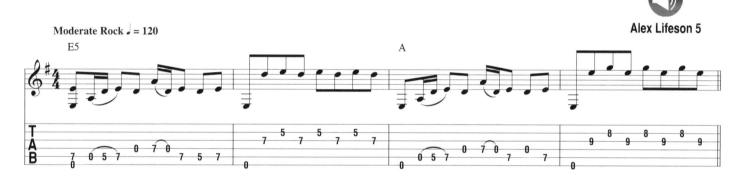

One of the characteristics of prog-rock bands is changing time signatures, and Rush is no exception. Again, Lifeson utilizes the technique to alter the perception of "time."

Performance Tip: Employ hybrid picking, utilizing the flat pick in conjunction with the right-hand middle finger, to access the C/A dyad in measures 1 and 3 and for the Am7 voicing in measures 2 and 4.

Alex Lifeson 6

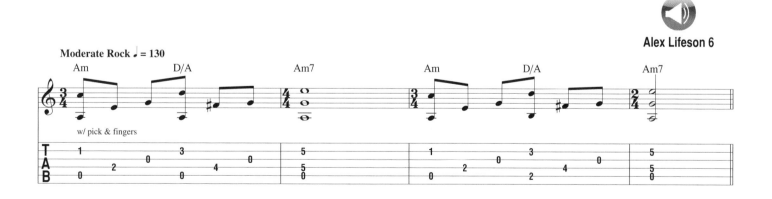

Brian Setzer of the Stray Cats performing in 1992.

(Ian Dickson/MediaPunch)

BRIAN SETZER
(1959–)

Similar to the Police, and with the same blond coifs, the Stray Cats were seen by some to be some weird, mutant punk group, when in fact, they were bent on reinvigorating rock with their version of primal, classic rockabilly. Led by virtuoso guitarist Brian Setzer, who ignored the punk manifesto of no solos and the avoidance of ostentatious technique, the Stray Cats brought swing back to pop music. Not surprisingly, Setzer would go on to become the modern "King of Swing" with his big band, following the breakup of the Stray Cats.

Brian Setzer was born on April 10, 1959, in Massapequa, Long Island. When he was six years old, he listened to the first Beatles and Stones albums, being particularly attracted to the rock 'n' roll covers on each. At age 8, he began playing the euphonium and would stay with the tuba family member for years while developing a taste for jazz by sneaking into clubs in Greenwich Village while underage. Seeing the Mel Lewis Orchestra at the Village Vanguard planted the idea that he would like to lead a large ensemble someday on guitar. At 14, he saw a photo of Eddie Cochran and began adopting the appearance of the '50s rockabilly icon by dressing with a slicked-back pompadour and the requisite T-shirt and baggy, cuffed jeans. Setzer began playing guitar circa 1975 and, showing great aptitude on the instrument, dropped out of school at 16 to be a musician. One of the earliest bands that he joined was the Massapequa Wildcats, performing blues and rockabilly. He also began singing and playing solo guitar as the Rockabilly Rebel in "old man" bars on the south shore of Long Island while taking jazz guitar lessons in Manhattan. Itching to have his own group, he brought in his younger brother Gary on drums and Bob Beecher on bass to form the rockabilly cover band the Tomcats. In 1978–79, while trying to make ends meet, he and Beecher also played with the more commercially successful, new wave Bloodless Pharaohs in Manhattan, fronted by keyboardist/singer Ken Kinnally.

Concurrently, local stand-up acoustic bassist Leon Drucker, the son of a classical double bassist, and drummer Jim McDonnell had also come under the allure of rockabilly music in the age of disco. They began showing up regularly at Tomcat gigs with the appropriate look and, around 1980, had become members of the trio known as Brian Setzer and the Tomcats. McDonnell states that many of the stages on which they performed were so small that he did not have enough room to set up a full drum kit, resulting in his iconic snare/bass drum/cymbal configuration, as well as allowing him to save space and be physically closer to the other two. He performed under the name "Slim Jim Phantom" and Drucker became "Lee Rocker" as the band underwent a number of name changes while building a following up and down the mid-Atlantic states. A series of bootleg live recordings documenting the Tomcats was issued in 1997 by Collectables Records, including early versions of "Rock This Town" and "Stray Cat Strut," along with rockabilly classics.

Pop music audiences in the U.S. were dumbfounded by the retro rockers who added punk and jazz flourishes to their sound. Consequently, when Setzer met a British bartender and rocker in a New York City club in 1980 and was told that rockabilly had never gone away in England, he decided to ditch the Pharaohs and try his luck with the Tomcats across the sea. In order to finance the venture, they went to "Music Row" on 48th Street in Manhattan to sell all their gear, in addition to Phantom's 1966 Pontiac, in order to purchase three one-way tickets to London. With the bartender freshly installed as their manager, they moved to the capital of the British Empire, sleeping in theaters and Hyde Park until their first gigs started coming in on borrowed instruments. By this time, they had been dubbed the "Stray Cats" by Rocker, as he thought it fit their image as "strays." As a fictitious group, the Stray Cats had previously appeared in the movie *That'll Be the Day* (1973), as well as its sequel, *Stardust* (1974).

Within a few months, the Stray Cats were seen by Brit rockers like the Stones, the Who, Led Zeppelin's Robert Plant, and neo-rockabilly guitarist Dave Edmunds from Rockpile, who wanted to produce them in order to preserve their authenticity. He got his chance when, after being pursued by Virgin and Stiff Records, they signed with Arista and recorded the charting *Stray Cats*. Released in February of 1981 in the U.K. only, the album featured the hit singles "Runaway Boys," "Rock This Town," and "Stray Cat Strut." Gigs in Europe and a tour of Japan, where hysterical enthusiasm for their rockabilly music rivaled Beatlemania, raised their profile considerably. The "Cats" were given a huge boost in visibility and import sales when the Stones had them open three dates in the U.S. on their North American tour in the fall of 1981. Concurrently, they made a quick trip to Montserrat, West Indies, to record *Gonna Ball*. The laidback locale and the speed at which they cut the tracks turned out to be a misstep, as it did not chart as well as their debut. However, during the same time frame, the Stray Cats went back to the U.S. and appeared on the TV show "Fridays." Following a U.S. TV appearance on the "Merv Griffin Show" in the early part of 1982, the band was signed to EMI America in the early spring. In the summer, they embarked on their first North American tour and EMI released the double-platinum *Built for Speed* (#2), a combination of songs from both Arista U.K. albums, including "Rock This Town" (#9) and "Stray Cat Strut" (#3). In addition, with their exaggerated pompadours, tattoos, and classic American cars, they fit right into the image-conscious times.

The platinum *Rant 'n' Rave with the Stray Cats* (#14, 1983) was their next release. Singles like "(She's) Sexy + 17" (#5), "I Won't Stand in Your Way" (#35), and "Look at That Cadillac" (#68)" and their image made them naturals for the newly emerging MTV. Despite the burgeoning success, "instant" fame and fortune created tension within the Stray Cats, as often happens. Phantom married blonde Hollywood star Britt Eklund, and Setzer was pursued for various side projects with Bob Dylan, Stevie Nicks, and Robert Plant. In late 1984, Setzer called it quits following the addition of Tommy Byrnes on second guitar and backup vocals and after a European and U.S. tour. He stated that he had nothing more to say in the genre and wanted to leave the Cats on a high note. However, others theorized that it was because of the rock-star posturing of the bassist and drummer. While Setzer commenced a solo career with Byrnes in tow, Rocker and Phantom ran off and formed a trio with guitarist Earl Slick. Setzer released *The Knife Feels Like Justice* (#45) in 1986 as his debut, containing a large number of guest and backup musicians and featuring a far more commercial roots-rock sound and topical subject matter. Unfortunately, it was poorly promoted by EMI, possibly because of the change from the rockabilly that had proven to be a viable commodity. Perhaps in a countermove, Setzer reconvened the Stray Cats the same year for *Rock Therapy* (#122), an album of mostly covers. He would do it again for *Blast Off!* (1989), followed by a tour with Stevie Ray Vaughan, for the Niles Rodgers-produced *Let's Go Faster!* (1990), for *Choo Choo Hot Fish* (1992), produced by Dave Edmunds, and finally, for the rock 'n' roll cover album *Original Cool* (1993). The Stray Cats would reunite many times over the years for special occasions and for immensely successful tours in 2007–08 and 2009.

Previously, in 1987, Setzer got to live out a childhood fantasy when he was cast to play Eddie Cochran in *La Bamba* while continuing his solo career and reuniting with Rocker and Phantom every so often for appearances and tours. In 1988, *Live Nude Guitars* (#140), featuring "When the Sky Comes Tumbling Down" (#36), was a glossier version of the Stray Cats' rockabilly sound. Although recorded in 1993, *Rockin' by Myself* wasn't released until 1998. The album illustrated Setzer's vaunted skills, as he performed virtually solo, including on banjo, with assistance from his brother Gary on second guitar. Setzer realized another long-held dream in 1994 with the release of *The Brian Setzer Orchestra* (#158), where he got to play loud and distorted guitar in front of a 17-piece big band on standards and originals in a manner similar to blues legend Gatemouth Brown in the '40s and '50s. It could not have come at a better time, as it kicked off the swing and jump-blues music craze of the late '90s. *Guitar Slinger* (with the orchestra) followed in 1996, featuring the Clash's Joe Strummer and a more eclectic mix of material, including a version of Stevie Ray Vaughan's "The House Is Rockin'." He hit his high point in 1998 with *The Dirty Boogie*

(#9), which featured the smash Louis Prima cover "Jump, Jive 'n' Wail" (#14), a song that defined the swing revival and won a Grammy for Best Pop Performance by a Duo or Group with Vocal. In addition, his slinky version of the '50s classic "Sleepwalk" won the Grammy for Best Pop Instrumental Performance. *Vavoom!* (#62), released in 2000, contained similar swinging covers and won a Grammy for Best Pop Instrumental Performance for "Caravan." A year later, he returned to his roots with a vengeance with *Ignition* (#152), featuring the trio-powered '68 Comeback Special with Mark Winchester (slap bass) and Bernie Dresel (drums).

In 2002, he returned with the Brian Setzer Orchestra for *Boogie Woogie Christmas* (#141), including a version of "The Nutcracker Suite" originally arranged for the Les Brown Orchestra in the '50s. The following year, the retro-rocking *Nitro Burnin' Funny Daddy* (#23), containing mostly originals sans horns, displayed his versatility in a number of ensembles and genres. In 2005, *Rockabilly Riot, Vol. 1: A Tribute to Sun Records* (#28) presented Setzer in his element and proved the undiminished vitality of his rockabilly chops. That same year, he and his orchestra followed with another Christmas album, *Dig That Crazy Christmas* (#56), containing carols, hip seasonal tunes, and originals. In 2006, *13* (#35), his 13th studio album containing 13 original tracks, reverted to his stripped-down rock 'n' roll band, with a guest appearance by Slim Jim Phantom. Seemingly fearless about tackling unexpected material with his orchestra, in 2007 Setzer, released *Wolfgang's Big Night Out* (#141), containing his arrangements of an expansive list of classical pieces re-imagined as rockabilly and rumbas, among other startling results. Shifting gears, to use an appropriate metaphor for a hotrod "cat," *Songs from Lonely Avenue* (2009) found the Brian Setzer Orchestra utilizing its leader's all-original songs to explore '50s film noir, R&B, and rock 'n' roll. Surprisingly, it took until 2011 for the virtuoso guitarist to record his first all-instrumental record, *Setzer Goes Instru-MENTAL!*, sporting rockabilly, jazz, and bluegrass classics, as well as originals. In 2012, *Brian Setzer's Rockabilly Riot! Live from the Planet* added to his oeuvre of live discs, which included *Christmas Comes Alive* (2010), *Don't Mess with a Big Band* (2010), *Red Hot & Live* (2007) with Brian Setzer and the Nashvillians, and *Jumpin' East of Java* (2001).

Fortunately for guitarists and guitar fans, Brian Setzer shows no indication of slowing down or reining in his prodigious talent or quest to evolve musically. Springing forth from a subgenre of American rock 'n' roll that originally enjoyed a brief, five-year run, he has built a decades-long career and an eclectic style that is timeless.

THE GUITAR STYLE OF BRIAN SETZER

Setzer knows swing and jump blues as well as rockabilly music. As such, he is smart and cool enough to know when and how to cop saxophone licks. Assimilating a classic from the mid-'50s put him back on the map as a solo artist after the Stray Cats breakup. Observe the use of the major pentatonic scale relative to the B♭ (I) and E♭ (IV) changes, respectively, with emphasis on the 6th (G and C), as opposed to the ♭3rd or ♭7th, which are more common in postwar electric blues.

Brian Setzer 1

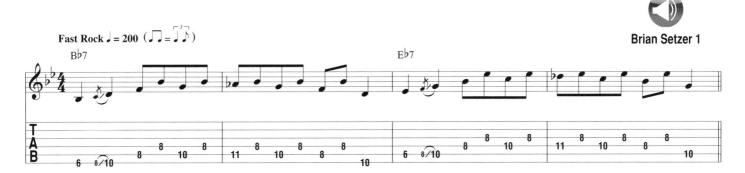

An eclectic mix of straight-ahead blues, jazz, and a nod to Gershwin via Grant Green contributed to a strutting early original Stray Cats tune. Note the sophisticated augmented arpeggio in measure 2, a favorite V chord of jazz, as well as hip blues musicians, from Wayne Bennett (with Bobby Blue Bland) to the Allman Brothers.

Performance Tip: Access the octaves in measures 3–4 with the index and ring fingers, low to high.

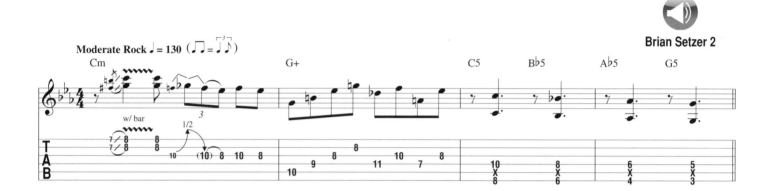

Brian Setzer 2

As a trio guitarist with the Stray Cats, Setzer was responsible for chordal accompaniment and fills, as well as solos. Again drawing on his knowledge of sax licks, he crafts a swinging embellishment that emphasizes the 6th (B) from the D major pentatonic scale.

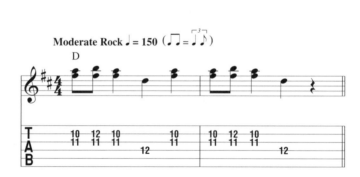

Brian Setzer 3

Here, Setzer relies on a classic blues triad and triple-stop pattern often employed as a turnaround when reversed. It not only adds harmony, but forward motion as it ascends and anticipation when it ends on an implied A7 voicing.

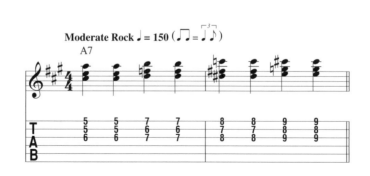

Brian Setzer 4

Measures 9–12 of a rocking 12-bar progression, this next example shows his intelligent combination of blues phrasing and Mixolydian mode notes relative to the V (E) and IV (D) chords before resolving to the tonic (A) chord via the root note, plucked from the composite blues scale. He then switches to the A major scale in what would be measure 12 of the final verse, ending with a classic rockabilly chord—a vibrant 6/9 voicing.

Performance Tip: Execute the 6/9 chord, low to high, with the middle, index (as a small barre), and ring (as a small barre) fingers.

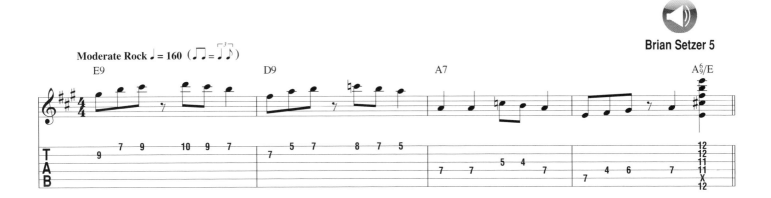

Setzer proves why he is one of rock's premier trio guitarists with advanced chords and swinging blues licks that accelerate into sizzling rock runs. With the ubiquitous rockabilly 6/9 chord anchoring the four-measure I chord (G6/9) phrase, Setzer cruises the composite blues scale like a hotrod '32 Ford burning rubber. In measure 3, dig the unusual note choices to create anticipation—the 3rd (B) to the ♭7th (F)—which are rewarded with slithery, descending pull-offs that flow into measure 4.

YNGWIE MALMSTEEN
(1963–)

Yngwie Malmsteen has seemingly unlimited confidence, seen as arrogance by many, and the chops to back it up. He put both attributes to spectacular use as he waved the banner high for neo-classical, heavy metal rock guitar in the '80s with blinding technique known as "shredding," inspired by legendary master Italian violinist Niccolo Paganini (1782–1840).

Lars Johan Yngve Lannerback was born on June 30, 1963, in a suburb of Stockholm, Sweden, to Rigmor and Lennart—a musical family in which Lennart, the father, and his brother and sister played instruments. He was described as an exceedingly difficult child who resisted Rigmor's efforts to interest him in music, though he would later attribute his love for Bach to having heard him, along with Beethoven, Mozart, and Vivaldi, at home from the age of 5 onward. He also credits his sister, Lolo Lannerbeck, who is a flautist, with providing most of his classical music education. However, in 1970 at the age of 7, he saw a TV special on the recently deceased Hendrix and was exceptionally impressed by his image, performance, and burning of a guitar. In an oft-quoted remark, he states, "The day Jimi Hendrix died, the guitar playing Yngwie was born."

Yngwie Malmsteen performs live at the Culture Room in Ft. Lauderdale, FL on May 28, 2006.

(© Larry Marano/Retna Ltd.)

Beginning on a Mosrite, by the age of 10, he had directed his previously untamed energy on obsessive practice, to the point that his fingers literally bled and would stiffen, requiring him to soak them in warm water in order to get them to move. Though essentially self-taught, he did take some theory lessons, learning to read and write music. His first band, Track on Earth, was a duo with a schoolmate on drums. Following the divorce of his parents, he took his mother's maiden name, Malmsteen, and altered "Yngve" to "Yngwie" to make it easier to pronounce outside of Sweden. Seeing a violinist perform Paganini's challenging *24 Caprices* on TV fueled an obsession with the flamboyant, 19th century virtuoso, who would serve as his personal and musical avatar. Additionally, the classically influenced rock style of Deep Purple's Ritchie Blackmore and Blackmore's Rainbow would prove to be a huge inspiration for the rapidly developing Malmsteen, along with metal guitarist Uli Jon Roth and Queen's Brian May.

Despite an endeavor that occupied his time and direction, Malmsteen was a behavioral problem in school. In 1978, following periods during which his mother allowed him to remain at home and practice, he quit. He was 15. For a while he had a job in a local music shop, where he fortuitously discovered an antique lute with a scalloped fretboard. Like Blackmore and his Stratocasters, Malmsteen had his guitar fretboards scalloped. Initially, it made them more difficult to play; however, as he discovered that scalloped frets precipitated a lighter touch, he eventually gained more facility, resulting in even more speed. He played in a succession of Swedish bands that featured his astounding technique in extended improvisations, but the public preferred pop music, leaving him greatly frustrated. In 1978, he recorded a stunning self-titled disc and sent it out to various record companies. However, the 19-year old fretboard wiz would not receive his deserved break until early 1982, when the demo found its way into the hands of Mike Varney of Shrapnel Records in Northern California. Initially specializing in heavy metal and the neo-classical genre, he recognized Malmsteen's extraordinary ability and invited him to come to the U.S. and join Steeler, an up and coming but obscure pop-metal band from Nashville who had settled in Los Angeles and become the darlings of the Sunset Strip crowd. Apparently, he was flown in at the last minute to add his parts to their undistinguished, completed tracks, including an unaccompanied, classically derived intro to "Hot on Your Heels," previewing the shape of things to come.

Looking for more challenging material to showcase his burgeoning talent, Malmsteen joined the Deep Purple/Rainbow-influenced Alcatrazz in 1983 and appears to maximum effect on *No Parole from Rock 'n' Roll* (#128), featuring "Island in the Sun," and the live *Live Sentence* (#133) in 1984. The latter was recorded in Japan, reportedly the only country enthusiastic about the band, and contains Malmsteen's ferocious "Evil Eye," which would appear on his first solo album. Intended to be an instrumental side project, *Rising Force* was a phenomenal debut, hitting #60 with his friend Jens Johansson on keyboards and Jeff Scott Soto on vocals, while winning the Best Rock Album award from *Guitar Player* magazine and receiving a Grammy nomination for Best Rock Instrumental Performance. Building upon and bypassing the technical virtuosity of Eddie Van Halen and the classical forays of Randy Rhoads, Malmsteen single-handedly ushered in the age of shredding with an onslaught previously unheard in any guitar genre. His revolutionary sweep picking, fat vibrato, classical progressions and melodies on iconic songs like "Black Star" and "Far Beyond the Sun" stunned rock guitarists everywhere and sent them scrambling after Paganini and Bach recordings. Conspicuously, he was replaced in Alcatrazz by Steve Vai.

The following year, Yngwie J. Malmsteen's Rising Force released the even more aggressive *Marching Out* (#54), with Soto delivering the maestro's less than compelling lyrics about demons and Vikings, and Anders Johansson, the brother of Jens, joining on drums. In 1986, the highly touted *Trilogy* (#44) closed out his seminal neo-classical metal era, with Malmsteen playing bass and Mark Boals on vocals, showing his growing commercial success as his compositional and lyrical skills vie to match his spell-binding chops. However, just when his "force" was "rising" ever higher, tragedy struck and brought the "guitar god" down to earth. In the early summer of 1987, he crashed his speeding Jaguar into a tree, severely injuring his right hand and suffering a blood clot on his brain, leaving him in a coma for a week and nearly killing him. While convalescing, his beloved mother died and it was revealed that his manager had ripped him off. Nonetheless, in a manner similar to Django Reinhardt, he displayed his unwavering perseverance, regaining his exceptional pick control and releasing his biggest hit to date, the hard-rocking *Odyssey* (#40), in 1988. That same year, Fender released a signature Strat. Vocalist Joe Lynn Turner replaced Boals and co-wrote the radio friendly single "Heaven Tonight" with the guitarist. Reining in his prodigious technique in the service of more commercial songs was a successful strategy, though his critics lambasted him for lacking passion and soul, without considering that he was still recovering from the accident. A world tour to support *Odyssey* followed, but *Trial by Fire: Live in Leningrad* (#128), recorded during a performance in the Soviet Union and containing a cover of Hendrix's "Spanish Castle Magic," would signal the end of Rising Force and, for all practical purposes, the beginning of the end of '80s hair bands. It was also the last album to feature the Johansson brothers, and upon the completion of the tour, Malmsteen moved back to Sweden to form a new, all-Swedish group.

Released in 1990, *Eclipse* (#112), featuring similarly accessible neo-classical material, showed Malmsteen in a holding pattern and would be his last album for Polydor Records, as he left their stable in a huff after their lack of promotion contributed to its poor showing in the U.S. At the same time, Malmsteen seemed poised to put the neo-classical metal music that made him famous behind him for good, coinciding with a drop in popularity of heavy metal in the '90s. Following the 1991 release of *The Yngwie Malmsteen Collection*, and before the 1992 release of *Fire & Ice* (#121) on Elektra Records, he was married and divorced from a Swedish pop star. An uneasy mashup of his signature neo-classical metal songs, with a blatantly commercial hair metal slant, *Fire & Ice* would be his one and only release for the label. The next two years saw more personal tragedy bedevil him, as Hurricane Andrew destroyed his home in Miami, his manager died of a heart attack, he broke his hand in a freak accident, he battled tendinitis resulting from his extreme practicing, and his future mother-in-law had him falsely arrested for holding her daughter hostage with a gun, though the charges would be dropped. However, *The Seventh Sign*, released in 1994 through Music for Nations in Europe and Pony Canyon in Japan, took a surprising change of direction towards heavy blues rock powered by Hendrix-derived wah-wah, along with his rote neo-classical playing, challenging longtime fans. Hot on its heels, the EP *I Can't Wait*, containing three studio tracks and two live ones from a Budokan, Japan concert, helped to make up for the previous recording hiatus.

Staying the course musically, in 1995, Malmsteen recorded the ostentatiously titled *Magnum Opus*, containing the predictable combination of hard rock and neo-classical guitar, along with sentimental pop ballads. In 1996, he took a brief hiatus from repeating the same format and gathered many of his former bandmates for *Inspiration*. With an emphasis on Deep Purple and Rainbow, the album featured covers of songs that had influenced him, including the classic rock of "Carry on Wayward Son" and "Manic Depression." He also reunited with singer Jeff Scott Soto and bassist Marcel Jacob for one song on their album *Human Clay*. Re-energized, he returned in 1997 with the all "original" *Facing the Animal*, featuring drummer Cozy Powell and consisting of his typical patented style, along with power ballads and more "inspiration" and fire, which were lacking in previous outings. *Double Live*, a selection of originals and Blackmore covers recorded in Brazil in 1998, revealed, if anything, his playing had become even faster and more overwhelming. Tragically, Powell died before the tour that produced the album. The year 1998 also saw the debut of his Fender Signature Stratocaster with scalloped fingerboard, based on his original 1972 model known as the "Duck" due to its yellow finish and Donald Duck decals on the headstock. The following year, *Alchemy* would close out the '90s, with Malmsteen using mystical themes including the single about UFOs/aliens, "Hangar 18, Area 51," around which to display his fully recovered, awesome fretboard power.

Two compilation CDs, *Young Person's Guide to the Classics, Vol. 1 and 2*, containing his personal selection of classical favorites, and the cryptically titled *War to End All Wars* were his way of welcoming the new millennium, and Malmsteen did not disappoint. For his debut on the U.S. label Spitfire, made available concurrently with the domestic release of the previous decade of albums, Malmsteen not only played electric and acoustic guitars, but bass and sitar as well. The acoustic track "Miracle of Life" seems to be a reference to him having recently become a husband and father. The album would be the last with longtime lead singer Mark Boals, who was replaced by former Rainbow frontman Doogie White in a move seen as an improvement by the fans. In addition, Patrik Johansson became the new drummer, a position he commands down to the present day. White made his debut on *Attack!!* (2002) with noted session and solo musician Derek Sherinian on keyboards, acquitting himself admirably in the style of the late Ronnie James Dio. Meanwhile, the guitarist unfailingly proves his virtuosity on the title track and "Baroque 'n' Roll," among others, even if to the point of overkill. In addition, he takes a rare lead vocal on the bluesy "Freedom Isn't Free." Also put out in 2002, *The Genesis* chronicled his musical exploits as a 17-year-old, some of which appears on bassist Marcel Jacob's *Birth of the Sun*.

In 2003, Malmsteen joined the G3 super guitar group with fellow string wizards Steve Vai and Joe Satriani, resulting in the live double-disc speed orgy *G3 Live: Rockin' in the Free World*, while also taking a short sabbatical from solo recording to guest with others. He returned to the studio in 2005 for *Unleash the Fury,* an enhanced CD with 18 original tracks and three videos on which he plays guitar, bass, sitar, guitar synthesizer, and some keyboards. The title references an ugly incident on an airplane that occurred in 1988 during the *Odyssey* tour. After a drunken tirade, Malmsteen passed out only to be awakened by an offended woman passenger pouring a jug of ice water over his head, to which he responded, "You've released the f---ing fury." The entire incident was captured on audio tape and released on the internet. That same year, he also presented his wildly ambitious *Concerto Suite for Electric Guitar and Orchestra in E Flat Minor, Op. 1* on DVD, which was filmed in 2001 with the New Japan Philharmonic and previously recorded and released in 1998 with the Czech Philharmonic in Prague. Completely composed and arranged by the rock virtuoso, it is an amazing accomplishment considered superior to past collaborations by others. Though Malmsteen has been criticized for his tone not complementing the sound of the orchestra, as well as for moments of sloppy playing, he should be cut some slack for performing the epic, authentic classical composition before a live audience.

Perpetual Flame came out in 2008 on his Rising Force label, with former Judas Priest lead singer Tim "Ripper" Owens, who many consider to be the best singer to stand next to Malmsteen since Soto, replacing White. An excellent example of the "medieval metal" that his loyal fans come to expect, the album confirmed how, in spite of his outsized ego, Malmsteen strives to maintain his own high standards of technical performance as he "unleashes the fury." Three tracks were made available for the video games *Rock Band, Rock Band 2*, and *Rock Band 3*. *Angels of Love*, an all-instrumental production of acoustic guitar arrangements of previously released material, along with one new track, followed in 2009. Malmsteen plays all instruments, including steel and classical guitars, guitar synthesizer, some electric guitar fills, and keyboards. Around the same time, the compilation *High Impact* was released, consisting of his most famous instrumental songs since 1993, including a vocal track and a surprising cover of Michael Jackson's "Beat It" with Owens on vocals. The second album with the new dynamic duo, the appropriately titled *Relentless*, came out in 2010 and maintains their excellent composing, playing, and singing save for the one misstep, "Look at You Now," "featuring" Malmsteen on vocals.

Currently a resident of Miami, Florida, during the 2011 baseball season, he played "The Star Spangled Banner" before a St. Louis Cardinals/Florida Marlins game at Sun Life Stadium. In the summer of 2012, he made a rare appearance in his native Sweden, headlining the Getaway Rock Festival in Gavle. In the early winter, he released *Spellbound*, on which he plays all the instruments, including singing lead.

Love him or hate him, Yngwie Malmsteen is an ongoing "rising force" of nature. He sums up his unwavering musical philosophy thusly: "People say, 'Slow down. Less is more.' How can less be more? More is more!"

THE GUITAR STYLE OF YNGWIE MALMSTEEN

In the following example, Malmsteen flashes his intimidating virtuosity in a single measure. Applying the harmonic minor scale over an Em harmony, he sears the frets of his Strat in a blur. Tellingly, he makes sure to include enough quick hits on the root (E), ♭3rd (G), and 5th (B) notes to anchor the tonality while also taking advantage of the half step between the major 7th (D♯) and root, which helps provide the scale with its unique, exotic flavor.

Yngwie Malmsteen 1

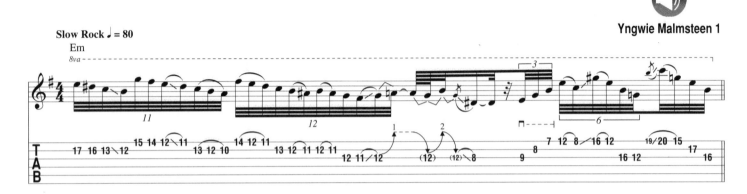

Once again, the harmonic minor scale provides the appropriate improvisational material for Malmsteen to construct fluid melodies, this time phrased in descending and ascending triplets over the Em and C/E changes. Observe how he avoids the C (♭6th) over the Em (i) chord while subtly inserting it in measure 2, over the C/E chord. In addition, be sure to notice how the long line of first-string notes in measure 3 creates anticipation for measure 4 (C/E) via the repetition of the C note. However, Malmsteen avoids resolving to the root in measure 4, instead opting to "dance" around it with the major 3rd (E) and ending with a bent and vibratoed D note as a way to produce anticipation.

Yngwie Malmsteen 2

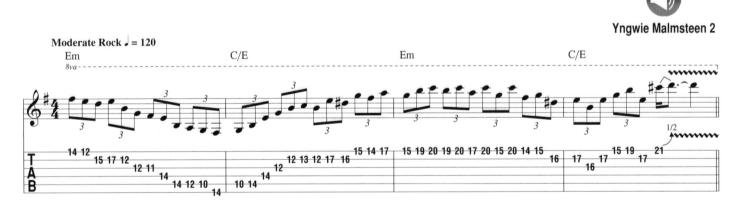

In measures 1–3, Malmsteen cleverly and intelligently employs the notes of the E major scale, beginning on C♯ (6th of E), in an ascending melodic motif that complements the C♯ (VI), B (V), and A (IV) chord changes. Check out how the last E note in measures 1 and 3, within the exact same pattern, functions as the ♭3rd and 5th of C♯ and A, respectively, while the D♯ in measure 2 is the major 3rd of B. In measure 4, he turns the tables with a surprising and stunning lick derived from the C♯ harmonic minor scale. Be aware that using "5" chords (or power chords), enables Malmsteen to take creative liberties with his scale choices, as power chords are neither major nor minor.

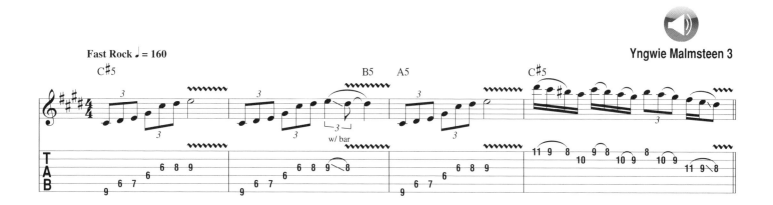

Though respected, feared, or even demeaned as an obsessed virtuoso, Malmsteen is capable of constructing elegantly simple but memorable riffs. In measure 1, the major 3rd (E#) and 5th (G#) denote C# major. In measure 2, the root (F#) and ♭3rd (A) line the minor tonality. In measure 3, four choice notes from the E# (F) diminished scale provide a striking melody over the E# diminished chord.

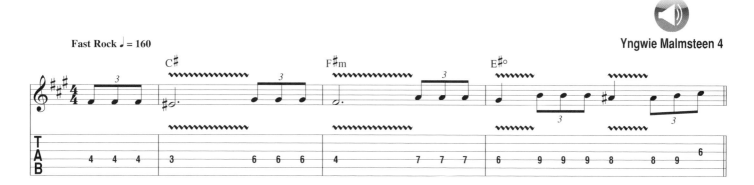

In this next example, Malmsteen utilizes an impressive combination of scale notes and chord tones to navigate the changes, which could be seen as drawn from the C Mixolydian mode. Again, the employment of power chords affords him latitude with respect to his note selection. For example, on beat 1 of measure 1, he plays what could be seen as a D minor arpeggio or merely a convenient run down/up the D minor pentatonic scale, using an index-finger barre at fret 10. For the return of the D5 change on beat 4 of measure 1, he utilizes the B♭, D, and F notes from the previous change, B♭5. Over the latter chord, they function as the root, major 3rd, and 5th, respectively, whereas over the former, they function as the ♭6th, root, and ♭3rd. Finally, don't miss the E major triad on beat 1 of measure 2.

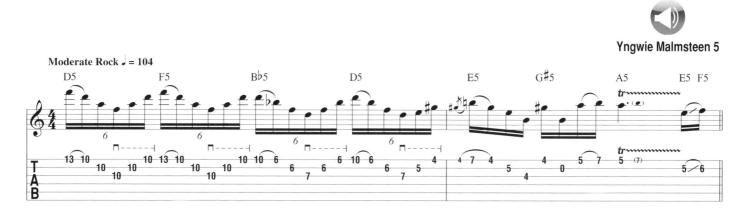

KIRK HAMMETT
(1962–)

Kirk Hammett has been the lead guitarist for the mega-metal stars Metallica through their most productive period and down to the present time. During his tenure, the band has won nine Grammy Awards and set a record with five consecutive albums debuting at #1 on the *Billboard 200* chart, among other awards and honors. Hammett is ranked #11 on the *Rolling Stone* list of the 100 Greatest Guitarists of All Time and #5 on the list of the 100 Greatest Metal Guitarists. The wah-wah pedal has been an element of his trademark sound, while his blistering, exceptionally clean execution, containing repetitive patterns building logically and dramatically with inventive melodies, has been a hallmark of Metallica, contributing to their huge fan base and his numerous personal honors as a top rock guitarist.

Kirk Lee Hammett was born on November 18, 1962, in San Francisco, California, to his Filipino mother, Teofila "Chefela" Oyao, and his Irish, Merchant Marine father, Dennis Hammett. His childhood was spent growing up in El Sobrante, where Les Claypool would become a classmate and friend. Piano lessons at 11 ended when he disliked his teacher. However, seeing a film about Jimi Hendrix compelled him to not only want to play like him, but to be him as well. At 15, his older brother's record collection, which contained UFO along with Led Zeppelin, Deep Purple, Black Sabbath, and KISS, also stoked his desire to begin playing guitar. His first instrument was acquired from a Montgomery Ward catalog, played through a homemade "shoebox" amp, and followed by a 1978 Strat copy. His attempts to find a signature sound by upgrading the pickups and hardware led to his purchasing a 1974 Gibson Flying V in emulation of UFO's Michael Schenker. As his self-taught skills increased, Hammett started to play with other musicians, revealing the shortcomings of his gear. In a tale that has become part of his backstory, he took a job at a local Burger King in order to buy a Marshall amp.

In 1980, Hammett formed Exodus, named for the 1958 Leon Uris novel about the creation of Israel. One of the earliest thrash metal groups, they were influential in the Bay Area, though Hammett only appears on their 1982 demo. However, Exodus, with Hammett, opened for Metallica on two occasions in what would prove to be fortuitous for the future "metal god." Metallica lead guitarist Dave Mustaine was becoming a problem in the band due to his substance abuse and violent behavior, and a replacement was sought in 1983. Mustaine would go on to found Megadeth, while the former manager of Exodus, who had become the road manager for Metallica, recommended Hammett as his replacement. In April, a call to California was placed, requesting him to fly to New York on his dime for an audition, which resulted in an immediate bond with lead singer/guitarist James Hetfield, bassist Cliff Burton, and drummer Lars Ulrich. Fifteen days later, he was playing onstage with Metallica for the first time and, within a month, was playing on their debut album, the triple-platinum *Kill 'Em All* (#155, 1983), featuring the virtuoso bass solo "(Anesthesia) Pulling Teeth" by Burton. Since the songs were already composed, including four co-written by Mustaine, Hammett mainly contributed solos, reflecting, in part, the previous lead guitarist's work. Following a tour to support the album, Hammett began taking lessons from *über*-teacher Joe Satriani in order to pump up his chops and expand his melodic sense with jazz, blues, and classical influences.

The six million-selling *Ride the Lightning* (#100) followed in 1984, with Mustaine receiving writer's credits for the last time, on the title track and the nine-minute instrumental "The Call of Ktulu." The album was heralded as a major step forward for the band and the first to feature Hammett as a writer, including the Metallica classic "Fade to Black," on which his shredding solo was justly applauded by guitar fans. In 1986, *Master of Puppets* (#29), also certified six-times platinum, became the breakout album for Metallica, receiving rave reviews beyond the world of metal music for its passion, musical quality, and political statements, owed in no small part to the contributions of Burton. A landmark of thrash metal and the first album to be certified platinum with virtually no radio or MTV exposure, *Master of Puppets* is often declared their artistic zenith and the greatest metal album of all time. In addition, Hammett was showcased on the instrumental "Orion" and became acknowledged as a bona fide guitar hero, reflected in the album ranking high on the list of greatest guitar albums. He recalls having more time to work on his parts and tone, even though he would sometimes have to wait for days, playing poker with Burton, as Ulrich got his parts down.

In 1986, Hammett played on the *Kill as One* demo for the San Francisco thrash metal band Death Angel. In September, while Metallica was on the Damage, Inc. Tour in Sweden, Burton swapped bus bunks with Hammett after drawing high card. Tragedy struck when the driver lost control of the vehicle, causing it to roll over several times and Burton to be thrown out and crushed to death underneath it. Hammett and the band were devastated, questioning whether they could continue without him. Deciding it's what Burton would have wanted, and with the support of his family, they agreed to soldier on. In the neighborhood of 40 bass players were auditioned, including Les Claypool, with Flotsam and Jetsam's Jason Newsted, who learned their entire set list, being chosen for the position. Nonetheless, the loss of Burton is felt by the band down to the current day. The tour with Newsted ended in early 1987 and an EP of covers of late '70s and early '80s British metal and punk tunes, *The $5.98 E.P.: Garage Days Re-Revisited* (#28), was released in the late summer.

In 1988, Hammett played second lead guitar on the title track of the EP *Kichigai* by the thrashcore band Septic Death. That same year, while diving further back into recording as a way to deal with the death of Burton, Metallica put out the eight-times platinum *...And Justice for All* (#6), with the instrumental "To Live Is to Die" dedicated to their late bassist. Their first time in the Top 10 was roundly acclaimed as "progressive metal," with the single "One" (#35) winning the Grammy Award for Best Metal Performance and Hammett's guitar solo ranking high on "Best of" lists. Some fans were dismayed when Metallica made an MTV video for the song, which went hand in hand with the overall commercial thrust of the endeavor. However, in a stupefying development, the album, which was nominated for a Grammy for Best Hard Rock/Metal Performance, lost out to *Crest of a Knave* by Jethro Tull, who never even bothered to show up. Undeterred by the snub from the Academy, Metallica entered the studio in the fall of 1990 to record the 16-times platinum *Metallica* (*The Black Album*) (#1), containing the hit singles "Enter Sandman" (#16), "The Unforgiven" (#35), "Nothing Else Matters" (#34), "Wherever I May Roam" (#82), and "Sad But True" (#98). Hammett was responsible for the killer, signature, broken-chord riff in "Enter Sandman," arguably their most popular song, while the album stands as their best-selling effort to date, with a wider variety of material giving the lead guitarist ample opportunity to show off his versatility. The success of the entire production, however, came at a personal cost, as the marriages of three band members failed during the process.

There followed nearly three years of touring before Metallica began work on their sixth album. Taking a year to write and record, the five-times platinum *Load* (#1, 1996) extended their run of unprecedented hits as the band evolved musically and sartorially. The former involved Hammett and Hetfield trying a more conventional, blues-based heavy metal style and sound, while the latter was evident in their trendy short haircuts. Musically, it was a boon to Hammett, who responded positively to the dynamic and more melodious material, displaying his expansive chops while contributing significantly to the more accessible (read: commercial) songs and willingly sharing soloing duties with Hetfield. Though some fans and critics decried what they saw as a conservative sell-out and negation of the revolutionary "take no prisoners" thrash metal power of their earlier music, the continued huge sales for Metallica confirmed the wisdom of their direction. Originally conceived as a double album, a decision was made to release the rest of the material from the *Load* sessions as a separate record in 1997. The quadruple-platinum *Reload* (#1) logically contained some of the same bluesy, Southern-rock influences of the preceding release and even featured Marianne Faithful on "The Memory Remains" as yet another indicator of their determination to expand and experiment, while the single "Better Than You" received a Grammy for Best Metal Performance. It would be the last studio release of new material to feature bassist Jason Newsted.

Kirk Hammett of Metallica

(Retna Ltd.)

In 1998, Metallica released *Garage, Inc.*, an album of covers featuring songs by classic rock and New Wave of British Heavy Metal bands that have influenced their music. Paired with a reissue of the rare collector's item *The $5.98 EP: Garage Days Revisited*, it debuted at #2, as Metallica could do no wrong at this point in their career. Two live recordings with the San Francisco Symphony Orchestra in the spring of 1999 further served to raise their profile above and beyond their metal audience. The video footage and two audio discs were packaged as the five-times platinum *S&M* (#2), including the entrance instrumental "The Ecstasy of Gold" by Ennio Morricone.

The new millennium began with Metallica taking a courageous stand against Napster, the online, peer-to-peer file sharing network, following their unauthorized theft of the Metallica demo "I Disappear." The band's intense and extensive legal actions helped end the company whose unlawful, unethical copyright infringements resulted in significant loss of income for recording artists and songwriters. A year later, Jason Newsted left Metallica, citing "private and personal" reasons, as the band prepared to record their next studio album of new material. The double-platinum *St. Anger* (#1) would not be completed until 2003, with long-time Metallica producer Bob Rock playing bass in the studio and on a handful of gigs. No stranger to criticism from fans and critics over the years, Metallica received a substantial dose for *St. Anger* due in part to a complete lack of guitar solos. Hammett stated that he was on board with the absence of his solos, as the goal for the project was to sound raw, like four musicians jamming live in a garage, with no unnecessary overdubs. Despite its strong initial showing, the record has faded in popularity and prominence over time. The title track won the Grammy for Best Metal Performance and bassist Robert Trujillo was hired as the replacement for Newsted, appearing in the DVD that accompanied the CD. After touring for two years to support the album, Metallica took an extended hiatus in 2005, interrupted by two shows opening for the Rolling Stones in San Francisco late in the year. In a rare appearance outside of Metallica in 2005, Hammett guested on Carlos Santana's "Trinity," from *All That I Am*.

In 2008, after a lengthy hiatus, the band released the thrashing *Death Magnetic* (#1), their fifth consecutive #1 disc, setting a *Billboard* record and continuing their string of smash hits, with wunderkind producer Rick Rubin replacing Bob Rock. It contains numerous, lengthy guitar solos from Hammett and Hetfield, in direct, almost violent, contrast to *St. Anger*, including the 10-minute instrumental "Suicide & Redemption." The album won a Grammy for Best Recording Package, while the single "My Apocalypse" won for Best Metal Performance. In addition, the album was released as downloadable content (DLC) on *Guitar Hero III: Legends of Rock,* highlighting Hammett and Hetfield, along with various offshoots of the game. Riding high, Metallica was inducted into the Rock and Roll Hall of Fame in the spring of 2009 with both Trujillo and Newsted present and onstage. Although not included in the induction, Dave Mustaine was invited by the band to attend the ceremony, but declined due to previous commitments. Though busy with his band, the lead guitarist moonlighted on the single "If Rap Gets Jealous," from Somali/Canadian rapper K'naan's album *Troubadour*. Meanwhile, the metal "road dogs" continued the World Magnetic Tour into late 2010.

In the fall of 2011, Metallica announced the release of the most unusual and divisive album of their career. The two-disc *Lulu* (#36), based on plays by German playwright Frank Wedekind, was a collaboration with legendary singer/songwriter/guitarist Lou Reed. Consisting mainly of spoken-word narration by Reed over Metallica backing tracks, with some vocal assistance from Hetfield, the response was mixed to say the least, with the overwhelmingly negative feedback being particularly vicious. The concept, hatched by Reed and Metallica in 2009 at the Rock and Roll Hall of Fame's 25th Anniversary Concert, did not actually commence until two years later. Though hinted at by Hammett in the early spring of 2011, when he announced cryptically that they would be making "not 100 percent a Metallica record. It's a recording project, let's put it that way," the true nature was not revealed to the public until the actual recording process had been completed. The single, "The View," was initially streamed online and likewise garnered mostly negative reaction. The near 20-minute "Junior Dad" closed the album and received the most positive response and reportedly reduced both Hammett and Hetfield to tears when they first heard the playback, as the latter had recently lost his father. Reed's response to their show of emotion was to laugh and comment, "That's a good one, huh?" Similarly, drummer Ulrich revealed that, at one point during the stressful recording, Reed challenged him to a "street fight." In the fall of 2013, Metallica released the 3-D concert film *Through the Never* in IMAX theaters. Though the prospect of a 10th Metallica studio album, with Rick Rubin once again producing, has been bandied about since the fall of 2011, it appears that one will not materialize sooner than 2015.

With his dedication to always improving and advancing his musicianship, Kirk Hammett stands as an inspiration to all guitarists. Thoughtful and intelligent as he is skilled, he paraphrases Socrates famous dictum: "A life lived unexplored is a life not worth living." Proving that "mastering" the guitar is an ongoing, lifelong pursuit, he continues to strive for additional excellence as Metallica forges ahead undeterred after 30-plus years in the music business.

THE GUITAR STYLE OF KIRK HAMMETT

Hammett is a master of the memorable Metallica riff. Often, they are part and parcel of his solos, thereby helping to drive the tune forward. One of their outstanding characteristics is the way he subtly alters the sequence of notes, instead of just repeating the same riff mechanically. Using the E Aeolian mode, Hammett creates a classic, ominous pattern fraught with uneasy anticipation, highlighted by emphasis on the ♭6th (C) and 5th (B) notes.

Performance Tip: Stretch from fret 12 to fret 17 on string 1 with the index and pinky fingers.

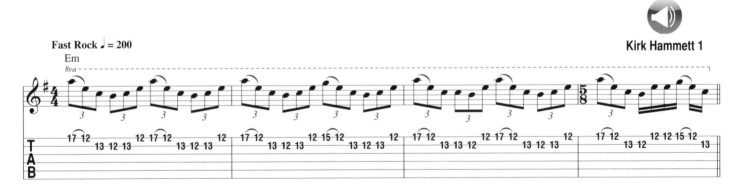

Another prime example of his hypnotic handiwork, likewise derived from the E Aeolian mode, consists of slippery, descending pull-offs to E (root of E5, major 3rd of C5, and 9th of D5) in measures 1 and 2 and F♯ (major 3rd of D5) in measure 3. However, on beats 3–4 of measure 4, over the F5 change, F♯ functions as the nasty, tension-producing ♭2nd from the F♯ Phrygian mode.

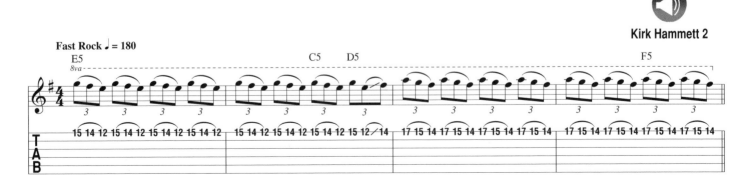

Hammett turns a bevy of garden variety power chords derived from the D major scale, clicking by at a fast clip, into a striking chordal accompaniment by phrasing in churning 6/4 time. Note that measures 1 and 3 are the same, as are measures 2 and 4.

Kirk Hammett 3

Hammett flaunts his virtuosity in a spectacular display of pick-tapping drawn from a slimmed-down version of the E Aeolian mode. Observe the F5 and F#5 changes on beat 4 of measures 2 and 4, respectively, as brief modulations for dynamic reasons, rather than discrete harmonic entities.

Kirk Hammett 4

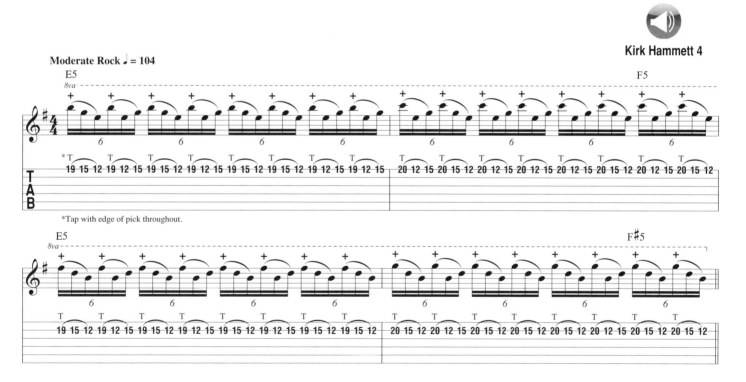

Richie Sambora performing with Bon Jovi in Hartford, Connecticut on March 6, 1989.

(Photo by Ebet Roberts/Cache Agency)

RICHIE SAMBORA
(1959–)

Richard "Richie" Stephen Sambora is a charter member of the select group of rock guitarists who, beginning in the '80s, made their mark by backing non-playing band leaders and lead singers. Though the creator of several excellent solo albums and boasting a long list of session credits, he is best known as the lead guitarist in Bon Jovi. While backing the revered New Jersey rock icon, Sambora has contributed numerous memorable riffs, solos, and even lead vocals while accumulating well-deserved accolades and honors for his melodic, blues-based style.

Richie Sambora was born on July 11, 1959, in Perth Amboy, New Jersey, to Joan and Adam and raised in Woodbridge Township. Like other notable rock guitarists, in 1970 at the age of 12, he was inspired to play by Jimi Hendrix, following the untimely death of the immortal "rock god." He was also influenced by other legends of the '60s and '70s, including Eric Clapton, Jeff Beck, George Harrison, Jimmy Page, Johnny Winter, and Joe Perry, as well as Stevie Ray Vaughan. An additional interest in classical guitar from an early age would later inform several of his classic intros with Bon Jovi.

While in high school, Sambora played in a number of local bands, and in 1978, was invited to play in a local club band named Shark Frenzy, where he would sing some lead vocals as well as play guitar. Two albums worth of original material were recorded, but not released until 2004. In 1980, following the breakup of the band, Sambora joined the Sayreville, New Jersey band Message, appearing on their self-titled, self-produced debut the same year. Signed to Led Zeppelin's Swan Song Records, the disc would remain unreleased until 1995. In 1982, they were chosen to open for a Joe Cocker tour, though a lack of financial resources forced them to bow out after only a few shows. Returning home, Sambora and bassist Alec John Such would meet local rockers John Bongiovi and the Wild Ones in a prophetic coincidence.

In 1983, with the help of his cousin, Power Station studio co-owner Tony Bongiovi, and following his original song "Runaway" being played on New York City radio stations, John Bongiovi assembled a new band. Included was bassist Such and his friend, guitarist Dave "The Snake" Sabo, who was never officially in the group and would later form Skid Row. Sambora, who had auditioned for KISS at one point, showed up backstage at a Bongiovi show and brashly informed the leader that he should be his lead guitarist. Thinking to call his bluff, Bongiovi instructed him to learn their songs and show up at a rehearsal. Sambora did as told, arriving early and nailing the material and the gig, thereby joining drummer Tico Torres and keyboardist David Bryan, along with bassist Such. Following a string of showcases and opening-act slots, the band was signed to Mercury Records in 1983 and the name was changed to "Bon Jovi." Their self-titled debut (#43) was released in January of 1984 with the singles "Runaway" (#39) and "She Don't Know Me" (#48). Receiving generally positive critical reviews, the keyboard-heavy music was alternately described as "hair metal," "hard rock," and "pop rock," while the accessible songwriting and appealing arena-rock sound forecast immense commercial success to come.

Released in 1985, the platinum *7800° Fahrenheit* (#37) referred to the melting point of rock and indeed saw the band and its music heating up, even though sales were a bit disappointing. The singles "Only Lonely" (#54) and "In and Out of Love" (#69) added to their "pop metal" evolution and Sambora contributed significantly, epitomized by his solo on the latter. A heady synthesis of hard rock, blues rock, and post-Van Halen pyrotechnics, it was his entre into the guitar-hero sweepstakes of the '80s and beyond.

Determined to take their game to the next level, Bon Jovi changed producers and hired professional New York songwriter Desmond Child to work with Jon Bon Jovi and Sambora on new material, resulting in 30 compositions. Additionally, in early 1986, they relocated to Vancouver, Canada, for a six-month writing and recording sojourn. At one point, the songs were played before New Jersey and New York teenagers for their feedback. The change in approach succeeded beyond even their ambitious dreams. Getting its name from a visit to a strip club, the 12-times platinum *Slippery When Wet* (#1) was released in the summer and would go on to become the top-selling album of 1987. Hit singles poured from the album like water, including fan favorites "You Give Love a Bad Name" (#1) and "Livin' on a Prayer" (#1), both co-written by Child, along with "Wanted Dead or Alive" (#7), featuring classic, signature guitar parts from Sambora. *Slippery When Wet* would become the first hard rock album to contain three *Billboard* Top 10 hits. Along with the notoriety due to the huge success of Bon Jovi, Sambora also received substantial media attention due to his relationship—and subsequent breakup—with Cher, whose self-titled "comeback" album he had appeared on and co-produced in the fall of 1987.

Released in the early fall of 1988, the seven-times platinum *New Jersey* (#1) confirmed the promise of Bon Jovi's previous release—they had arrived as superstars with staying power. Proving the perception, the album produced five *Billboard* Top 10 hits—"Bad Medicine" (#1), "I'll Be There for You" (#1), "Born to Be My Baby" (#3), "Lay Your Hands on Me" (#7), and "Living in Sin" (#9)—three of which were co-written with Desmond Child. That accomplishment broke their own record for a hard rock disc and still stands today. Sambora continued to be the prominently featured soloist, flashing his cool flamenco chops on "Wild Is the Wind." The band embarked on an exhausting two-year tour through 1990. In the early fall of 1989, however, Jon Bon Jovi and Sambora played "Livin' on a Prayer" and "Wanted Dead or Alive" with acoustic guitars on the MTV *Video Music Awards* show, with the performance being credited with launching the *Unplugged* craze.

Band members took a much-needed break from one another while Jon Bon Jovi wrote and created the soundtrack for *Young Guns II* in 1990. Following suit, Sambora played a cover of "The Wind Cries Mary" for the soundtrack to *The Adventures of Ford Fairlane.* In 1991, he released *Stranger in This Town* (#36), his first solo album. The recording featured 12 original, heavily blues-based songs and a large backing group that included drummer Tico Torres and keyboardist David Bryan from the Bon Jovi band. "Ballad of Youth" (#63) was the highest-charting single, but the album failed to resonate with Bon Jovi fans, despite admirably displaying Sambora's love of and feel for the blues and even featuring a guitar solo by his hero, Eric Clapton, on "Mr. Bluesman." A tour to support his efforts ensued before the fall of 1992, when Bon Jovi members reconvened for a meeting to clear the air over past grievances, agreeing to move forward with a new record. The double-platinum *Keep the Faith* (#5), featuring the hit singles "Bed of Roses" (#10), "In These Arms" (#27), and the title track (#29), signaled a turn to more "mature" rock music, as exemplified by Jon Bon Jovi's new, short haircut. Desmond Child co-wrote two compositions and the team of Jon Bon Jovi and Sambora contributed five, while the leader authored the bulk of the remaining tunes. The vague comparison to the blue-collar, "serious" music of Bruce Springsteen, made as an attempt by Jon Bon Jovi to evolve while recapturing his lost fans in the U.S., produced mixed results.

In the fall of 1994, *Cross Road* (#8), a greatest hits collection with two newly recorded tracks, "Always" (#4) and "Someday I'll Be Saturday Night," was released, with the former single, a power ballad, selling over three million copies to become the top-selling single in the group's history. More good news followed when the band scored the Best Selling Rock Band honors at the World Music Awards. High on their meteoric climb up the ladder, Sambora married TV star Heather Locklear in early winter. Despite the ongoing success of Bon Jovi, however, bassist Alec John Such was fired following years of threatening to quit and replaced in an unofficial capacity by Hugh McDonald, who had played on the original version of "Runaway."

The platinum *These Days* (#9) was released in the summer of 1995 and continued the "dark side" trend for Bon Jovi by way of a larger variety of influences, including R&B, soul, and the blues, all of which are close to the heart of Sambora, as well as more serious subject matter. The appropriately titled singles "This Ain't a Love Song" (#14), "Something for the Pain" (#76), featuring Sambora contributing a section of lead vocals, "Lie to Me" (#76), "These Days," and "Hey God" highlighted the shift in tone. Despite lower sales, critical response to an album favoring ballads and songs with a social conscious was mostly positive and acknowledged as being more mature and stronger musically. After another successful and expansive world tour, the band members unanimously agreed that a two-year break would be in everyone's best interest as a way to decompress from the rigors of the virtual non-stop recording and touring. In 1996, Sambora played on two tracks on legendary pioneer rocker Bo Diddley's *A Man Amongst Men*. Also during the interim, in 1998, Sambora was again backed by a large cast of supporting musicians for his second solo album, *Undiscovered Soul* (#174), which contained 12 original tunes and a broader swath of pop and mainstream rock material, in addition to blues rock. Although proving himself an adequate lead singer and composer, it was his emotional and tasty guitar work that shone through.

It would take until early summer 2000 for Bon Jovi to get the double-platinum *Crush* (#9) out to their fans. "It's My Life" (#33), featuring Sambora using a talk box, "Thank You for Loving Me" (#57), and "Say It Isn't So," with Sambora contributing to lead vocals, telegraphed a return to the pop formulas of their salad days. The album not only introduced the veteran Jersey icons to a new, younger audience, but was rewarded with a Grammy nomination for Best Rock Performance by a Duo or Group and seen as a triumphant "comeback" for the group. During their obligatory world tour to support the recording, they took time out to compile their first live album, *One Wild Night Live: 1985-2001* (#20).

A plan for the band to take a vacation following shows in the summer of 2001 was interrupted by the murderous terrorist attacks of 9/11. Springing into action, Jon Bon Jovi and Sambora recorded Public Service Announcements for the Red Cross, cut a version of "America the Beautiful" for the NFL, and performed on the *America: A Tribute to Heroes* telethon. Meanwhile, the band appeared at the Concert for New York City at Madison Square Garden. In 2002, Sambora contributed a song to the soundtrack to *The Banger Sisters.* In the spring, Bon Jovi, still influenced by the events of 9/11, began working on material for their eighth studio album. The gold *Bounce* (#2) seemed to resonate more outside of the U.S., as reflected in higher sales of the album and its singles: "Everyday," "Misunderstood," "All About Lovin' You," "Bounce," and "The Distance." Containing the loud, distorted guitars of Sambora and the growly vocals of Jon Bon Jovi, the critical and commercial response tended to be negative, with the album seen as an inexplicable step backwards following the encouraging reception to the cheery *Crush.* However, in retrospect, it is now viewed positively by many fans as their hardest-rocking album. Following the requisite supporting tour, Bon Jovi had planned on making a live acoustic album. Instead, in the late fall of 2003, they decided to re-imagine, rewrite, and record a dozen of their biggest hits for *This Left Feels Right* (#14), including some as acoustic versions.

Two years passed before Bon Jovi produced their ninth album, the platinum *Have a Nice Day* (#2), featuring the singles "Who Says You Can't Go Home" (#23) and the title track (#53). The former would be re-recorded as a duet with Sugarland's Jennifer Nettles, hitting #1 on the country charts. In fact, the album was recorded in the summer of 2004, but release was delayed due to disagreements by the group and the record company over material that would be deleted, added, and altered. Closer to *Bounce* than *Crush* in political content, and with a heavy arena-rock sound, it received mixed reviews. Nonetheless, the fans remained loyal and turned out in huge numbers to see the band on a tour grossing third behind only the Rolling Stones and Madonna.

The surprise success of the country version of "Who Says You Can't Go Home" intrigued Jon Bon Jovi enough to try a "Nashville" album, *Lost Highway* (#1), in the early summer of 2007, featuring "(You Want to) Make a Memory" (#27, #35 Country), "Lost Highway," "Till We Ain't Strangers Anymore" (#23) with LeAnn Rimes, "We Got It Going On" with country duo Big & Rich, and "Whole Lot of Leavin'," written by Jon Bon Jovi for Sambora. The song was about the death of the guitarist's father, his divorce from movie star Heather Locklear, a custody battle, and his struggle with alcohol abuse, resulting in his entering rehab in

L.A. in early summer. Unfortunately, in the spring, Sambora had been driving drunk in Southern California with his young daughter and her friend in his car and was arrested. Though named for a Hank Williams classic, the vibe on *Lost Highway* is thoroughly post-Garth Brooks, modern country music and was nominated for a Grammy for Best Pop Vocal Album in 2008. The wildly successful world tour to promote the album was the highest grossing of 2008, again confirming their lasting appeal despite the critics.

Barely a year later in the late fall of 2009, Bon Jovi followed *Lost Highway* with the gold *The Circle* (#1). The Grammy-nominated single "We Weren't Born to Follow" (#68) was re-recorded when fans decried what they considered the lack of a proper guitar solo, resulting in Sambora adding his signature style. "Superman Tonight" and "When We Were Beautiful" were initially written for a greatest hits collection, but released as an online download in conjunction with the documentary *When We Were Beautiful*, which debuted at the Tribeca Film Festival in lower Manhattan. The album was yet another return to "rock 'n' roll," to the obvious delight of Sambora, while continuing the politically and socially conscience lyric themes of Jon Bon Jovi, known for his liberal views and Democratic Party contributions. Prior to the release of the album, David Axelrod, President Barack Obama's former chief advisor, had a framed copy of the lyrics to "Work for the Working Man" hanging in his office. Though the critical reception to the record was again mixed, the Circle Tour was the highest grossing of 2010.

Almost three decades into their career, a time when other top veteran rock bands might be resting on their laurels and on cruise control, Bon Jovi kept pushing forward and were richly rewarded. In the fall of 2010, two greatest hits albums featuring a total of four new songs came out on the same day: the single-disc *Greatest Hit* and double-disc *Greatest Hits: The Ultimate Collection*, with the latter containing the same disc as the former record, in addition to a second disc of fan favorites. In 2011, during their Bon Jovi Live tour, Sambora missed 13 shows while he again entered rehab, which occurred just a week after he had completed probation for the drunk driving charges from 2008. While he was away, session pro Philip "Phil X" Xenidis took his place, instrumentally and vocally. In the fall of 2012, the live Bon Jovi video album *Inside Out* (#196), first shown in theaters, was made available on iTunes.

Less than a year later, *What About Now* (#1) maintained Bon Jovi's amazing string of consecutive top-charting albums (three), and their fifth overall. Featuring the singles "Because We Can" (#15 Adult Contemporary) and the title track, the album sold better overseas, perhaps due to the increasingly fragmented U.S. pop audience. As usual, the music was roundly panned by the critics for being "soft rock," despite the "weighty" topics. The album was recorded in the midst of Sambora working on his third solo disc, *Aftermath of the Lowdown* (#149), which saw the light of day in the early fall of 2012. Ranging even wider in styles than his previous solo outings, with influences as disparate as Aerosmith, David Bowie, and Coldplay, the album is impossible to pigeonhole and is seen as his most obvious attempt to distance himself from Bon Jovi. In the early spring of 2013, during the Because We Can Tour, Sambora abruptly left citing personal reasons, seemingly a reference to his fashion company. Phil Xenidis again was brought in to sub as Sambora and Jon Bon Jovi traded pointed charges in the press. The latter inferred that the guitarist had fallen off the wagon again and entered rehab, while the former fired back at the singer: "It is my opinion… Jon wants to see if he can pull off the stadiums by himself. He is making it very difficult for me to come back." In early 2014, Sambora announced that he had quit to spend time with his teenage daughter from his marriage to Heather Locklear and to care for his ailing mother. He also traveled to Australia to perform with guitarist Orianthi at the Soundwave Festival.

In a vaunted career of over 30 years, Richie Sambora has proved his worth as the strong right hand of Jon Bon Jovi, as a versatile sideman, and as a solo artist with as yet still unrealized potential. Fans of bruising rock rhythms, inventive, memorable hooks, and expressive soloing can only hope he and Jon will make peace and continue as one of the great vocalist/guitarist tandems of all time.

THE GUITAR STYLE OF RICHIE SAMBORA

Though he has certifiable post-Van Halen chops and can shred with the best of them, Sambora has a mean blues streak that underpins his playing. Observe how he not only phrases with blues-approved mojo in the most minimal of means, but also intelligently navigates the chord changes. In measure 1, he bends the 6th (A) to the major 7th (B) of the C major harmony for a decidedly non-blues effect that nonetheless sweetens the major tonality. In measure 2, releasing it back to A and embellishing with slinky vibrato, it functions as the 5th of D. In measure 3, over the Em harmony, C is bent to D (♭7th) and followed by the open B and G strings (5th and ♭3rd, respectively). Measure 4 contains the fretted pitches G and E followed by a one-octave dive bomb of the open G string to complete the delineation of the Em chord.

Richie Sambora 1

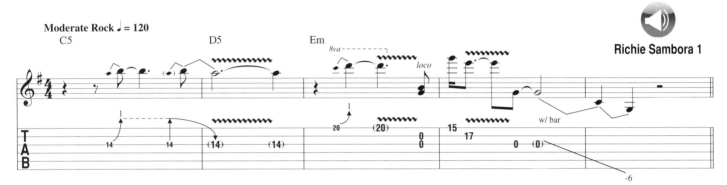

Again proving that "less is more" from where he stands and plays (i.e., next to Bon Jovi), Sambora creates a memorable four-measure blues "head" on strings 3–4 of the root-position C minor pentatonic scale. The minimal lick in measure 1 is recycled in measure 3, with the 4th (F) bent one step to the 5th (G) and ending on the raspy ♭3rd (E♭) for musical tension. Meanwhile in measure 2, the ♭3rd (E♭) is bent a quarter step to the evocative "true blue note" before resolving to the root (C).

Richie Sambora 2

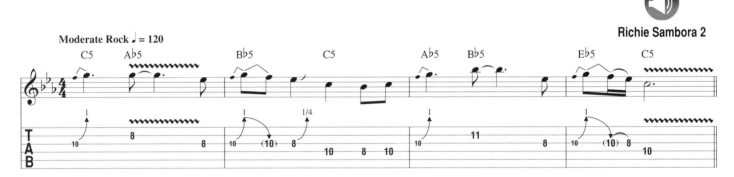

Sambora finds a comfortable and familiar home in the root position of the C♯ minor pentatonic scale, where he indulges his blues "jones" by fluidly bending to a variety of pitches with gusto. Check out the way he employs the bent C♯, which functions as the root in measure 1 and as the major tonality-defining major 3rd in measure 2. In measure 3 over the E5 change, he produces palpable tension by bending the 9th (F♯) to the "true blue note" in between the minor 3rd (G) and major 3rd (G♯) before resolving to the classic E/B (root/5th) dyad.

Richie Sambora 3

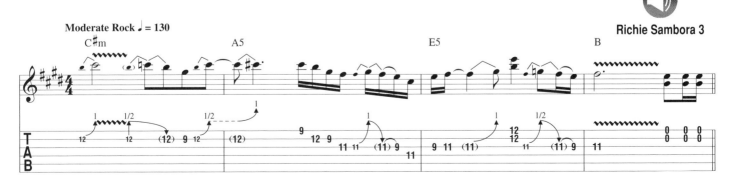

In this next example, Sambora utilizes bluesy phrasing before unleashing his classic broken-chord pattern. Following the bend (and release) from the 4th (G) to the 5th (A) to create musical tension, Sambora layers on more tension by picking the signature descending 16th notes relative to the D Dorian mode before resolving conclusively and satisfactorily to the D/A chord.

Richie Sambora 4

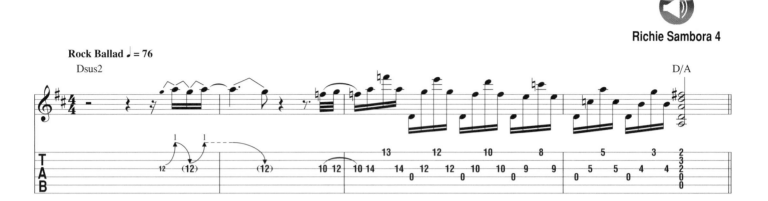

Sambora flies through the chord changes in total command of his faculties as he negotiates the blues-rock progression with inventiveness and cool logic. In measures 1–2 over the A5 change, he combines bluesy licks from the A minor pentatonic scale, including the bend to the "true blue note" in between the minor 3rd (C) and major 3rd (C♯) in two dynamic octaves, with the root (A) note. Do not miss the likewise dynamic gliss on string 2, which moves from A to E and B. In measure 3 over the C5 chord, he bends the major 7th (B) to the root (C) and ends with the 6th (A) and 5th (G), which are derived from the C major scale. In measure 4, hip, R&B-style chord melody nails the G5 harmony on beat 1, followed by the 5th (D), 3rd (B), 9th (A), root (G), and 3rd (B) from the G major scale.

Richie Sambora 5

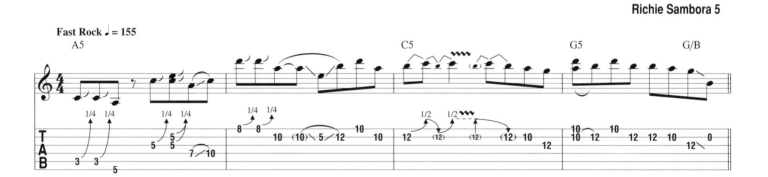

NUNO BETTENCOURT
(1966–)

As one of the greatest and most original post-Van Halen shredders, Nuno Bettencourt utilized his virtuosity and gift for melodies and rhythms most prominently with Extreme to expand beyond '90s heavy metal stardom into progressive hard rock, funk, alternative, and pop-rock genres, among others. His ability to adapt to a wide variety of artists and styles during his career has allowed him to continue to evolve and grow beyond his initial pursuits.

Nuno Duarte Gil Mendes Bettencourt was born on September 20, 1966, in Praia da Vitoria, Terceira, Azores, Portugal, to Aureolina da Cunha Gil de Avila and Ezequiel Mendes Bettencourt. When he was four years old, Bettencourt's family moved to Hudson, Massachusetts, where he lived until the age of 25. As a youngster, he was more interested in playing soccer and hockey than music. However, as a teenager, he experimented with the drums, bass, and keyboards before coming under the influence of Eddie Van Halen while a freshman in high school. He first tried to learn the guitar from his brother Luis, but found he could progress faster on his own. Obsessed with the instrument, he abandoned sports and would often skip school to practice seven hours a day, eventually dropping out of high school to pursue a career in music. He bounced around the Boston area in a number of bands, often with his brothers Luis and Roberto, including the hair metal act Sinful. Though all the bands lead to a dead end, Bettencourt used his practice time wisely, absorbing inspiration, tone, and technique from Queen's Brian May, as well as groups as diverse as the Beatles, the Scorpions, Led Zeppelin, Al Di Meola, and Paco de Lucia, among others.

In 1985, at the age of 19, Bettencourt made the most important career move of his young life. Sinful played a show with Dream, containing singer Gary Cherone and drummer Paul Geary, and the Berklee School of Music band In the Pink, with bassist Pat Badger. After the highly competitive groups engaged in a dispute about the dressing room arrangements, the four musicians decided to form a new group. The name "Ex-Dream" was eventually altered to the more evocative "Extreme." Bettencourt and Cherone set to writing songs together and the band gigged locally, developing a following and being named the Outstanding Hard Rock/Metal Act at the Boston Music Awards in 1986–87. In 1988, they were signed to A&M Records and their self-titled debut (#80) of original songs was released in 1989 and featured Bettencourt playing synthesizer, piano, and percussion, in addition to guitar. Sales of the pop metal record with the glam-rock image were modest and their music showed the pervasive influence of Van Halen and Queen, particularly, as heard in the three-part harmonies and melodic guitar solos, in addition to metal riffs, shredding solos, and funky, syncopated rhythms. One of the four singles, "Play with Me," was featured on the soundtracks to both *Bill & Ted's Excellent Adventure* and *Jury Duty*. Including riffs based on Mozart's *Rondo Alla Turca* and a blazing solo hinting at Bettencourt's virtuosity to come, it would become a fan favorite.

In 1990, the double-platinum *Extreme II: Pornograffitti* (#10) was the bust-out recording for the band and it confirmed Bettencourt as a new "rock god." His intro to "He-Man Woman Hater"—"Flight of the Wounded Bumblebee," based on the Rimsky-Korsakov classical composition "Flight of the Bumblebee"— is a staggering guitar showcase. Seemingly contradictory to the main thrust of the album, the two acoustic tracks, the ballad "More Than Words" (#1) and the rocking "Hole-Hearted" (#4), were the highest charting of the five singles released, with the former becoming one of their classics. However, "Get the Funk Out," with a horn section, was emblematic of their term to describe their music, "funky metal." Coming at the tail end of the '80s metal era, the record helped display the broad range of music welled up inside Bettencourt. Consequently, in 1991, readers of *Guitar World* magazine voted Bettencourt Best New Talent.

Nuno Bettencourt of Extreme performing in 1992.

(Ian Dickson/MediaPunch)

In the spring of 1992, while in the middle of recording their third album, Extreme made an appearance at the Freddie Mercury Tribute Concert at Wembley Stadium in London, where Brian May gave them a laudatory introduction in gratitude for their appreciation of Queen. The concert was reportedly broadcast to as many as one billion people worldwide, providing unprecedented publicity for Extreme and exposing them to a broad audience beyond their core metal fans. In the early fall of 1992, the gold *III Sides to Every Story* (#10) came out to positive reviews and is considered a high point by the band and their fans. Divided into three sections, "Yours," "Mine," and "The Truth," Beatles references abound on the concept album reflecting Cherone's evolving religious views. Bettencourt, the arranger and musical guru of the band, burns on the funky hard rock of the first section, while pop songs grace the second section, and an 80-piece orchestra, recorded at Abbey Road studios, provides grandiosity to the ambitious art-rock "cantata" in the third section. However, their ascendancy as a major force unfortunately coincided with the rise of grunge as a popular rock trend in the early '90s and sales far below the previous release reflected the reality of the shift.

In 1994, during the recording of their fourth album, drummer Geary left Extreme to pursue a career in music business management. He was replaced by Annihilator drummer Mike Mangini, who appears on three tracks on *Waiting for the Punchline* (#40), which was released in January of 1995. Responding to the new wave of grunge rock, the album is raw, stripped down, and funky, with a nod to alternative rock, in direct contrast to *III Sides to Every Story.* As clearly stated in the single "Hip Today," the album was more a cynical reaction to the transient nature of the sounds emanating from Seattle than an attempt to jump on the bandwagon. Lyrically, it's a "concept" record, with the theme appearing to be the questioning of faith, as addressed in the first track, "There Is No God." Unfortunately, even the always-extraordinary guitar work of Bettencourt, who sometimes solos without a rhythm guitar track, could not save it from selling less than the previous disc. In 1996, Extreme amicably called it quits, with Bettencourt heading off for a solo career and Cherone joining Van Halen for a brief tenure.

In February of 1997, Bettencourt treated his fans to his first solo album. Five years in the making, *Schizophonic* likewise contained the pervasive influence of alternative rock, along with progressive rock and even country rock. Listed on the cover as simply "Nuno" and dressed in drag in the photo, Bettencourt wrote or co-wrote all the tunes while singing lead and playing guitar, bass, and drums on most tracks. Cherone contributed one lead vocal and Mangini played drums on two tracks. Reviews were generally positive, but sales were slack. In 1998, Bettencourt formed Mourning Widows, the name being derived from graffiti that the guitarist had seen written on a church wall back in Portugal. Besides guitar and lead vocals, Bettencourt played drums under the name "Billy Vegas" and was backed by his nephew, Donovan Bettencourt, on bass. Their self-titled debut recalled the heavy funk rock of Extreme, as well as the requisite grunge and alternative rock influences, and was best received in Japan and New England. The subsequent supporting tour featured New York drummer Jeff Consi. Two years later, in the early fall of 2000, Mourning Widows followed their self-titled debut with *Furnished Souls for Rent*, which again featured Donovan Bettencourt as well as Consi, and received about the same critical and commercial response.

Looking to create the proper musical environment to express his music and get it out to the public, in 2002, Bettencourt formed Population 1. The self-produced, self-titled release boasted him playing virtually all the instruments. In order to tour, he enlisted Joe Pessia (rhythm guitar), Steve Ferlazzo (keyboards), Philip Bynoe (bass), and Kevin Figueiredo (drums) as his backup. In 2004, the same band minus Bynoe, with Pessia moving over to bass, put out the EP *Sessions from Room 4* and an East Coast tour was embarked upon in the fall. In 2005, Bettencourt took some time off for a short Extreme reunion in the Azores and Boston, along with a few dates in Japan. That same year, a legal challenge was mounted against Population 1, forcing a name change to Near Death Experience and then to DramaGods, with *Love* being the sole disc created under the latter incarnation. The DramaGods successfully toured Japan in the summer of 2006 and appeared at the Udo Music Festival with a high-profile lineup that included Jeff Beck, Santana, the Doobie Brothers, KISS, the Pretenders, and Alice in Chains, among others.

In early 2007, despite receiving the most encouraging response post-Extreme, Nuno saw his DramaGods band breakup as he, Ferlazzo, and Figueiredo were invited to join Satellite Party, a band led by former Jane's Addiction vocalist Perry Farrell. Released in the spring, *Ultra Payloaded* (#91) would be their only studio release. The album contained a large assortment of guest artists, as well as a 30-piece orchestra, though Bettencourt co-produced and is prominently featured on guitar, bass, and keyboards. In the summer of 2007, during the tour in support of the album, Bettencourt left the project amicably, citing creative differences, and with Figueiredo in tow, rejoined Gary Cherone and Pat Badger in Extreme. In the summer of 2008, *Saudades de Rock* (#78), which is loosely translated from Portuguese as "Nostalgic Yearnings of Rock," became the group's fifth album. Well-received critically, the vintage energy and power of the music harkens back to the basic production of *Waiting for the Punchline*, with funky metal, including the satirical "Comfortably Dumb," tender ballads, and a smattering of country rock. Two tours, the Take Us Alive World Tour and the East Meets West Tour, carried the band through 2008 and 2009, respectively, with the final gig, the House of Blues in Boston in late summer 2009, recorded for the CD/DVD *Take Us Alive*, which contains material that spans their entire career.

Though further plans for Extreme to record with top rock producer Rick Rubin were bandied about in 2010, they appear to be in a continual holding pattern, if not another full-fledged hiatus, as Cherone plays in Hurtsmile with his brother and guitarist Joe Pessia. Going all the way back to 1990, Bettencourt has recorded with an impressive array of other artists, including Janet Jackson, Dweezil Zappa, Robert Palmer, and Toni Braxton. Since 2009, Bettencourt has backed Barbadian pop diva Rhianna, playing lead guitarist on tour and on the records *Loud* (#3, 2010) and *Talk That Talk* (#3, 2011). Though they would seem an unlikely combination, the pop diva gives her virtuoso instrumental foil plenty of room to move, and he burns brightly with explosive passion. While awaiting another Extreme "reunion," the opportunity to hear his inspired creativity should more than satisfy his fans.

THE GUITAR STYLE OF NUNO BETTENCOURT

Bettencourt taps harmonics an octave above the fretted note at a brisk tempo fully illustrative of his exceptional chops. While the left hand voices the E and B major triads, the right hand taps harmonics to produce a dynamic "orchestral" effect.

Performance Tip: With the middle finger of your right hand, tap 12 frets higher than the left-hand fingers while holding the pick between your thumb and index finger.

Nuno Bettencourt 1

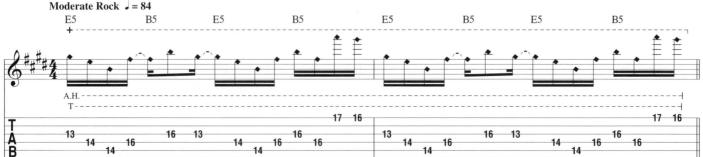

In a display of his concept of funk, Bettencourt crafts inventive, ascending syncopated riffs with notes from the C major scale and the C Mixolydian mode, along with passing tones. Notice the way musical anticipation is created in measures 1–2, landing on the ♭7 (B♭). Measure 3 adds more subtle tension by employing the same relative intervals, but beginning on string 6 instead of string 5. Then, on beats 3–4 of measure 4, the riff dynamically reverses direction and ends on the tension-producing 4th (F).

Nuno Bettencourt 2

A significant aspect of his artistry is the way Bettencourt is just as capable of picking sensitive acoustic lines and broken chords as he is at bending the frets on his electric axe, with no diminishment of expressiveness. Observe how he mostly uses the G note on string 1 as a pedal point relative to all the changes while conclusively indicating tonality with the bass notes as often heard in classical and flamenco guitar music.

Performance Tip: Unless one is a fingerstylist playing with bare right-hand fingers, hybrid picking is virtually the only recommended technique for plucking notes in the upper and lower registers simultaneously. While holding the pick between the thumb and index finger, pick the bass-string notes with the plectrum, utilizing the middle and ring fingers for the notes on the upper strings.

Nuno Bettencourt 3

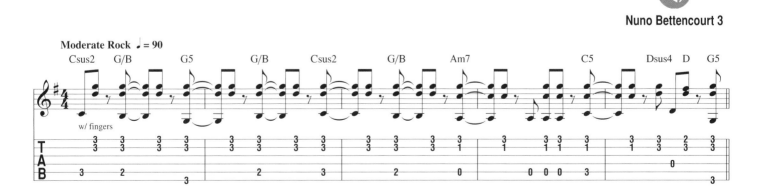

Bettencourt clearly relishes intelligent patterns that indicate tonality via the subtle manipulation of as few as one note moved one fret. Check out how in measure 1, he raises the 5th (B) of Em to the root of C and then reverses the process in measure 2, where he lowers the 9th (C) of B7♭9 to the root of B.

Nuno Bettencourt 4

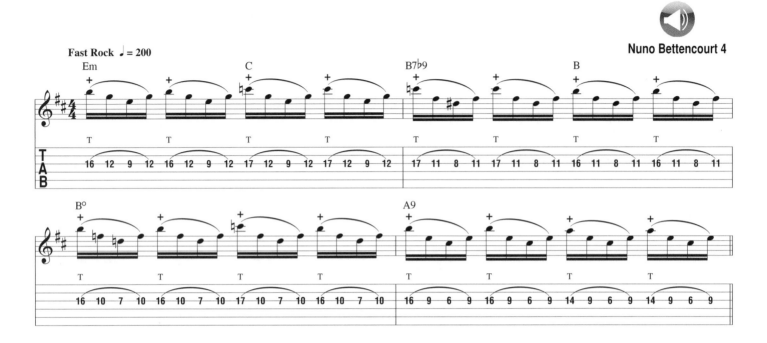

Bettencourt unleashes his flaming picking chops with an onslaught of rippling sextuplets relative to the A5 and D5 chords. Be aware that he plays the A Dorian mode in measure 1, stepping "up" to the D Mixolydian mode in measure 2.

Nuno Bettencourt 5

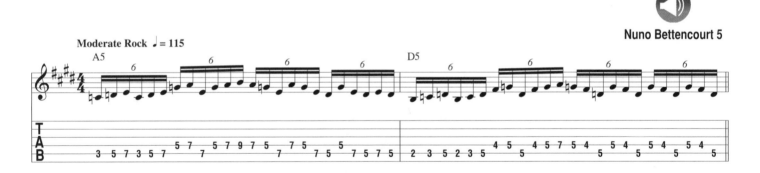

JOE SATRIANI
(1956–)

As an unsurpassed instrumentalist *and* a most influential teacher, Joe "Satch" Satriani occupies rarified territory in the annals of rock guitar. While possessing the requisite virtuoso chops to become a bona fide guitar hero, he is also blessed with an ear for unique compositions, melodies, and arrangements. His great love of the guitar and his determination to continue to explore the creative possibilities sets an inspiring example for all.

Joseph Satriani was born into the musical family of Italian immigrants Katherine and John Satriani on July 15, 1956, in Westbury, New York. An uncle who lived in Spanish Harlem played accordion, his mother played and taught jazz piano, his older brother blew blues harmonica, and a sister strummed folk guitar and gave music lessons. At the age of 9, Satriani began playing drums, followed by singing in choirs and in his early bands. In a perhaps apocryphal story, he decided, as had many other notable guitarists, to promptly quit the football team and dedicate himself to playing the instrument on the day in 1970 when Jimi Hendrix died. The "Voodoo Child" would exert the greatest influence on Satriani and continues to do so down to the present day, though Muddy Waters, Albert King, Led Zeppelin, and Jeff Beck also figure in his list of idols. Though modest in the telling, he clearly practiced to the point of obsession to achieve his enormous skills while studying music theory and playing in high school groups. In addition, he went out on the road with Top 40 bands at the age of 17. Following in the footsteps of his mother and sister, he also began giving guitar lessons while attending college to study music, as well as taking private lessons from jazz guitarist Billy Bauer and jazz pianist Lennie Tristano. One of his students was Steve Vai, a high school classmate. The two had similar music goals and aspirations and would become fast friends, with the mentored eventually doing a solid favor for his mentor.

In 1978, Satriani relocated to Berkeley, California, with the goal of furthering his musical career. Before long, he was teaching guitar in a San Francisco music store, a position that he would hold for approximately 10 years. During that time, he would instruct and inspire a future who's who of rock royalty, including Metallica's Kirk Hammett, Primus' Larry LaLonde, Counting Crows' David Bryson, Testament's Alex Skolnick, Third Eye Blind's Kevin Cadogan, Charlie Hunter, and Andy Timmons, among many others. One of the first bands that Satriani joined in San Francisco was the Squares, whose drummer, Jeff Campitelli, would develop a long-term professional relationship with the guitarist. In 1984, Satriani independently released a self-titled EP, originally on vinyl only, worthy of investigation due to the inventive ways in which he produced all the sounds with just his guitar, including tapping on the pickups with an Allen wrench to produce percussion and detuning his guitar to simulate a bass. The most important result of the endeavor, however, was to secure a recording contract.

In 1986, Satriani released on Relativity Records his first LP, the self-produced and self-financed *Not of This Earth*, featuring 10 original instrumentals, backed by Campitelli and John Cuniberti. Though not widely heard, it nonetheless made its mark on his fellow guitarists who enjoyed his unusual compositions, robust tone, and quicksilver jaw-dropping licks. That same year, he was asked to join the revamped Greg Kihn Band and appears on *Love and Rock and Roll*, which unfortunately spelled the end of Kihn's commercial success as a power-pop proponent. However, the upside was that Kihn graciously helped to pay the outstanding credit card debt rolled up by Satriani for his own album. In a related example of his resourcefulness, Satriani was hired by Blue Öyster Cult to clean up guitar tracks in the studio for the epic production of *Imaginos* (#122), including playing on "The Siege and Investiture of Baron von Frankenstein's Castle at Weisseria," in exchange for his own studio time.

Joe Satriani performs at the Macomb Music Theatre on September 22, 2013 in Mt. Clemens, Michigan.

(© Chris Schwegler/Retna Ltd.)

That same year, Satriani was the beneficiary of the generosity of his former student Steve Vai, who had scored a plum gig with David Lee Roth. During the course of his coverage in the guitar press, Vai made a point of singing the praises of Satriani, leading to his landmark second album, the platinum *Surfing with the Alien* (#29, 1987). It revealed him to be an astounding contemporary rock guitarist while also demonstrating new vitality for instrumental music and opening the door for others to follow. The song "Ice 9" refers to an element in the Kurt Vonnegut book *Cat's Cradle*, acknowledging his keen interest in sci-fi and fantasy fiction, while the hit single "Satch Boogie" (#22 Mainstream Rock) and the sci-fi title track (#37 Mainstream Rock) likewise confirmed a surprisingly lucrative audience for "non-commercial" instrumental rock. The 10 originals showed a modern master who could compose sophisticated and sensitive melodies, as well as shred with stunning force while enjoying consummate command over his tone and production. With his professional profile noticeably raised, Satriani guested on and produced records for other artists.

In 1988, he released the gold four-track EP *Dreaming #11* (#42), which contained only one studio song, "The Crush of Love" (#6 Mainstream Rock), in addition to three live numbers that were recorded while on tour. Unfortunately, the tour was a bust financially and bleeding money so profusely that he considered calling it quits. Literally out of the blue, and in the nick of time, he was called to audition for the lead guitar spot on Mick Jagger's short tour in support of his second solo album, *Primitive Cool*. Jagger's exceptional generosity in helping promote the still struggling, emerging guitar star, including a significant solo spot in the show, would provide a needed boost to his career.

In 1989, Satriani followed *Dreaming #11* with the spectacular *Flying in a Blue Dream* (#23). The 18 original tracks received rave critical reviews due to the sheer audacity of his vision and execution. On an album ranging from stomping blues rock to spacey sci-fi, six songs featured his lead singing before closing with "Into the Light," a moving emotional tribute to his beloved father, who passed away during the recording sessions. Further increasing his visibility and credibility, "One Big Rush" was selected for the soundtrack to Cameron Crowe's *Say Anything*. After a three-year layoff, Satriani let loose with the gold *The Extremist* (#22), named for the DC Comics series, his highest-charting, most successful album and one of his most popular to date. Meanwhile, the three singles—"Friends" (#12), "Summer Song" (#5), and "Cryin'" (#24)—scored impressively on the Hot Mainstream Rock Tracks chart. The hard-driving, bluesy rock of "Summer Song" received an added boost when Sony used it in a commercial for their Discman portable CD player around the release date, as well as on the soundtracks for PlayStations 1 and 2. The 10-song, all-instrumental set shows the uninhibited guitarist "painting" with an even broader and richer "palette of colors." While expanding his arsenal of instruments to include banjo, harmonica, Dobro, keyboards, bass, and mandolin, he also increased his pool of backup musicians to include Matt Bissonette (bass), Matt's brother Gregg Bissonette (drums), Paulinho da Costa (percussion), Doug Wimbish (bass), Simon Phillips (drums and percussion), and Brett Tuggle (keyboards), among others.

As word of his vaunted skills spread, Satriani became a sought-after hired guitar slinger. In 1991, he appeared on rock legend Alice Cooper's *Hey Stoopid* (#47), playing on five songs, including the title track (#78). The next year, he let rip on the title track to *Break Like the Wind* by the satirical, semi-fictional band Spinal Tap. The gold *Time Machine* (#95) was released by Satriani in the fall of 1993 as a two-record set, with the first disc containing new and unreleased studio tracks, including four songs from his 1984 EP, and the second disc consisting of live recordings from 1988 and 1992. The latter disc confirmed beyond a doubt that he was fully capable of executing his demanding compositions in "real time" while still featuring his outrageous, virtuosic improvisations. During the late fall, he was invited to play with Deep Purple after Ritchie Blackmore walked out on them in the midst of a European tour. Thrilled at the chance to perform with the classic rock legends, he stayed on through the winter of 1994 and into a summer European tour, after which he was asked to join the band on a permanent basis. However, his recent signing of a long-term solo record deal prevented him from doing so, leading to Steve Morse taking the lead guitar chair. It has been reported that, prior to recording *Joe Satriani* (#51) in 1995, the fret master was listening to Eric Clapton's blues anthology *From the Cradle*, resulting in a more straightforward affair shorn of effects and overdubbing, while presenting a heavier, soulful blues vibe. The presence of Andy Fairweather Low (rhythm guitar) and Nathan East (bass), previous backers of "Old Slowhand," would seem to confirm suspicions. On an album of creative blues and jazz improvisations, the single "(You're) My World" (#30 Hot Mainstream Rock) stands out as the most commercial entry.

Showing ambition, unusual creativity, and entrepreneurship, in 1995, Satriani envisioned an ongoing world concert tour involving a star-studded array of guest guitarists playing with him in pairs, dubbed "G3." The name is derived from *Ghidorah, the Three-Headed Monster*, a 1964 Japanese horror film. In 1996, the first lineup went out with Steve Vai and Eric Johnson. Subsequent tours were convened in 1997–98, 2000–07, and 2012. Several guitarists have appeared more than once, including Vai (11), John Petrucci (6), Eric Johnson (3), Robert Fripp (2), and Steve Morse (2). To date, four albums from select tours have been released: *G3: Live in Concert* (1997), *G3: Live in Denver* (2004), *G3: Rockin' in the Free World* (2004), and *G3: Live in Tokyo* (2005).

In 1998, Satriani resumed his solo career with *Crystal Planet* (#50), containing the single "Ceremony" (#28 Hot Mainstream Rock). Reuniting with Stuart Hamm (bass) and Jeff Campitelli (drums), Satriani sounds reinvigorated, again pushing musical boundaries and his chops with a seven-string guitar. Many consider it to be his best work since *Surfing with the Alien*. Two years later, he was pushing the stylistic and technological envelope even further with *Engines of Creation* (#90), featuring guitars electronically altered via computer programs, digital software, and synthesizers, except on the track "Until We Say Goodbye," which received a Grammy nomination for Best Rock Instrumental Performance. Confoundingly, Satriani has the unenviable distinction of receiving 15 Grammy nominations without winning, second only to R&B musician Brian McKnight, who has 16.

Entering the new millennium, in 2002, Satriani looked forward with electronica, world, and techno music on *Strange Beautiful Music* (#140). He also took a glance back to the roots of rock with a cover of the 1959 Santo & Johnny instrumental classic "Sleepwalk," featuring guest guitarist Robert Fripp. With the backing of the Bissonette brothers once again, Satriani plays banjo, sitar, keyboards, and autoharp. The record was well-received by his long-time fans as he put the focus back on playing the guitar with a more traditional sound. Also in 2002, he was invited to play in the short-lived Planet Us with former Van Halen members Sammy Hagar and Michael Anthony, guitarist Neal Schon, and drummer Deen Castronovo. The group played live just four times, with Satriani appearing only the last time in the early spring of 2003, as a Van Halen reunion intervened.

In 2003, Satriani played lead on "Train Kept A-Rollin'," from the Yardbirds' new *Birdland*. With the release of *Is There Love in Space?* (#80) a year later, Satriani once again explored previous territory, though this time it was his own, circa *Surfing with the Alien*, as well as some of the more exotic Eastern themes of his last release sans the digital hardware. It also includes vocal numbers, which are passable, but not his strong suit. The combination seemed to satisfy Satriani's creative desire, as well as his audience's need for his "classic" style of guitar rock. His son Z.Z. appears on "Bamboo" playing bowed bass. Four years later, Satriani would sue Coldplay, charging them with substantially ripping off "If I Could Fly" on their song "Viva la Vida." His case would be dismissed in 2009, with Coldplay admitting to no wrongdoing, though an out-of-court settlement may have occurred. Listeners may decide for themselves, but the similarities seem coincidental due to similar chord progressions, which are not copyright protected.

Rolling along in his now-familiar stylistic groove, *Super Colossal* (#86) seems to have kept everyone happy in 2006, and if they needed more, he also presented his fans with a live two-disc set, *Satriani Live!*, also available as a separate DVD. On the studio album, Satriani also plays all the bass parts and keyboards in a manner that harkens back to earlier recordings, providing for a cohesiveness serving his vision. The "kicker" on the album is the last track, "Crowd Chant," featuring Satriani playing short bluesy riffs in a raucous "call and response" manner with an in-studio "crowd" over a drum track. The ending theme, however, is based on *Pavane in F-sharp Minor, Op. 50* by Gabriele Fauré. Not unlike Gary Glitter's "Rock and Roll, Part 2," it has been appropriated by some NFL and NHL teams to celebrate touchdowns and goals, respectively, as well as being featured on *NHL 2K10* and *Madden NFL 11*. Two years later, Satriani reunited with the bassist Matt Bissonette for the majority of tracks on the cringe-worthy *Professor Satchafunkilus and the Musterion of Rock* (#89). Containing little actual funk, it showcased more of his melodic and expressive instrumental rock, albeit with noticeably mature emotion, along with the requisite virtuosic shredding for which he is well-known and respected. Concurrently in the early spring of 2008, Satriani launched the Guitar Center Sessions tour, featuring in-store performances, autograph signings, and Q&A sessions, continuing to boost his profile and presence.

In the late spring of 2008, 20 years into his solo career and with his creative juices flowing, it was announced that Satriani had joined Sammy Hagar, Michael Anthony, and the Red Hot Chili Peppers' Chad Smith in a stomping hard rock band named Chickenfoot. They played their first gig in the winter and their gold, chart-busting, self-titled debut (#4) arrived in the late spring with "Oh Yeah" (#21 Mainstream Rock) and "Sexy Little Thing" (#40 Mainstream Rock). The commercial response speaks for itself and Satriani reveled in his new role as rhythm guitarist behind the fun-loving hard rock singer, yet some criticism focused on the seeming incompatibility of the four disconnected playing styles. Though the overwhelming technical expertise of Satriani may seem converse to the looser, house-rocking Hagar and Anthony, the members have bonded as a band and remain enthusiastic.

In the fall of 2010, *Black Swans and Wormhole Wizards* (#45), an album in contrast to the "party-hearty" concept of Chickenfoot, maintained the commercial viability of Satriani's unique brand of instrumental rock. Though still containing a fair share of boogie, the progressive rock glances back to *Surfing with the Alien*, but with the restraint that comes with growing maturity and the confidence to not have to blow everyone away to prove his superiority. In the late winter of 2010, he dipped into his apparently endless cache of live performances to release the double-CD/DVD *Live in Paris: I Just Wanna Rock*. Recorded in 2008, it contains a selection of his fan favorites, along with a few from *Professor Satchafunkilus and the Musterion of Rock*. Then in early spring 2012, the concert film *Satchurated: Live in Montreal* was released to theaters worldwide in both 3-D and 2-D formats, followed by a CD/DVD/Blu-ray release a month later. Containing footage from a December 2010 concert at the Metropolis Theatre, the release contained a huge chunk of songs plucked from *Black Swans and Wormhole Wizards*. In 2011, Satriani appeared as himself in the hit baseball film *Moneyball*, playing "The Star-Spangled Banner" in a tribute to one of his heroes, Jimi Hendrix.

With all the principals having honored their other obligations in order to record, Chickenfoot set free *Chickenfoot III* (#9) in the early fall of 2011. Humorously skipping over "II" so as not to have the sophomore jinx befall them, the neo hard rockers sound even more like a band, enjoying the music, camaraderie, and audience acceptance that gave "serious" critics apoplexy. "Big Foot" (#40 Rock Songs) and "Different Devil" were released as singles and a short U.S./European tour ensued in the late fall with veteran drummer Kenny Aronoff subbing for Chad Smith. In the summer of 2012, a longer U.S. tour was conducted, followed in the late fall by the release of the live album *LV*.

Satriani returned to his solo career in the spring of 2013 with *Unstoppable Momentum* (#42), backed by the classic rock ensemble of Mike Keneally (keyboards), Chris Chaney (bass), and the legendary Vinnie Colaiuta (drums), rather than the large roster of session musicians employed on previous releases. Displaying his unquenchable thirst to stretch beyond his already broad boundaries, the disc features a welcome element of swing rhythms, along with his usual, but by no means ordinary, knack for melodies and compositional strength over flash. With the title of the album an apt description of his energy and ambition, Satriani took off on an extensive European tour in the summer, followed by a North American tour in early fall. Clearly, more solo and Chickenfoot albums will follow for the inspiration, enjoyment, and edification of fans and guitarists alike. Always a teacher at heart, in the summer of 2014, he participated in the G4 Experience, a week-long guitar camp featuring fellow guitarists Paul Gilbert and Andy Timmons, in addition to keyboardist Mike Keneally.

THE GUITAR STYLE OF JOE SATRIANI

One of the hallmarks of Satriani's overpowering style is the employment of advanced altered voicings in a rock context. For example, the C9#11(no3rd) chord allows him to add the tart #11 (F#) note to the C major scale (resulting in C Lydian) for extra musical tension in measure 1, as well as over the C major triad in measure 2. Also notice his emphasis on the major 7th (B) for a quick hit of consonant melody.

Performance Tip: The pick taps/slides in measure 2 require a deft touch, with light-gauge strings and low action contributing to the effect.

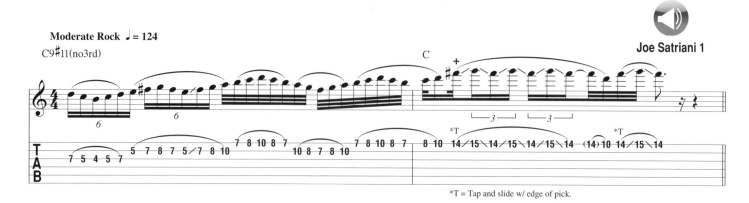

Though Satriani is well known as a shredder par excellence, he is fully capable of throttling back his prodigious note production. Along with relatively fewer notes, observe his sophisticated scale choices. In measure 1, the #4th (A#), or b5th (Bb), creates tension among the E major scale degrees, implying E Lydian. He utilizes the E Aeolian mode's dissonant melodic quality in measure 2, where the b7th (D) helps to emphasize the Em7 tonality and the note C complements the b13th chord alteration. Almost functioning as a melodic motif, Satriani slyly inserts the #4th (A#) into the E major scale in measure 3, simultaneously implying E Lydian. A "measure" of his brilliance is shown in measure 4, where he executes an unusual descending pattern derived from the E Mixolydian mode, resolving to the root (E).

No one would ever mistake Satriani for a blues guitarist. Nonetheless, he understands the roots of rock well enough to use bends to his expressive advantage. In addition, and in conjunction with the E minor pentatonic scale, he showcases fluid blues-rock phrasing. Given the rapid tempo, his note selection is based more on dynamics and forward motion than on targeting chord tones, with the root (E) in measure 1 a significant exception.

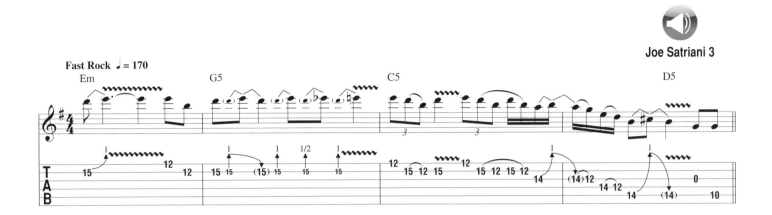

"Satch" rocks the "boogie" with the A composite blues scale (blues scale plus Mixolydian mode) at a blazing tempo. John Lee Hooker may not have recognized the roots of his pioneering efforts, but it still contains the spirit of the genre, albeit in an exceptionally contemporary vein. In measure 4, check out the unusual pull-off from the fretted C (♭3rd) to the open G string (♭7th), which manages to mash together two of the "blues" notes.

In this last example, Satriani brilliantly and subtly alters repetitive 16th notes to acknowledge chord changes. In measure 1 over G5, he plays the 3rd (B), root, and ♭7th (F), followed by the ♭7th (B♭), 5th (G), and major 3rd (E) over C5, which is maintained into measure 2. Despite the fleet tempo, he makes the same three notes work over the very brief B♭5 and A5 changes in measure 3 before completing the measure with a return to the same three notes as in measure 1 (over G5). Though the G5 harmony is maintained in measure 4, Satriani opts to try a new set of notes on alternate beats: the 4th (C) added to the root and ♭7th (F).

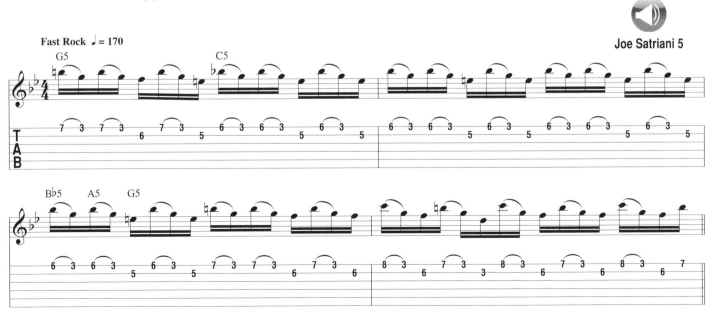

Steve Vai performs at the House of Blues in Chicago, Illinois on September 21, 2007.

(© Rob Grabowski/Retna Ltd.)

STEVE VAI
(1960–)

It is only proper that Steve Vai follows his mentor and friend Joe Satriani in the chronology of great rock guitarists. Not only was he the prize student of Satriani, but he has gone on to carve out his own chunk of the rock. As an amazing virtuoso with exceptional theoretical knowledge and sight-reading ability, the multiple award winner in a variety of categories stands out as the epitome of devastating power, melodic sophistication, and inventive, eclectic compositions.

Steven Siro Vai was born on June 6, 1960, in Carle Place, New York, into the Italian-American family of Theresa and John. An early interest in music led to his parents providing him with accordion lessons. Watching as his parents listened to *West Side Story* while at the same time his older sister listened to Led Zeppelin had a profound effect on the future guitarist. Hearing Zeppelin's "Heartbreaker," and then seeing the band at Madison Square Garden in 1973, when he was 13, convinced Vai that the guitar was *it*. Consequently, he purchased an inexpensive model at a garage sale. Realizing the guitar was more than a passing fancy, his parents accepted the change, springing for a better quality instrument and encouraging their son to pursue his interest. Jimmy Page, Jimi Hendrix, Jeff Beck, Brian May, Ritchie Blackmore, and Glen Buxton (Alice Cooper) were early influences. In 1974, he started taking lessons from high school alumnus Joe Satriani and would go on to play in the bands Circus, Rayge, and Bold as Love, along with one called the Steve Vais. Upon graduation in 1978, he spent one year at Berklee College of Music in Boston, where he played in Axis and Morning Thunder while being drawn to the genre mashup music of Frank Zappa.

By this time, his music-reading skills were highly developed and he transcribed Zappa's drum and percussion composition "The Black Page," an extraordinarily difficult challenge, and sent it off to the iconoclastic rock guitarist, along with a tape of his own playing. Zappa was so impressed that he engaged the music major to transcribe guitar solos from *Joe's Garage* and the *Shut Up 'n' Play Yer Guitar* series. Vai would leave Berklee in 1979 and, in the early fall, went to work for Zappa as his transcriber. In 1980, at the tender and impressionable age of 20, he was invited to a band rehearsal for an audition, scoring the gig after a "brutal" musical test of his ability. A subsequent tour found the guitarist pushing past the limits of his maturity and physical endurance. He would add guitar parts to *Shut Up 'n' Play Yer Guitar* (1981), *Tinsel Town Rebellion* (1981), *You Are What You Is* (1981), *Ship Arriving Too Late to Save a Drowning Witch* (1982), and *The Man from Utopia* (1983), among others, credited variously with "Impossible Guitar Parts," "Strat Abuse," and "Stunt Guitar." Despite Zappa affectionately referring to Vai as his "little Italian virtuoso," the rising guitar star found being around the chronically cynical leader a seriously negative influence, leading to depression and leaving the band in 1982, as well as making significant changes in his lifestyle and philosophical outlook. In addition, in 1983, he recorded the self-produced *Flex-Able* in his "Stucco Blue" backyard studio in Sylmar, California, and saw it released the following year on Relativity Records to sales of 250,000 with virtually no promotion. A year later, *Flex-Able Leftovers* was released as an EP, though in two limited editions of 1,000 copies each. While showing an obvious compositional and lyrical debt to Zappa, the albums also hinted at where his virtuosity, intelligence, and uninhibited exploration would take him.

During the next two years, Vai played and contributed vocals to the Out Band, the Classified, and 777, all of which contained future notable bassist Stu Hamm. In 1985, Vai caught a break when, against the wishes of lead singer Graham Bonnet, he was asked to join Alcatrazz after Yngwie Malmsteen had quit. Following a tour of Japan, *Disturbing the Peace* (#145, 1985) was released to negative criticism and would be their only record with Vai, though the tepid pop-rock band would at least help to prepare him for his following ventures. Later that year, he would seem to again be out of his element. As a session musician alongside ex-Cream drummer Ginger Baker and jazz drummer Tony Williams, he added lead guitar parts to Public Image Ltd.'s *Album* (#115), a group led by former Sex Pistols singer John "Johnny Rotten" Lydon. Also in 1985, Vai stepped outside his role as rock guitar hero to play satanic Jack Butler in the mythological blues film *Crossroads*, where his dark looks and charismatic presence were an ideal fit.

Better days were about to arrive, musically. At the behest of friend and virtuoso bassist Billy Sheehan, Vai joined the David Lee Roth band, a supergroup that also featured former Maynard Ferguson drummer Gregg Bissonette. Their debut recording, the double-platinum *Eat 'Em and Smile* (#4), featuring "Goin' Crazy" (#66), "That's Life" (#85), and "Yankee Rose" (#16), was a smash hit. Any doubts that listeners may have had as to whether Roth would try to show the Van Halen band the error in letting him go were quickly dispelled by the riotously hard pop-rocking affair. Vai and Sheehan executed breathtaking unison runs and riffs, with the former letting everyone know that he was every bit the virtuoso instrumentalist as EVH, with his own mojo to boot. Though another commercial blockbuster, *Skyscraper* (#6, 1988), sporting the acoustic ballad "Damn Good" (#2 Mainstream Rock) and the sizzling "Hot Dog and a Shake," created controversy among fans and reviewers due to its shiny pop sheen, apparently produced in compliance with Roth's outsized ego. Citing creative differences, Sheehan left after recording the album to form Mr. Big, and Vai would soon be cutting out as well, effectively pulling the plug on the popular supergroup. Despite the break up, both Vai and Sheehan came away from the project as rock superstars, confirmed for the former via Ibanez's creation of the Jem 777 signature series of guitars.

In 1989, Vai released the gold instrumental album *Passion and Warfare* (#18), featuring the rocking "I Would Love To" (#38 Mainstream Rock) and fan favorite "For the Love of God." Recorded in his "Mothership" home studio, the album was based on a series of dreams that he had as a child, describing it as "Jimi Hendrix meets Jesus Christ at a party that Ben-Hur threw for Mel Blanc." Many believe *Passion and Warfare* represents his best work, highlighting his flair for composition, often derived from his spiritual views, personal philosophy, and sense of humor, in addition to his unsurpassed, fret-melting technique. Concurrently, he had Ibanez produce the Universe seven-string guitar and he joined the British heavy rock band Whitesnake, formed in 1978 by former Deep Purple lead singer David Coverdale. Second guitarist Vivian Campbell had split due to "creative differences" and lead guitarist Adrian Vandenberg, who had written the majority of the material for a forthcoming album, seriously injured his wrist, preventing him from playing. Remembering Vai from *Crossroads*, Coverdale sought out the "devilish" guitarist and Vai proceeded to learn and play all the guitar parts on the platinum *Slip of the Tongue* (#10). A huge Whitesnake world tour followed in 1990, including a headlining appearance at the Monsters of Rock festival in England, with both Vai and the recovered Vandenberg sharing axe duties. Despite the success, however, Coverdale would end the band after the tour, leaving Vai to pursue his solo career. In addition, Vai made himself available for session work, guesting on the track "Feed My Frankenstein" from Alice Cooper's *Hey Stoopid* (1991), an album also featuring Joe Satriani.

Vai went through a period of reflection and intense discipline before following *Passion and Warfare* with *Sex & Religion* (#48) in 1993. In contrast to his acknowledged masterpiece, his third effort has been criticized for the excessiveness of lead singer Devin Townsend, the uninspired backing band, and the lackluster vocal-rock material. In fairness to bassist T.M. Stevens and drummer Terry Bozzio, particularly, Vai has admitted to cramping the creativity and input of the stellar sidemen in his desire to have his concept performed to his unyielding vision, leading to constant conflict during the recording process. Ultimately, it may have just been his inexperience at leading a band. Consequently, Stevens and Bozzio bolted the project after the recording process and Vai went out on the road with Townsend and session musicians. Perhaps stung by his experience as a band leader, in 1994, Vai began writing and recording with Ozzy Osbourne, resulting in "My Little Man" appearing on the double-platinum *Ozzmosis* (#4, 1995). Unfortunately, his guitar parts were replaced by Zakk Wylde and Osbourne has been quoted as calling

Vai a "mechanic." On the bright side, also in 1994, he received his first Grammy award for Best Rock Instrumental Performance, scoring the honor for the song "Sofa," from the album *Zappa's Universe*, a tribute to the late composer/guitarist.

During the lengthy sessions for his next full-length disc, Vai opted to fill the void in 1995 by putting out a seven-song EP, *Alien Love Secrets*. A virtual solo project, with minimal contributions from drummer Deen Castronovo and organist Tommy Mars, the guitarist plays bass, keyboards, and programmed drum tracks in a virtual trio format. The instrumental recording contains tributes to Jimi Hendrix, including "Tender Surrender" (based on "Villanova Junction"), and most obviously, "The Boy from Seattle." In 1996, Vai enjoyed the first of his record 11 appearances in the G3 concert series founded by Joe Satriani while also releasing the ambitious *Fire Garden* (#106), featuring 18 songs divided into two parts, or "phases," with Phase 1 containing mostly instrumentals and Phase 2 containing Vai's vocals save for one cut. Vai described *Fire Garden* thusly: "Being as dense as it is, this CD may best be experienced by devouring it in pieces, but those with a strong constitution may dare to consume it whole as is."

In direct contrast to *Fire Garden* in all ways, *Flex-Able Leftovers* was re-released in 1998 with the "leftovers" from 1984, along with five newly-recorded bonus tracks. Included in the extra material is the pseudo-rap vamp "F--k Yourself," which compelled the record company to put a "Parental Advisory" sticker on most packaging. A questionable stab at humor in the manner of Frank Zappa, with Vai giving a credible imitation of his mentor's voice, the song nonetheless features a lengthy solo that functions as a tasty sampler of the Vai style.

Released in 1999, *The Ultra Zone* (#121) resembles *Fire Garden* inasmuch as eight of the songs are instrumental tunes and the remaining five vocal numbers are sung by Koshi Inaba from the Japanese band B'z. Included amongst the instrumentals are proper tributes to Zappa ("Frank") and Stevie Ray Vaughan ("Jibboom"). That same year, Vai founded his own record label, Favored Nations, to not only release his own music, but that of a wide variety of artists whom he respects. Over time, it would grow to encompass Favored Nations Acoustic and Favored Nations Cool (jazz). Vai rang in the new millennium with the unusual concept record *The 7th Song: Enchanting Guitar Melodies (Archives Vol. 1)*. Except for three new compositions and a "hidden" track, all the songs appeared as track 7 on one of his previous albums. "Those songs sounded a bit out of place on the original album, but when I put them all together, it creates a beautiful, flowing musical experience," Vai said of the compilation.

In 2001, Vai released the stunningly creative, two-disc *Alive in an Ultra World*, recorded during the Ultra Zone Tour. Save for one track previously appearing on *Fire Garden*, it consists of 16 live tracks, with 15 written during soundchecks in order to honor the countries visited on the tour. For the next four years, Vai took a break from creating new studio albums and instead explored various other musical opportunities. Also in 2001, he produced *No Substitutions: Live in Osaka* for guitarists Steve Lukather and Larry Carlton, sharing their Grammy for Best Pop Instrumental Album. In the summer of 2002, he participated with the Metropolitan Symphony Orchestra in the world premiere of *Fire Strings*, a 20-minute, atonal concerto for electric guitar and 100-piece orchestra composed by Ichiro Nodaira and performed at the Suntory Hall in Tokyo, Japan. In 2004, Vai played with the Metropole Orchestra of the Netherlands on a program of his orchestral arrangements and compositions. In early 2005, Vai premiered the *Blossom Suite*, a duo composition for electric and classical guitar, in Paris with classical guitarist Sharon Isbin. Also in the early part of the year, *Real Illusions: Reflections* (#147) signaled his return to the studio to continue his ongoing solo career. Though he had been experiencing steady commercial decline since *Sex & Religion*, Vai was determined to express his personal artistic vision and crafted a new-age "rock fable," featuring Billy Sheehan on bass, Gregg Bissonette on percussion, and a horn section. The first installment of a planned trilogy, the concept album employs interconnected "vignettes" to advance a story line described in the CD booklet as "a multi-layered mélange based on the amplified mental exaggerations of a truth-seeking madman who sees the world through his own distorted perceptions," with further extrapolation available on his website. Also in 2005, Vai became an official supporter of the non-profit Little Kids Rock organization, which provides instruction and free instruments to public school children.

In 2006, Vai toured the U.S. and Europe with Zappa Plays Zappa, a tribute band led by Frank Zappa's eldest son, Dweezil, and in 2008, won a Grammy for Best Rock Instrumental Performance for "Peaches En Regalia," from the album *Zappa Plays Zappa*. It was his third Grammy overall. In the summer of 2007, Vai put out the two-disc *Sound Theories, Vol. I & II* (#45 Top Independent Albums), compositions recorded with the Metropole Orchestra in 2004–05. Also in 2007, Vai, along with a group of fellow musicians and friends, "confessed" to those he may have hurt in the past on the Dream Theater cut "Repentance," from *Systematic Chaos*, while in 2009, he sat in with the band during their Los Angeles stop on the Progressive Nation Tour.

In 2012, Vai released *The Story of Light* (#78) as the second installment of a trilogy, seven years after the first one, *Real Illusions: Reflections*. According to Vai, the extraordinarily complicated story concept will not be fully understood until all three albums are available, stating, "I wanted it to span a long period of time," adding that "it is probably going to be one of my life's greatest works." The respectable chart position would suggest that his fans were not daunted by the challenging spiritual album containing a duet with singer/songwriter Aimee Mann, a surprising cover of legendary country bluesman Blind Willie Johnson's "John the Revelator" (sung by Beverly McClellan from "The Voice" and backed by a gospel choir), and the use of Russian rather than English on the title track. In 2013, Vai guested on the track "Carnage Asada," from the album *Late for Nothing* by metalcore band Iwrestledabearonce. The title is a play on the name of a popular Mexican grilled steak dish, "carne asada," hence an appropriate track for the vegetarian Vai.

Steve Vai possesses unparalleled, singular dedication to and unshakeable confidence in his art, always forging ahead in his quest to push the limits of creativity. Like an ancient alchemist, he mixes his carefully chosen combination of guitars, amps, and effects into a sonic brew, using his enormous talent to captivate listeners with a potent musical spell.

THE GUITAR STYLE OF STEVE VAI

Vai is an exceptionally knowledgeable and trained rock guitarist capable of extremely sophisticated melodic, harmonic, and rhythmic concepts. Nonetheless, he is more than intelligent enough to know when to streamline his scale choices—in this case, A major—to best express his musical ideas.

The D Dorian mode is mined for hidden gems as Vai phrases in his innovative and idiosyncratic way. On beats 3–4 of measure 1, he descends an Am triad, but here, over a Dm7 harmony, the notes function as the 9th (E), ♭7th (C), and 5th (A), respectively. Then, on beat 2 of measure 3, he wisely inserts the gnarly ♭5th (A♭) on strings 5 and 3 for brief musical tension before returning to the scale's harmonious A natural.

Performance Tip: Use sweep picking for the ascending runs in measure 3.

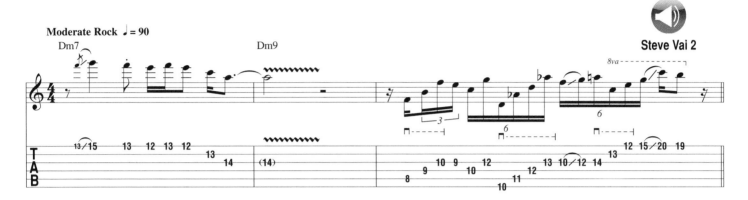

This next exercise is another example of his angular phrasing while tearing through rhythmically challenging licks. Note that the only time the E Dorian mode is theoretically indicated, as opposed to the minor pentatonic scale, is on beats 3–4 of measure 2, where the 6th (C♯) and 2nd, or 9th (F♯), appear and function as the major 7th and major 3rd of the D major harmony, respectively.

Performance Tip: Sweep picking is once again highly recommended for the vertical runs.

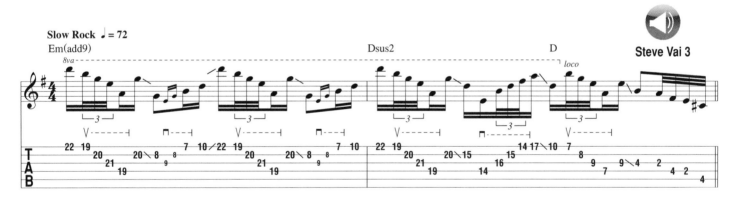

To compliment his signature, twisting, quicksilver, aggressive lines, Vai offers gentle, graceful melodies that are produced with minimal notes. Of course, the C♯ (♯4th) in measures 3 "tweaks" the ear with its bluesy dissonance; however, it's quickly counteracted by the sweet 6th (E) in measure 4, achieved via a one-and-a-half-step bend.

Performance Tip: Execute the second-string bends with the ring finger, backed by the middle and index.

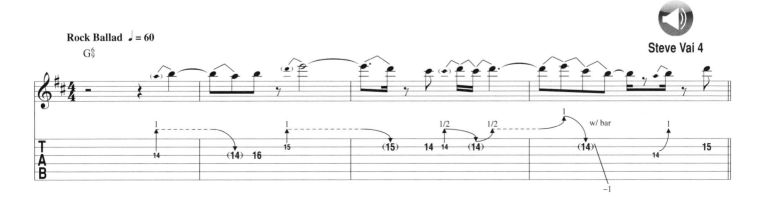

Over the same G6/9 harmony as in the previous example, Vai displays his intuitive grasp of musical drama. An ascending run up the G Lydian mode begins with dynamic syncopation (measure 1) before giving way to a fluid, melodic line (measure 2) and climaxing with a soaring bend to the gritty #4th (C#), fueled by sensuous vibrato (measures 3–4).

Steve Vai 5

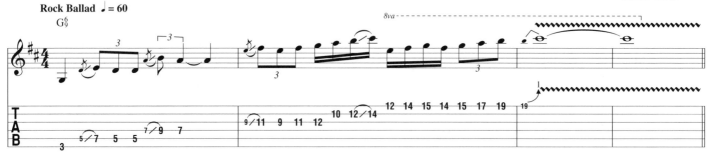

SLASH
(1965–)

In the late '80s, Slash burst on to the scene as a bona fide guitar hero in the hard-rocking Guns N' Roses with a combination of classic, high-energy, blues-rock soloing, arena-rock riffing, and a bold image and attitude. Though the latter has, at times, threatened to overwhelm his considerable talents, his explosive passion remains his memorable calling card.

Saul Hudson was born on July 23, 1965, in Hampstead, London, England, to Ola, an African-American clothing designer, and Anthony, an English art director and album cover designer. An infinitely quotable and intelligent individual, Slash once stated: "As a musician, I've always been amused that I am both British and black, particularly because so many American musicians seem to aspire to be British, while so many British musicians, in the '60s particularly, went to such pains to be black."

As a very young child, Slash was raised by his father and paternal grandparents after his mother relocated to Los Angeles, California, shortly after his birth in order to further her career. When Slash was 5, he made his first musical appearance in public, playing drums in a school Christmas pageant. Around the same time, he and his father moved to Los Angeles to be with his mother, living for a time in Laurel Canyon among the rock elite of the day. His mother made an effort to make up for lost time with her young son by taking him to her work, where he met music and film stars. In 1974, his parents separated and Slash chose to live with his mother, though his father's abuse of alcohol and antisocial behavior would contribute to his son becoming, in his own words, a "problem child."

In 1979, at the age of 14, Slash was hit by the "lightning bolt" of music while listening to the Aerosmith album *Rocks*, in the company of an older girl who he coveted. Starting in junior high school, he was in and out of trouble, including for theft, while relieving some of his aggressive tendencies by becoming a competitive bicycle motocross (BMX) racer. While in school, Slash met future Guns N' Roses drummer Steven Adler with whom he would listen to music and go to see Van Halen, a major influence, in concert. Adler played guitar and the two decided to form a band with Slash on bass, despite Slash having never played an instrument. The "band" never happened, but Slash still wanted to play the bass, so armed with a one-string flamenco guitar, he proceeded to take lessons at a music school. However, hearing his teacher play the classic rock of the Stones, Cream, and especially Led Zeppelin, inspired him to play guitar. With the nylon-string guitar restrung, he began teaching himself from a rock guitar book and borrowed $100 from his beloved maternal grandmother to buy a Gibson Explorer copy. He was given his nickname by noted character actor Seymour Cassel because "he was always on the go, zipping ["slashing"] from one place to another and never sitting still." To the detriment of his schoolwork, he began practicing "12 hours a day," dropping out of high school in the 11th grade.

In 1981, while still in high school, Slash formed his first serious band, Tidus Sloan, a slang term for people asked to leave a drunk's house. For the next two years, they played instrumental versions of early Black Sabbath, Rush, Led Zeppelin, Deep Purple, the Stones, and the Police, as neither Slash nor anyone else wanted to sing. When the band broke up, Steven Adler, who had been woodshedding the drums, was back in the picture and suggested they start a new band called "Road Crew." With bassist Duff McKagan completing the rhythm section, they began working up original material but were unable to find the right lead singer and disbanded in 1984. Slash would next replace lead guitarist Chris Weber in Hollywood Rose, featuring lead singer Axl Rose, after they had recorded a five-song demo financed by Weber's father, thereby compelling rhythm guitarist/singer Izzy Stradlin to quit in a snit. Other lineup changes followed, including Adler taking over the drum throne, and the band split up. In 1985, Slash briefly played with Black Sheep, a local band run by music avatar Willie Basse, who was known for having the hottest guitarists. In addition, Slash auditioned for Poison, but lost out to C.C. DeVille. While Slash believed he could nail the music, the makeup and "glam" clothes were a sticking point, and Poison frontman Bret Michaels remembers thinking that Slash's Aerosmith influence would not have been right for them, anyway. Meanwhile, Rose went off to sing with L.A. Guns.

Hollywood Rose reformed in 1985 with Rose, Stradlin, Weber, bassist Steve Darrow, and L.A. Guns drummer Rob Gardner. Weber would eventually leave, with L.A. Guns' Tracii Guns taking over lead guitar and Ole Beich replacing Darrow, and the name would change to "Guns N' Roses." However, Beich would be bumped for McKagan and Tracii Guns' absence at rehearsals would convince Rose to bring Slash back to assume the lead guitar chair. Then in the late spring of 1985, Gardner quit and was replaced by Adler, completing the "classic" Guns N' Roses lineup. Several Hollywood Rose compositions would find their way onto future recordings. Within days, a short West Coast tour was organized and, for the next 10 months, they set about building a following on the Hollywood club scene with prime gigs at the Troubadour and the Roxy. The music industry took notice and in the early spring of 1986, they were signed to Geffen Records and released the four-song EP *Live?!@ Like a Suicide*, containing two originals and two cover songs. Canned audience applause was added to create the illusion of an exciting live performance.

In the summer of 1987, the 18-times platinum *Appetite for Destruction* (#1) burst onto the scene, blowing away the hair metal and pop pap of the '80s with raw, reckless abandon driven by Slash and Stradlin and the pounding rhythm section, along with the convincingly sleazy attitude of Rose. All three of the album's singles—"Welcome to the Jungle" (#7), "Sweet Child O' Mine" (#1), and "Paradise City" (#5)—reached the Top 10. In retrospect, the track "Mr. Brownstone," slang for heroin, sounded an ominous warning. A 16-month tour of the U.S. and Europe was embarked upon to support the hit record, with the band going from opening act to headliner. Released in 1988, *GN'R Lies* (#2) went platinum five times and is considered their second studio album, though technically it's an EP, with four of the eight tracks snatched from *Live?!@ Like a Suicide*. The four remaining tracks contain acoustic guitar accompaniment, with the maudlin "Patience" (#4) released as the single. Despite the high chart position, the record is seen as catalog filler and a step down from the power and hard rock cred of their blockbuster debut. Far more troubling, however, was the misogyny, homophobia, and racism inherent in some of Rose's lyrics, not to be excused as poetic license or artistic irony like "Money for Nothing" by Mark Knopfler of Dire Straits, for example. An aura of uncertainty and uneasiness began to pervade their concerts: Rose assaulted a security guard, called out his bandmates about their heroin use from the stage at their first gig opening for the Stones, and riots broke out at two shows. In time, they would be referred to as "The Most Dangerous Band in the World," an appellation beyond hyperbole.

In 1990, during recording sessions for their next release, keyboard player Dizzy Reed was added to GN'R and Adler was fired due to his substance abuse, replaced by Matt Sorum from the Cult. The two-disc *Use Your Illusion I* (#2), containing the Top 10 singles "Don't Cry" (#10), "Live and Let Die" (#2), and "November Rain" (#3), and *Use Your Illusion II* (#1), with "You Could Be Mine" (#29), "Knockin' on Heaven's Door" (#12), and "Yesterdays" (#72), debuted simultaneously in the early fall of 1991, eventually selling 14 million copies combined. Although the double release set records, the direction of the band continued to veer away from the thrilling intensity of *Appetite for Destruction*. Nonetheless, the maturity and variety of the vast new material—heavy metal, classical, classic rock 'n' roll, punk, and even the blues—scored high with critics and fans.

Unfortunately, but perhaps predictably, their 28-month tour was marred by the increasingly psychopathic behavior of Rose, resulting in Stradlin quitting in the late fall of 1991 and being replaced by Gilby Clarke. The tour's last show, in the summer of 1993 in Argentina, would also be the last time Slash, Sorum, and Clarke would perform live with Rose. The swan song with Slash would arrive in the late fall

Slash performing live in the early 1990s.

(© Ian Tilton/Retna UK)

with the release of *The Spaghetti Incident?* (#4), a collection of punk, glam rock, and classic rock covers mainly recorded during the *Illusion* sessions, with Stradlin's parts re-recorded by Clarke. "Ain't It Fun" (#8 Mainstream Rock), the doo-wop classic "Since I Don't Have You" (#69), and the Nazareth cover "Hair of the Dog" (#19 Mainstream Rock) were released as singles. As perhaps his final outrage with the current GN'R lineup, Rose requested the inclusion, as a hidden track, "Look at Your Game, Girl," a song written by mass-murder perpetrator Charles Manson. Ironically, the band's performance on the album was their most driving, straight-ahead hard rock since *Appetite for Destruction.*

In 1994, Slash initiated a side project, Slash's Snakepit, with Sorum and Clarke from Guns N' Roses, Alice in Chains bassist Mike Inez, and lead singer Eric Dover. With songs earmarked originally for GN'R, the platinum *It's Five O'Clock Somewhere* (#70) became their debut album in early 1995. As expected and to the delight of his fans, Slash plays a ton of his signature blues-rock guitar, though critics knocked the songwriting. Following a tour with a different rhythm section, Slash ended the band in 1996 and toured for the next two years with Slash's Blues Ball, playing blues-rock covers with lead singer/harmonicist/keyboardist Teddy Andreadis, rhythm guitarist Bobby Schneck, saxist Dave McLarem, bassist Johnny Griparic, and drummer Alvino Bennet. Meanwhile, from 1994–96, new material was being composed and recorded for GN'R, with Slash accusing Rose of including little to no input from him, and vice versa. The release of a cover of "Sympathy for the Devil" on the *Interview with the Vampire* soundtrack, against Slash's wishes, and escalating tension with Rose finally pushed Slash to quit Guns N' Roses in the fall of 1996.

In 1999, after the dissolution of Slash's Blues Ball, he resurrected his Snakepit for *Ain't Life Grand* with a core group that consisted of Griparic and singer Rod Jackson, rhythm guitarist Ryan Roxie, and drummer Matt Laug. It sold less than their debut and critical response was tepid, once again due to the clichéd songwriting, but also because Slash seemed to have taken a gracious backseat to his bandmates. In the summer of 2000, they embarked on a world tour opening for AC/DC, followed by their own headlining tour. However, by 2002, Slash was ready for another change. That year, he hooked back up with Duff McKagan and Matt Sorum with the idea of putting a band together. Izzy Stradlin was likewise to be involved, but bowed out when informed that they were looking for a separate lead singer and was replaced by Dave Kushner. Former Stone Temple Pilots singer Scott Weiland, a "wild card" due to his serious past and present drug abuse and take-charge personality, was eventually tapped for the gig and the supergroup Velvet Revolver was born. Released in the summer of 2004, the double-platinum *Contraband* (#1) was roundly praised by most critics and proved the star guitarist's commercial viability away from GN'R, even with Weiland taking the upper hand in the songwriting minus Slash, including "Slither" (#1 Mainstream Rock and Grammy winner for Best Hard Rock Performance), "Fall to Pieces" (#67), and "Dirty Little Thing" (#8 Mainstream Rock). Despite the substance abuse of all but Kushner, a nearly two-year-long world tour was undertaken. Their sophomore effort, *Libertad* (#5), released in the summer of 2007 with the singles "She Builds Quick Machines" (#2 Mainstream Rock) and "The Last Fight" (#16 Mainstream Rock), would not fair nearly as well as the debut. Another single, "Get Out the Door," would presciently be the last to feature Weiland, as he split in the spring of 2008 to rejoin the reformed Stone Temple Pilots. Slash and his band were determined to find a new singer and carry on, going so far as to write and record a group of new songs by the early winter of 2011. However, later in the early spring, following a one-gig reunion with Weiland in January 2012, Slash announced that due to their inability to find a new, suitable singer, they would be taking a few years off from the band to pursue individual projects.

In the early fall of 2008, following Weiland's departure, Slash had begun work on his first solo album. It took almost two years to complete the project, but in the early spring of 2010, *Slash* debuted at #3, backed by Stradlin, McKagan, and Adler, along with an all-star cast of vocalists, including Ozzy Osbourne, Iggy Pop, Dave Grohl, Chris Cornell, Lemmy Kilmister, Adam Levine, Fergie from the Black-Eyed Peas, M. Shadows from Avenged Sevenfold, and Myles Kennedy from Alter Bridge. The singles "By the Sword" (#25 Mainstream Rock), "Back from Cali" (#24 Mainstream Rock), and "Beautiful Dangerous" (#11

Heatseekers Songs) further confirmed his status as a certifiable hit maker, and in the summer, he headed out on tour with Kennedy on lead vocals and rhythm guitar. In the late spring of 2012, Slash released his second solo album of his patented L.A. hard rock, *Apocalyptic Love* (#4), with a band known as "Slash featuring Myles Kennedy and the Conspirators." Along with the singles "You're a Lie" (#12 Rock Songs) and "Standing in the Sun" (#28 Rock Songs) and positive reviews, Slash proved to himself and the public that, with a cooperative lead singer, he could lead a successful band. Around the same time, Guns N' Roses was inducted into the Rock and Roll Hall of Fame, with Slash and his fellow former members appearing and playing, except for Rose and Stradlin, as Kennedy stepped up and sang on the selection of GN'R classics.

In the spring and summer of 2013, Slash and his Conspirators burned their way through a world tour, with bassist Todd Kerns backing lead singer Kennedy on a half dozen tunes. When his signature Marshall SL5 debuted in 2013, it joined his six signature Les Paul and three signature Epiphone guitars, Marshall AFD100, Marshall JCM 2555, Cry Baby SW95, Cry Baby SC05, MXR Octave Fuzz, and AmpliTube Slash as gear honoring his talents and contribution to rock music. Now clean and sober for eight years and counting, and with the ghosts of Guns N' Roses laid to rest, Slash finds himself at the top of his game.

THE GUITAR STYLE OF SLASH

Besides his fiery, blues-rock lead lines, Slash is known and admired for his use of tasty dyads, or double stops. Note the wide variety of 3rds and 4ths under his command relative to the E major chord, including G#/D (3rd/♭7th) and G#/E (3rd/root) from the E Mixolydian mode in measures 1 and 3. He also adds some dynamic bluesy grit in measure 2 with B/G (5th/♭3rd) and the classic D/B (♭7th/5th) "dominant" dyad favored by blues and blues-rockers everywhere. Performing the same function to an even greater degree is D/G# (♭7th/3rd) in measures 3–4.

Slash 1

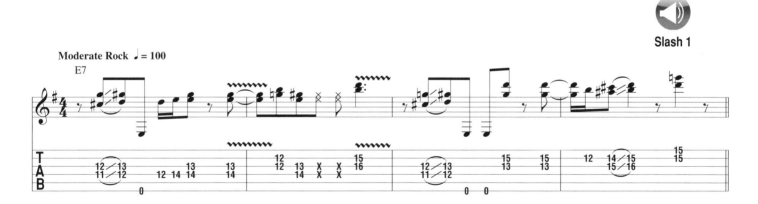

One of the "secrets" to his success is his regular and skillful employment of the major pentatonic scale. Like many rock, blues, and country guitarists, he frequently accesses it by playing in the relative minor pentatonic position. Evident in measures 1–2, with the B minor pentatonic at fret 7 relative to D major, the classic triple-stop form indicates the D major triad via the oblique bend of E (2nd) to F# (major 3rd) while simultaneously acknowledging the F#5 change by sustaining the root (F#). Also check out measure 3, where Slash uses notes mainly from the D composite blues scale (blues scale plus Mixolydian mode) to function as the b3rd (A), b7th (E), b5th (C), 4th (B), and root (F#) of F#5. Two kickers are the C# and D from the D major scale, which function as the 5th and b6th of F# and likely represent him thinking D major scale fingerings.

> **Performance Tip:** In measures 1–2, barre strings 2–1 at fret 10 with the pinky, bending the E note on string 3 with the ring finger, backed by the middle and index. In measure 3, place the ring finger on fret 12 of string 1, catching the B note at fret 12 of string 2 with the same finger.

Again utilizing the versatile composite blues scale, Slash flies through the root position in the key of A, making sure to confirm the major tonality by including the major 3rd (C#), hammered, in true blues fashion, from the minor 3rd (C). Adding to the fluidity of his execution are the pull-offs involving the G (b7th), F# (6th), and E (5th) notes on string 2 and the Eb (b5th), D (4th), and C notes on string 3.

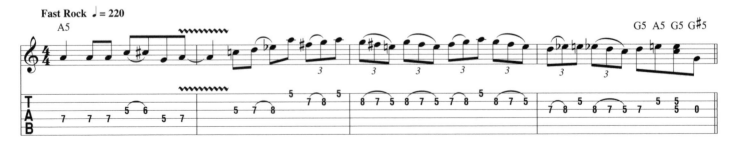

Slash is feted as one of hard rock's most melodic guitarists. Accessing the F major scale in D minor pentatonic positions allows him to phrase with familiar and friendly fingerings. Though not known for literally playing, navigating, or negotiating the changes, observe how he perhaps intuitively emphasizes appropriate notes nonetheless. In measure 1 over Fmaj7, they include the root, major 3rd (A), and major 7th (E). In measure 2 over Dm, they include the root and ♭3rd (F). In measures 3–4 over C major, they include the root, 3rd (E), 4th (F), and 5th (G).

Slash 4

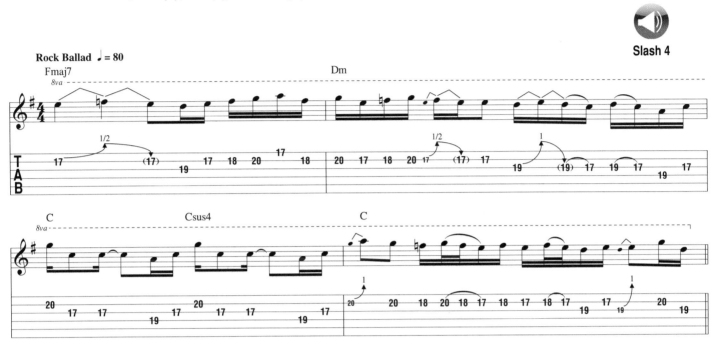

Slash upgrades the G major pentatonic to the G major scale by improvising in the root-octave position of the E Aeolian mode, which functions as the relative minor scale of G major. Like the previous example, he smartly implies chord changes with a clever combination of consonant and dissonant notes, creating musical tension and anticipation: the root and major 3rd (B) in measure 1 (over G5), the major 3rd (E) and 5th (G) in measure 2 (over C5), the "sophisticated" 13th (D) and 9th (G) in measure 3 (over the F5), as well as the root over C5, and the 3rd (B) and 4th (C) in measure 4 (over G5).

Slash 5

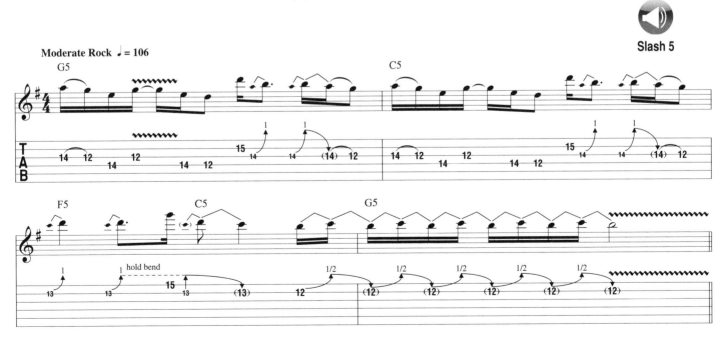

ZAKK WYLDE
(1967–)

Though most famous for his long association with Ozzy Osbourne, Zakk Wylde has also enjoyed a successful career playing heavy metal, doom metal, hard rock, and Southern rock on his own. A veritable "Viking" in his hard-partying lifestyle, he is revered by his fans for his overpowering speed, big tone, killer riffs, and ability to get the most out of the minor pentatonic scale. His aggressive, passionate playing stands out in a genre more "noted" for gymnastic scale manipulation.

Jeffrey Phillip Wielandt was born on January 14, 1967, in Bayonne, New Jersey, to Mr. and Mrs. Jerome Wielandt. He grew up in nearby Jackson, where he began playing the guitar at the age of 8, but he really wanted to play football instead, and his guitar teacher thought it best to let him go. At the age of 14, he began working in a music store, regained his desire to play, and took lessons for two years from LeRoy Wright, the son of the high school football coach whom Wylde cites as an excellent rock guitarist. Around 15, he discovered that many of his heroes, including Jimmy Page, Randy Rhoads, Gary Moore, Keith Richards, and Eric Clapton, all played Les Paul guitars at some point in their careers and he was smitten for life. Harboring the dream to someday play with his idol, Ozzy Osbourne, he built his skills through daily marathon practice sessions and also took lessons from a jazz and a classical guitarist. He soon developed a reputation as the local hotshot influenced by John Sykes of Whitesnake, Randy Rhoads, Van Halen, Tony Iommi, Jimi Hendrix, and Al Di Meola. In 1984, as a senior in high school, he played in Stone Henge, performing Black Sabbath and Rush covers. Upon graduation in 1985, he worked at menial jobs while a member of a succession of bands. Joining Zyris gave him the chance to begin writing originals to go with their Zeppelin and Sabbath covers and he decided to take the professional name of "Zakari Wyland," inspired by Dr. Zachary Smith from the TV show *Lost in Space.* In addition to gigging locally, his progress was such that he augmented his day job at a gas station by giving guitar lessons in Jackson.

One night in 1986, a rock photographer heard Wylde playing with Zyris and mentioned how Ozzy was looking for a guitarist to replace Jake E. Lee, who had been hired after Randy Rhoads' tragic death. He volunteered to pass on Wylde's press kit containing a tape of "Mr. Crowley" and the solo from "Crazy Train," among others. Surprisingly, he got a call from Sharon Osbourne to audition in Los Angeles and he flew out, figuring he had nothing to lose. He played "I Don't Know," "Crazy Train," "Suicide Solution," and "Bark at the Moon," along with some acoustic and classical guitar, but was sent home and had to fly back out a second time to be informed that he had the gig. Appropriately enough, it was the outrageous Ozzy who suggested that he change his last name to "Wylde." Consequently, the "Godfather of Heavy Metal" officially introduced his new lead guitarist and co-songwriter at the end of 1987 in New York City.

Wylde made his first recorded appearance with Ozzy on the double-platinum *No Rest for the Wicked* (#13) in the early fall of 1988. Critical response was positive, as Ozzy's fifth solo album was hailed as his best since *Blizzard of Ozz* eight years earlier. The subsequent tour included original Black Sabbath bassist Geezer Butler, only adding to the dream situation for Wylde. The live EP *Just Say Ozzy* (#58) followed in the early spring of 1990. Purportedly recorded in London, it seems to have the same crowd noise as a concert in Philadelphia from the No Rest for the Wicked Tour in 1989. Wylde co-wrote three tracks, while the EP also contains two Sabbath covers. A high point in the Ozzy/Wylde collaboration was reached with the quadruple-platinum *No More Tears* (#7) in 1991. Four singles cracked the Top 10: the title track (#5 Mainstream Rock), "Time After Time" (#6 Mainstream Rock), "Road to Nowhere" (#3 Mainstream Rock), and "Mama, I'm Coming Home" (#2 Mainstream Rock). In addition, "I Don't Want to Change the World" scored a Grammy for Ozzy for Best Metal Performance. Critical approval was virtually unanimous, including from *Entertainment Weekly* of all places, due to Ozzy showing a more "sensitive" side, and Wylde's soaring, cathartic solo on the title track has proven to be a fan favorite. Presciently, a hint of Southern rock had crept into his soloing.

Zakk Wylde and Black Label Society in Las Vegas, Nevada on June 5, 2014.

(© RTNGDP/MediaPunch)

The tour to support the album was touted as Ozzy's farewell tour, or "No More Tours," as he was planning to call it a career, and it was an artistic and commercial success, with the band also going to the studio during breaks to cut new tracks to be included on a proposed live album. Instead, the platinum two-disc *Live & Loud* (#22), containing a recording of "Changes" (#9 Mainstream Rock) from the tour, was released in 1993, exposing the explosive playing of Wylde to an international audience. Previously in 1992, while still a member of Ozzy's band, Wylde formed Lynyrd Skynhead with two members from White Lion in order to play Southern rock covers—he even got to fill in for Dickey Betts with the Allman Brothers Band for one memorable gig in 1993, which is available on bootleg recordings. The next year, Wylde changed the name of his band to "Pride & Glory," recording one surprisingly well-regarded album of Southern-fried boogie, blues, metal, and acoustic tracks featuring the leader on piano, banjo, mandolin, and harmonica, in addition to guitars, with James LoMenzo on bass and Brian Tichy on drums. Though garnering precious little commercial payback while touring with name acts, the bruising chords and searing solos, along with appealing songs, bode well for future Wylde projects. While leading Pride & Glory, Wylde would meet and become fast friends with fellow metal monster "Dimebag" Darrell Abbott.

After a four-year "retirement," Ozzy returned to the studio, adding former Yes keyboard wizard Rick Wakeman to the band for the double-platinum *Ozzmosis* (#4) in 1995—a change indicative of the pop leanings of the album, including Wylde playing through a synthesizer. Two singles, "Perry Mason" (#3 Mainstream Rock) and "See You on the Other Side" (#5 Mainstream Rock), made it into the Top 10, while "I Just Want You" hit #24. Though the contemporary pop production and the lengthy, melodramatic songwriting were criticized, Wylde was praised for his consistently hot licks. However, Wylde wouldn't record with Ozzy again until 2001, as he was replaced by former Randy Rhoads student and David Lee Roth guitarist Joe Holmes due to his dithering about whether to join Axl Rose in Guns N' Roses. When Wylde dallied too long, Ozzy felt the need to fill the guitar chair, despite his liberal policy towards band members participating in other projects. Ironically, Wylde was crossed off the short list for the GN'R lead guitar position due to what he reports as miscommunication regarding his compensation. At the same time, his record company was pressing for new product and Wylde complied with his solo debut, *Book of Shadows*, in 1996. Backed by LoMenzo and drummer Joe Vitale, it contains a range of boogie, blues, country, and acoustic folk rock that he had been composing away from Ozzy.

In 1998, Wylde toured Asia as a featured member of Ozzy's backing band, though they were all let go following shows in Japan. The same year, Wylde recorded *Sonic Brewery* with drummer Phil Ondich and Alice in Chains bassist Mike Inez in a band tentatively called "Hell's Kitchen," but ultimately became the debut of "Black Label Society." Three different versions of the album would be released for various reasons, including the cease-and-desist order from the Johnnie Walker whiskey company due to the album's cover infringing on their trademarked bottle label. The all-original album, with merely a taste of his Southern rock pretensions, proved his unapologetic love of skull-cracking hard rock and metal, with ferocious solos taking precedent over song composition. A year later, Black Label Society, consisting of just Wylde on guitar, piano, and bass and drummer Ondich, followed with *Stronger Than Death*, which lived up to its title, rocking equally hard and redefining "heavy." The recording tends to favor the lower frequencies, as do his vocals, and his "patented" pinch harmonics are in great abundance. Star baseball catcher Mike Piazza, then playing for the New York Mets, was hanging with the band during the recording and his ad-libbed backing "vocals" are heard on the title track.

In 2001, BLS released the two-CD *Alcohol Fueled Brewtality Live!! + 5*, consisting of a live set recorded at the famous Troubadour in Hollywood, plus five new studio tracks, including a cover of Neil Young's "Heart of Gold" and Sabbath's "Snowblind." Guitarist Nick Catanese and bassist Steve Gibb, son of Bee Gee Barry Gibb, are featured on disc 1, while drummer Craig Nunenmacher backs Wylde on both. The same year, Wylde found time to play on Ozzy's platinum *Down to Earth* (#4), containing "Gets Me Through" (#2 Mainstream Rock) and "Dreamer" (#10 Mainstream Rock), but did not contribute as a songwriter, as the leader only used songs previously written with Joe Holmes, who had left the band prior to the album's recording. In addition, in 2002, Wylde accompanied Ozzy on the Merry Mayhem Tour with Rob Zombie, and appears on the resultant CD/DVD *Live at Budokan* (#70), with Wylde's blistering performances hailed as the high point of the endeavor. He also found time that year to release the third BLS album, *1919 Eternal* (#149), backed by bassist Robert Trujillo on two tracks and drum duties shared by Nunenmacher and Christian Werr. Five of the 14 tracks were songs Ozzy nixed for his *Down to Earth* album, as he felt they would make it sound like a Black Label Society album. Originally entitled *Deathcore WarMachine Eternal*, the change to *1919 Eternal* was made following the terrorist attacks of 9/11 and refers to the year Wylde's father, a WWII vet who had recently died, was born. While with Ozzy in 2002, Sharon Osbourne became concerned about Wylde's excessive drinking and convinced him to check into rehab. Wylde complied, but judged it a scam and left.

Cranking out an album a year, in 2003, BLS (Wylde and Nunenmacher) released *The Blessed Hellride* (#50), featuring Ozzy singing on "Stillborn" (#12 Mainstream Rock). Banging old-school metal ruled the day—changing pop and rock tastes be damned—as Wylde roared as loud as ever, in addition to the occasional "tender" ballad. Like clockwork, a year later, *Hangover Music Vol. VI* (#40), an acoustic guitar-driven affair containing grunge influences and the single "House of Doom" (#33), made its appearance with bass duties handled by the trio of Joe LoMenzo, John "JD" DeServio, and Mike Inez (except "No Other," which was left over from *The Blessed Hellride*). A glance back to *Book of Shadows*, the album included "Layne," a tribute to the late Layne Staley of the influential Alice in Chains, and Wylde performing a solo piano version of Procol Harum's "A Whiter Shade of Pale." At the end of 2004, Wylde's close buddy "Dimebag" Darrell, formerly of Pantera and Damageplan, was shot and killed onstage in Ohio by a deranged fan—a horror that would stun the rock world and devastate Wylde.

In 2005, *Mafia* (#15), featuring bassist LoMenzo and the Mainstream Rock hits "Suicide Messiah" (#24), "Fire It Up" (#35), and "In This River" (#32), proved to be one of the most successful BLS albums. Though it was written months before his tragic murder, the latter song came to be a tribute to Dimebag Darrell. Also in 2005, the BLS compilation *Kings of Damnation: 98–04* was released, confirming for one and all the extraordinary fretboard wizardry of Wylde. In 2006, Wylde had his handprints and signature memorialized on the Hollywood Rockwalk, a ceremony attended by Ozzy, among other rock glitterati. That same year, Catanese (guitar), DeServio (bass), and Nunenmacher (drums) joined Wylde for BLS's *Shot to Hell* (#21), a fan-friendly mix of beer-powered metal and softer ballads, including the singles "Concrete Jungle" (#29 Mainstream Rock) and "Blood Is Thicker Than Water" (#31 Mainstream Rock). BLS appeared at Ozzfest in 2006, with Wylde also backing Ozzy on some shows. Concurrently, Ozzy announced his intention to cut his first record of new material in six years, with Wylde invited back into the fold to wail and write. Released in 2007, the gold *Black Rain* (#3), featuring the singles "Not Going Away" (#14 Mainstream Rock), "I Don't Wanna Stop" (#1 Mainstream Rock), and "Black Rain" (#19 Mainstream Rock), would be the virtuoso rock guitarist's last album to date with the "Godfather of Metal." Significantly less "heavy" than his earlier recordings, despite Wylde providing the usual bombast, *Black Rain* displays psychedelic overtones reminiscent of mid-period Beatles and an age-appropriate maturity due in part to Ozzy's smash reality TV show and sobriety. With exceptions, the album was overwhelmingly pilloried in the rock press, even though it achieved considerable, if unanticipated, commercial success. Also in 2007, Wylde performed a solo piano version of "In This River" for the debut of the plaque for the late Dimebag Darrell on Hollywood's Rockwalk.

In 2008, during the Black Rain Tour with Ozzy, Wylde cut his right hand during a show in Sao Paulo, Brazil, and continued playing while it bled—an incident that added to his near-mythical stature among fans. In 2009, the BLS compilation *Skullage* (#111) was released, consisting of selections from each of the BLS albums, as well as one each from *Pride & Glory* and *Book of Shadows*. Also included are live tracks and a DVD. In the summer, Wylde was hospitalized for blood clots in both lungs and a leg, necessitating the cancellation of BLS's appearance on the Pedal to the Metal Tour. Adding to his problems, in 2010, Ozzy fired Wylde, without telling him directly, due to the guitarist's drinking problem. In response, Wylde, under doctor's orders, went on the wagon and began taking medication to deal with a blood disease.

In 2010, with new drummer Will Hunt, *Order of the Black* (#4) showed Wylde defiantly refusing to change his bone-crunching, hard-rocking style and his fans rewarded BLS handsomely in return. Also in 2010, he stretched his wings, joining Ludacris as a guest on My Darkest Days' video for "Porn Star Dancing." In 2011, BLS continued their breathless pace of album releases with *The Song Remains Not the Same* (#41), a title that takes an ironic twist on the legendary live album by Led Zeppelin. The album was an appealing combination of acoustic versions of songs that first appeared on *Order of the Black*, eclectic covers of "Junior's Eyes" (Sabbath), "Helpless" (CSNY), "Bridge Over Troubled Water" (Simon & Garfunkel), and "Can't Find My Way Home" (Blind Faith), and a guest vocal from country artist John Rich of Big & Rich. It received high marks from the critics for its variety and attention to songcraft, with Wylde even being acknowledged for his vocals.

An Irish Catholic and self-proclaimed "Soldier of Christ," Wylde played classical guitar in the Vatican in 2011, while in the midst of a tour of Italy. In the summer of 2012, he joined the Ozzy and Friends Tour, replacing the canceled Black Sabbath tour. Capping a typically busy year for the big bruiser, he had his uncensored, rude, crude, and hilarious autobiography, *Bringing Metal to the Children: The Complete Berzerker's Guide to World Tour Domination*, published. In the early fall of 2013, Wylde admitted that if Pantera ever decides to reunite, he would be happy to honor the memory of Dimebag Darrell, though it is an extreme long shot. That same year, he released BLS's two-disc, semi-live *Unblackened* (#72), consisting of acoustic versions of previous compositions, as well as studio tracks. In the spring of 2014, *Catacombs of the Black Vatican* (#5) became the ninth BLS studio album. Joining Wylde and bassist John DeServio was newcomer Chad Szeliga, formerly of Breaking Benjamin. The sheer power of Wylde's will, along with his skull-cracking solos, confirmed his unstoppable forward momentum.

Beyond technical prowess, which all great rock guitarists possess to varying degrees, it is the strength of their commitment to their musical principles that raises them to the pantheon of true "rock gods." Zakk Wylde continues to bull his way forward unimpeded with uncompromising, aggressive hard metal. His forays into Southern rock and creative cover versions of classic rock only add depth to his unapologetic, macho style.

THE GUITAR STYLE OF ZAKK WYLDE

Relatively speaking, Wylde is capable of dialing it down, especially when in "good ole boy" mode. Check out how he wisely follows the changes with the appropriate scale and selection of notes. In measure 1 over C5, he utilizes the C composite blues scale (blues scale plus Mixolydian mode) to confirm the tonality via the major 3rd (E) and the 5th (G). In measure 2 over G5, he slips comfortably into the G major pentatonic scale, fingered as the root-octave position of the E minor pentatonic scale. In measure 3 over the D5, Wylde manufactures a D major tonality dyad, A/F#, by bending E (2nd, or 9th) to F# (major 3rd) in conjunction with the A (5th) note.

Performance Tip: In measure 3, bend the E to F# with the ring finger, backed by the middle and index, while maintaining the A note with the pinky.

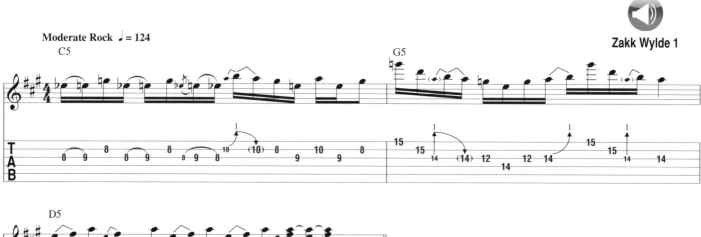

Few rock guitarists will pass up an opportunity to let rip over a slow tempo and dramatic chord changes, and Wylde is no exception. With the root-octave position of the E Aeolian mode as his improvisational "ammunition," he fires round after round of 32nd-note "bullets," with subtle emphasis on "target" notes. In measure 1 over Em, he lays on the root (E), followed by the 5th (G), major 3rd (E), 9th (D), and major 7th (B) over C. In measure 2 over G, he plays the major 7th (F#), 6th (E), root (G), 5th (D), and major 3rd (B), followed by the 9th (E), root (D), 6th (B), and 5th (A) over D.

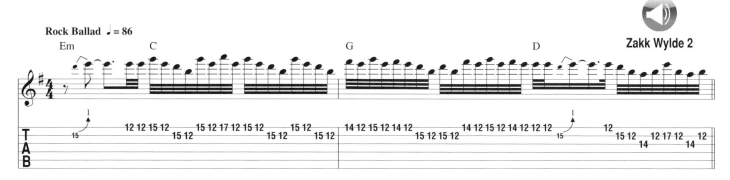

Wylde demonstrates his prowess at creating powerful and inventive repetitive riff patterns to skillfully define tonality. In measure 1, he uses an edited form of the C major scale, emphasizing the note D, which functions as the 4th of A5, for musical tension. In measure 2, with the harmony modulated up a half step to Bb5, he alters his scale to an edited form of the Bb major scale, with the addition of the note E (#4th). On beats 1–2, he emphasizes the D note, which functions as the major 3rd, for consonance and to define the major tonality. However, on beats 3–4, Wylde highlights the note E to ratchet up the tension for what follows.

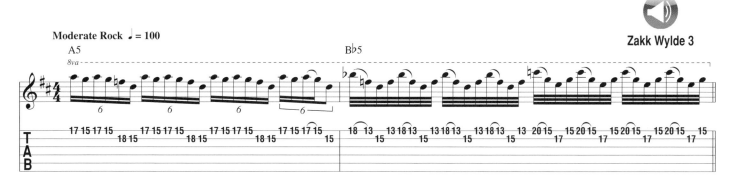

Showing his softer, gentler side, Wylde creates memorable melodies from the G major scale, fingered as the E Aeolian mode, or E relative minor scale. Within the parameters of his scale choice, he negotiates the chord changes with subtlety and sensitivity. In measure 1 over G5, he makes sure to emphasize the root (G). In measure 2 over Fmaj7#11, he lays on the root (F), 5th (C), and major 7th (E) leading tone. In measure 3 over G5 and Em7, he plays the major 3rd (B) and root (G) for the former change, while employing the minor tonality-defining b3rd (G) for the latter change. In measure 4 over Fmaj7, Fmaj7sus2, and C chords, Wylde makes the notes F and C function as the root and 5th of the first two chords, while the root (C) is joined by the major 3rd (E), 4th (F), major 7th (B), and 9th (D) over the third chord.

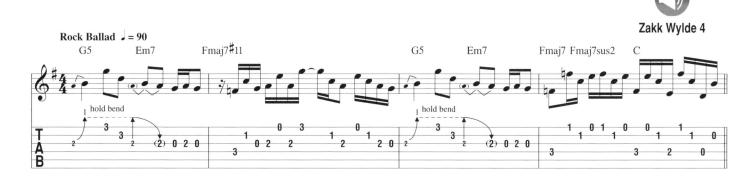

In addition to exhibiting his flair for melody in a rock ballad, Wylde demonstrates his sense of dynamics and drama. Additionally, he shows his ability to employ a motif: the sweet B–D–C–B phrase from the G major scale in measures 1 and 3 (over G, C, and C/B). In measure 2 over Am7 and C, he establishes the initial tonality with the root (A), sets up the C chord with its 5th (G), and then bounds up the G major scale, fingered as the relative E minor scale, with nimble 16th notes. In measure 4, he dramatically trims his note choices down to the essentials: the root (A) and the 5th (G), respectively.

Zakk Wylde 5

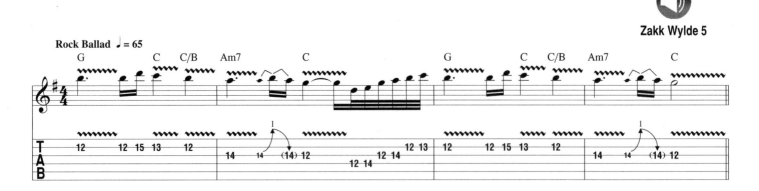